RURAL REVOLUTION
IN FRANCE

RURAL REVOLUTION
IN FRANCE

The Peasantry in the Twentieth Century

GORDON WRIGHT

Stanford University Press

Stanford, California

1964

Stanford University Press
Stanford, California
© 1964 by the Board of Trustees of the
Leland Stanford Junior University
All rights reserved
Library of Congress Catalog Card Number: 64-13356
Printed in the United States of America

Preface

THIS is not the book I intended to write when I began to reflect on French peasant problems a dozen years ago. It is not even the book I intended to write when I returned to the subject in 1960, after a long interruption. One's perspective is likely to change in the course of a decade, and to alter one's approach to any historical problem. But in this case it is not so much the author as the subject matter that has been transformed.

Agrarian France first drew my attention because I knew so little about it, and because I found it hard to learn very much from books. Most of the standard works on modern France mentioned the peasantry, and many indulged in resounding generalizations about the peasants' role in French society and politics. But some of these generalizations completely contradicted others, and few seemed to be based on anything more solid than folk wisdom and prejudice.

A year devoted to research in France (1950–51) led me to at least one firm conclusion: that a cautious historian or social scientist would do well to avoid the quicksands of the peasant problem. Rural France is almost infinitely diverse, and almost any generalization about the peasantry becomes partially false as soon as it is formulated. Any attempt to view peasant issues in the large, therefore, runs the risk of turning into another superficial essay, based on intuitive judgments and personal biases. One escape from the impasse might have been a series of precise but limited soundings into certain particular aspects of the peasant problem. Another might have been a study in depth of a single village, as a kind of microcosm of French rural society. Such books as *Les Paysans et la politique* (1958) and Laurence Wylie's remarkable *Village in the Vaucluse* (1957) demonstrate the value of those two approaches. But a nagging curiosity about general trends, combined with a streak of native bullheadedness, led me to persist in trying to see the problem in the large.

Since 1950, agrarian France has been transformed. Among other things, it is no longer the *terra incognita* that it used to be. Scholars were the first to rush into the quasi-vacuum that used to exist, but journalists followed in their wake as it became clear that something was really happening in the countryside. Thanks to the work of both professions, we know far more about rural France than we knew ten years ago. Yet the very speed of recent developments in French agriculture has created a new subject for the historian, whose stock in trade is the process of change.

Some observers hold that France has been experiencing a real rural revolution, more rapid and significant than anything the country has known since the nineteenth-century industrial revolution. If this is true, how did it come about, and what does it seem to portend for the France of the next half-century? This book has evolved into a general essay that tries to view these rural developments in historical perspective; that tries to explain what has been happening during the last thirty years, and why.

It is not easy to provide a dependable base for this kind of general essay. Some intuitive judgments are unavoidable. But I have tried to root those judgments in something deeper than my own prejudices. One source of information has been the printed page; I have dug rather extensively into the files of agricultural publications, both in provincial archives and in Paris. But newspapers and books are by no means adequate for such a topic. The historian, declared Sainte-Beuve a century ago, "does not travel enough; he fails to seek out living traditions at their source, to poke among ashes of the past that are smoldering still." I have attempted to profit by Sainte-Beuve's admonition, and to combine direct observation with documentary research in roughly equal proportions. In 1950–51, I spent several months in eight rural departments of France, selected as representative of differing patterns of economic or social structure, political behavior, and tradition. I returned to four of these regions in 1960, and added two others that I had not visited before. Much of my time was spent talking to officials of farm organizations and other knowledgeable observers of the rural scene— government officials, agronomists, journalists, politicians, parish and "missionary" priests. Whenever possible, I attended meetings of agrarian organizations, ranging from national congresses of the farmers' syndicate (FNSEA) to regional sheep-raisers' conventions and local conclaves of the Young Catholic Farmers (JAC).

My obligations are more than ordinarily heavy; indeed, the list will seem pretentious for so brief and general a book. The Social Science Research Council helped to finance my first year of research in 1950–51. The Committee on Public Affairs at Stanford University contributed to the cost of a return visit to France in 1960. Part of the final draft was written in residence at the Center for Advanced Study in the Behavioral Sciences. I cannot properly express my indebtedness to the many French informants who were kind enough to receive me in 1950–51 or 1960 (or both), and to devote a great deal of valuable time to answering my questions and showing me around. With rare exceptions, they responded with remarkable frankness, honesty, and patience. The Notes indicate the source of such oral information only when it has seemed to me that a direct citation would not embarrass my informant. A list of these informants is included in the Bibliography; my sincere thanks go to each of them.

The Appendix is a revised and somewhat condensed version of two separate essays originally published in the *Yale Review* (Spring 1952 and Autumn 1962). I should like to thank the editors of that quarterly and Yale University Press for permission to reprint them in altered form. I am indebted to the following persons for their aid in running down illustrations: MM. Archambault and Hérisson of *La Nouvelle République* (Tours); Pierre Bringé of the Ministry of Agriculture; A. S. Chapman of the United States Embassy in Paris; Madame René Colson; and the Secretariats of the APPCA and the CNJA. Marcel Faure, editor of *Paysans*, graciously authorized me to reproduce several maps from that review. Finally, the editorial labors of Miss Pauline Wickham and J. G. Bell of the Stanford University Press should not go unmentioned.

G. W.

Contents

Abbreviations

APA	Amicale Parlementaire Agricole
APPCA	Assemblée Permanente des Présidents des Chambres d'Agriculture
CDAP	Comités de Défense et d'Action Paysannes
CETA	Centre d'Etudes Techniques Agricoles
CFTC	Confédération Française des Travailleurs Chrétiens
CGA	Confédération Générale de l'Agriculture
CGPT	Confédération Générale des Paysans Travailleurs
CGT	Confédération Générale du Travail
CNAA	Confédération Nationale des Associations Agricoles
CNJA	Cercle (later Centre) National des Jeunes Agriculteurs
CNMCCA	Confédération Nationale de la Mutualité, de la Coopération, et du Crédit Agricole
CNP	Confédération Nationale Paysanne
CUMA	Coopérative pour l'Utilisation des Machines Agricoles
FNMCA	Fédération Nationale de la Mutualité et de la Coopération Agricole
FNPA	Fédération Nationale de la Propriété Agricole
FNSEA	Fédération Nationale des Syndicats d'Exploitants Agricoles

FO	Force Ouvrière
IVCC	Institut des Vins de Consommation Courante
JAC	Jeunesse Agricole Chrétienne
MRP	Mouvement Républicain Populaire
ONIC	Office National Interprofessionel des Céréales
RFD	Rassemblement des Forces Démocratiques
RGR	Rassemblement des Gauches Républicaines
RPF	Rassemblement du Peuple Français
SAFER	Sociétés d'Aménagement Foncier et d'Etablissement Rural
SIBEV	Société Interprofessionnelle du Bétail et des Viandes
SNPBR	Section Nationale des Preneurs des Baux Ruraux
UCSAF	Union Centrale des Syndicats des Agriculteurs de France
UNEF	Union Nationale des Etudiants Français
UNSA	Union Nationale des Syndicats Agricoles

DEPARTMENTS OF CONTINENTAL FRANCE

RURAL REVOLUTION
IN FRANCE

I
The Peasant Heritage

"IN THE LAST RESORT, and at bottom, France is a Peasants' Republic."[1] This judgment by a noted British historian dates not from the mid-nineteenth century (when more than half of all Frenchmen tilled the soil) but from the mid-twentieth (when only one Frenchman in four or five still lives by agriculture). It reflects a viewpoint cherished even more warmly by Frenchmen than by foreign observers. For generations now, French writers, historians, and politicians have consistently asserted its truth—usually with pride, though occasionally with impatience and regret. Few Western nations cling so strongly to their agrarian origins, or extol the rural virtues with such ritualistic fervor. "In France," remarks François Mauriac, "Cybele has more disciples than Christ."[2] No other industrialized nation has kept so large a proportion of its total population on the soil; nowhere else do so many city-dwellers regard their peasant ancestry as a mark of distinction.

Perhaps this peasantist* dogma should be classed as an item of political folklore; but even so, its shaping influence on French

---

* Some readers may object to such barbarous neologisms as "peasantism" and "peasantist," but I have found no better terms to describe the belief that peasant life possesses unique moral qualities, and that the strength of any society comes from its broad small-peasant base. "Agricultural fundamentalism," which is used by some American rural sociologists, conveys a similar idea.

political and social attitudes remains quite genuine. A nation that continues to think of itself as peasant, and that exalts what it believes to be the rural virtues, is likely to confront some special problems of adjustment in the industrial age. Problems of agricultural adjustment are world-wide in the mid-twentieth century, but they take on added poignancy in a country that has clung to its peasantist ideal, and that has managed to insulate many of its farmers against economic and social change. They grow even more complex when peasantist doctrine becomes entangled with political or philosophical-religious issues, and when the varying pace of rural evolution creates quite different agrarian structures within the same nation.

The consequences of France's "rural lag" are not easy to assess. To many Frenchmen, the peasantry has always been "the sheet anchor, the keel, of the ship of France"; to a smaller group of critics, a more accurate metaphor would be "a sailboat in the age of steam." A much-quoted rural philosopher of the Third Republic asserted that "France's peasant soul is essential for her wealth, her genius, and her destiny"; but his contemporary, the impatient Marxian Jules Guesde, held that "the only way to make the peasants fecund is rape."[3] In our own day, social scientists and journalists continue to debate the role and influence of the peasantry. Are the peasants eternal victims of injustice, or ultimate masters of the state? Are they shapers of the nation's destiny, or passive objects in the historical process?

* *

The written record is filled with ambiguities and encrusted with legend. As the historian-demographer Louis Chevalier puts it, "One need only compare, in the best-known historical syntheses, the chapters devoted to domestic, industrial, or international policy with the usually brief chapter devoted to agricultural policy. . . . At once the documentation becomes less precise, less relevant; the total plan breaks up into a series of disparate remarks; care for exact analysis gives way to approximations, to descriptions loaded with detail and indifferent to what is essential. . . . The history of our agriculture seems to be written on the margin of our history as a whole, and almost in a different language."[4]

But if Chevalier's strictures are generally valid, he does overstate his case. A few scholars of real stature—in particular Marc Bloch and Georges Lefebvre—have done notable work in this historical wilderness.[5] Thanks to their efforts, it is possible to sketch the main outlines of France's agrarian history, from the Middle Ages down through the Revolution, and to challenge some of the oldest and hardiest legends about France's peasant heritage.

One of these legends holds that modern France's agrarian history really begins with the Revolution, which completely transformed the country's rural structure. The great estates of the privileged orders, according to this view, were parceled out among the peasantry, so that an amorphous mass of landless serfs was transmuted into a nation of proudly independent smallholders. In fact, by no means all the large estates were broken up by the Revolution; some were sold relatively intact, and others remained in the hands of their noble owners or were recovered by those owners after the restoration. Nor did smallownership begin with the Revolution; its origins can be pushed back at least into the Middle Ages, and its existence was widespread before 1789. Nor did all peasants, or even most peasants, get their own plots of ground during the Revolution; a large proportion remained landless throughout the nineteenth century. Many peasants did get land for the first time, or added to their existing holdings, or secured firmer legal title to what they already possessed. But no one can say how many landless peasants became owners during the Revolution, or how much acreage passed into the hands of the peasantry rather than into those of bourgeois speculators. Clearly there were wide regional variations in the pattern, just as there had been in pre-Revolutionary times. The one certainty is that all peasants gained relief from the irritating remnants of the feudal age, manorial dues and obligations, and that they obtained political equality in principle. Yet even here some qualification is necessary. In certain regions (notably in the west), a kind of *de facto* feudal relationship between aristocratic landlord and peasant tenant survived for generations, into our own time.

There is another legend that does not stand up any better under close analysis: the myth that the peasantry, both before and after the Revolution, constituted a solid and largely undifferentiated bloc with common interests and aspirations. In fact, a clear distinction between *laboureurs* and *manouvriers* (or *brassiers*) had emerged as early as medieval times. This distinction, though economic in nature, was not based entirely on land ownership; some of the manouvriers possessed small bits of soil, while a good many laboureurs were large tenants rather than owners. But the laboureurs were markedly more prosperous than the mass of marginal peasants; they were village capitalists, possessing equipment, draft animals, and a cash reserve from which to make loans (often at usurious rates). The manouvriers, on the other hand, tilled their soil by hand, and often worked part time or full time for a neighboring laboureur or aristocrat. In the eighteenth century, many of them began to take employment in the rural textile industry, which allowed them and their families to spin and weave at home.

By the time of the Revolution, the line between manouvriers and laboureurs had become less distinct. Many laboureurs had been forced down into the manouvrier group (or were threatened by such a fate) owing to the growth of rural capitalism after

1750. France, like England, experienced its enclosure movement; and some large landowners set out to broaden their holdings in order to engage in large-scale modernized agriculture.
The more prosperous laboureurs could join in this process of
aggrandizement; many of the weaker ones were its victims.

During the Revolutionary decade, the chief point of conflict in the countryside was the issue of preserving or abolishing
such remnants of the medieval rural structure as the right to
graze animals on all village land after the harvest, or to collect
firewood on the village common land. The manouvriers clung
desperately to these ancient privileges, which might mean the
difference between subsistence and starvation. Their precapitalist
and stubbornly traditionalist attitude resembled that of the urban
sans-culottes—those half-bourgeois, half-proletarian artisans and
shopkeepers of Paris and Lyon who became ferocious revolutionaries but who doggedly opposed the socio-economic changes
dictated by emergent capitalism. In the end, the manouvriers
were more successful than the sans-culottes in protecting their traditional rights—perhaps because the exponents of the new capitalist economics were weaker in the countryside than in the cities,
perhaps because most of the laboureurs joined the manouvriers
in their resistance to change. Thus rural France emerged from
the Revolution with the myth of peasant unity strengthened
rather than exposed.

Still a third legend that springs from the Revolutionary
epoch concerns the excessive subdivision of the soil. Not only
are many farms in modern France uneconomically small, but
these small farms (as well as larger ones) are often split into
dozens of tiny parcels, sometimes contiguous but more often
scattered through one or more communes. Aerial photographs reveal the most bizarre patchwork patterns; land surveys provide
us with such appalling examples of parcelization as the famous
commune in the Loire valley where approximately 5,000 acres

were divided into 48,000 plots. All this is often held to be the product of that great Revolutionary monument, the Napoleonic Code, which abolished primogeniture in favor of the principle of equal inheritance, and presumably forced every peasant to split his holdings among all his sons. Conservatives have been particularly outraged at the effects of what Frédéric Le Play called Napoleon's "land-chopping machine" (*machine à hacher le sol*). A closer look, however, suggests that the Code had only limited consequences, for the abolition of primogeniture affected no one but the aristocracy. For commoners, equal inheritance had been customary in most parts of France long before Napoleon's time—and so had peasant devices for evading that principle. If excessive parcelization was an evil in rural France, Marc Bloch once remarked, the responsibility for it probably went back to neolithic man.

* *

Few periods in French agrarian history are so obscure as the half-century that followed the Revolution. Even the statistical evidence is sparse, for agricultural surveys were rare and their findings dubious.[6] Smallownership had certainly increased as a result of the Revolutionary upheaval, but large holdings persisted in many regions, and the landless farm population probably continued to exceed the number of landowners. If there was any dominant trend during this period, it was toward a steadily increasing subdivision of the soil. The number of farms in operation reached a peak of about 3.5 million during the 1880's.[7] The cause seems to have been, quite simply, the growing pressure of population on the land. France's rural population reached its all-time peak in the late 1840's, and even the drift to the cities that set in thereafter did not do much to relieve the pressure until the end of the century. Most of the peasantry, therefore, remained on a marginal standard that permitted at best only slight and sporadic improvements in living conditions and agricultural techniques.

Along with population pressure, several other factors seem to have contributed to the perpetuation of rural misery. One of these was the decay of the rural textile industry as urban factories began to displace the old system of home spinning and weaving on consignment. A major source of supplementary income for peasant families thus dried up by the mid-nineteenth century. A second factor was the sporadic continuation of the eighteenth-century enclosure movement, which challenged the peasants' ancient rights in the village common lands, and which increased class antagonisms between prosperous and poor peasants. Still another source of tension was the continuing inclination of the urban bourgeoisie to buy rural property, primarily in order to gain social status. The effect was to drive up land values at a time when peasant land hunger was intense.

As usual, there were sharp regional differences in this whole process of socio-economic change—a change caused chiefly by the advance of capitalist methods. The process went farthest and fastest in northern France, from the Paris basin to the Belgian frontier; it was probably speeded there by the growth of industry, which sucked away much of the excess rural population to the towns and cities and provided a large local market for the region's farm products. The rich soil and the flat terrain of the area were ideal for large-scale mechanized farming; and even where small farming persisted (as in the Nord department, adjoining the Belgian frontier), the proximity of urban markets and the example of progressive Belgian and Dutch agriculture encouraged rapid advances in agricultural productivity. In western, central, and southern France, the process of change was far less striking. These regions continued to be dominated by smallownership and share tenantry (*métayage*); except for a few islands of prosperity, they remained traditionalist in techniques, and continued to suffer from rural overcrowding. The modern contrast between the efficient and prosperous northeast and the underdeveloped, largely stagnant west, center, and south first emerged in clear fashion in the early nineteenth century.

The disturbances of the 1840's reflected these socio-economic changes. In the northeast the peasantry played a largely passive role in 1848 and after, whereas in central and southern France rural disorders began to occur as early as 1846, when the most severe economic depression of the century set in. There was a sporadic wave of food riots, as well as demonstrations against the enclosure of common lands and against the new professional skills that were undermining rural industry. In 1848, disorders continued to unsettle these areas; they were directed now against usurers, against large landowners, or against the Second Republic's emergency surtax. So widespread was the unrest that the government was forced to fall back on armed repression—which in turn alienated many peasants and drove them into the arms of Louis Napoleon as a potential savior. When Louis Napoleon failed them, some turned to new saviors. In the 1849 elections, there was a sharp rise in the "red" (i.e., republican socialist) vote in many villages; and the same regions in 1851 joined in violent resistance to Louis Napoleon's *coup d'état.*[8]

The historian Michelet, shortly before 1848, complained that French governments since the Revolution had systematically ignored the interests of agriculture in favor of those of industry. The Second Republic, although it was led by Parisian politicians, made a serious attempt to redress this balance. It decreed the establishment of peasant-elected *chambres d'agriculture* in each department of France, to represent the peasant population in its relations with the state and to further agricultural progress. It also drafted a sweeping program of agricultural education, intended both to give farmers some elementary professional training and to train a corps of highly skilled agricultural technicians. And it initiated, for the first time, a study of the problem of tenantry, with a view to protecting tenants against unscrupulous landlords. These projects, which were soon jettisoned by Louis Napoleon, stand out as the most farsighted agrarian reforms advanced by any French government during the nineteenth century.*

During the Second Empire, the rapid expansion of industry, banking, and commerce speeded the drain of population from country to city, and provided some relief from the terrible weight of rural population pressure. Napoleon's turn toward freer foreign trade in 1860 also inaugurated an experiment which, had it been continued, might have effected a fundamental change in French agriculture. No agrarian pressure groups yet existed to fight for a return to tariff protection; and one important segment of the farm population, the winegrowers, favored the free trade policy because it gave them access to foreign markets. The prosperity of the 1850's reconciled most of the peasantry to the regime; and even though Napoleon III provided few constructive reforms for agriculture, he enjoyed massive rural support until almost the very end of his reign.

Contemporary observers of French rural life in the middle of the nineteenth century emphasized its dreariness. Zola's novels and Millet's paintings show us country living at its worst. Left-wing critics like Karl Marx railed bitterly at the smallholding system that had transformed sixteen million peasants into "troglodytes" hovering on the margin of existence. Friedrich

---

* The Second Republic's agricultural reforms are rarely mentioned in studies of the period, though they certainly deserve careful analysis. The common charge that these urban politicians ignored the peasantry seems quite distorted. Among other things, they founded a National Institute of Agronomy, which was later revived by the Third Republic. Louis Blanc's Luxembourg Commission also projected some interesting experiments in communal agriculture.

Engels, after a brief journey through the provinces late in 1848, claimed to have noted everywhere "the same narrow-mindedness, the same complete misunderstanding of urban, industrial, and commercial conditions, the same political blindness, the same ignorance of everything that lies outside the village . . . ; in short, one must have known the French peasants of this year 1848 to experience the full force of their unmanageable stupidity." Ernest Renan, after an unsuccessful try for a rural seat in parliament in 1869, angrily summed up his reaction thus: "A government that is cheap, unimpressive, disinclined to interfere; an honest desire for liberty; a great thirst for equality; a total indifference to the nation's glory; an absolute determination to make no sacrifice for nonmaterial interests—there is the peasant spirit, in my opinion."[9]

Although each of these critics had his axe to grind, their judgments had at least some foundation in fact. The continuing isolation of rural communities until the later nineteenth century checked the inflow of any vigorous currents of change. Education —even of the most elementary sort—had spread in a slow and irregular fashion; as late as 1880, 16 per cent of all Frenchmen and 25 per cent of all Frenchwomen were still unable to sign their own names to marriage contracts.[10] Since most of the illiteracy was rural, perhaps one-third of the peasant population was unable to read and write. Nine-tenths of all Frenchmen in the census year 1861 were living in the department of their birth, and probably most of them had never been more than fifty miles from home. The nearest approach to a farmers' organization, the Société des Agriculteurs de France (1868), was established and run by a small group of landed aristocrats, whose interest in the mass of peasants was paternalistic at best. The peasants themselves possessed no organization through which they might undertake common action, either for self-help or for political purposes.* Marx, a shrewd sociological observer, caught at least part of the truth in his caustic analysis of French peasant society as "a nonhomogeneous and nonunified agglomeration of autonomous units of autarchic production. A smallholding, a peasant and his family; alongside them another smallholding, another peasant and another family. A certain number of these families form a village, and a certain number of villages, a department. Thus the great mass of the French nation is made up of a simple addition of units bearing the same name, just as a sack filled with potatoes forms a sack of potatoes."[11]

Yet the apparent stagnation of rural life in the middle of the century concealed the fact that the way was being prepared for some rather fundamental changes. The use of the ballot at regular though infrequent intervals after 1848 provided the peasants with the rudiments of a political education. The slow spread of literacy contributed to this process, though the full impact of rural education was not to be felt until after 1880. Meanwhile, the penetration of many parts of the countryside by the new railway network was foreshadowing a real social revolution. Again, it was not until the 1880's that the secondary rail lines were built, giving access to the back country; but with their completion the isolation of the rural village became a thing of the past. Men, ideas, products, could at last flow easily both into and out of the village; the way was cleared for the peasantry to become active rather than passive participants in national life.

Meanwhile, even more quietly and just as slowly, some technological changes were filtering into the countryside. In

* A considerable number of local study groups, as well as a network of organizations known as *comices agricoles*, had existed since the early nineteenth century. But the *comices* had few functions except to award prizes at local fairs, and the study groups were made up of large landowners rather than common peasants.

the region northeast of Paris, where the agricultural revolution of the eighteenth century had produced its chief effect, the process continued throughout the nineteenth century: concentration of land in larger units, mechanization, increased use of fertilizers, experimentation with new crops (notably the sugar beet). And in a less dramatic way, changes were coming to some of the more backward regions as well. From about mid-century, agronomists introduced the practice of "liming" the soil in certain infertile regions of central and western France; within a generation, vast areas of "acid" soil that had lain unused or had served only as low-grade natural pasturage were reclaimed for the plow.[12] Chombart de Lauwe points out that 1,500,000 acres were cleared in Brittany alone—an operation as remarkable, in his opinion, as the concurrent colonization of Algeria.[13] This increase in cultivable soil in some of France's most backward regions, along with a gradual trend away from cereals and toward livestock, considerably improved the position of agriculture in those regions. By 1870, rural France, though still sunk deeply in tradition and routine, was on the way to entering the modern age.

2
Prelude to Activism: The Beginnings
of Peasant Organization

THE REPUBLIC that Frenchmen established in 1870, and that lasted for almost three-quarters of a century, was neither installed nor managed by the peasantry; yet most Frenchmen believed that its stability depended on its broad peasant base. Without the conversion of the bulk of the peasantry to republicanism in the 1870's the regime could not have been consolidated; without the peasants' continuing support, it could not have endured. Two-thirds of the nation's population was still classed as rural when the Third Republic was founded, and the proportion did not fall below half until the census of 1931. Not all rural residents were farmers, but the proportion of farmers in the total active population did remain high throughout the whole life of the republic. It exceeded 50 per cent in 1870; it still stood at about 45 per cent in 1900; and it probably approximated 35 per cent in 1930.[1]

Throughout this era, French politicians, publicists, and social theorists were almost unanimous in extolling the smallowning farmers as the bulwark of the republic. Jules Ferry, in a fine burst of after-dinner rhetoric in 1884, declared, "The republic will be a peasants' republic or will cease to exist." In 1934 Edouard Herriot invited an audience to salute "the peasant, whose silence does not signify absence of thought, who ranks as the greatest of French philosophers, who might be described as our silent master." Necessity as well as honest conviction forced the political leaders of the age to keep agrarian interests in mind; for the peasants' massive electoral power was magnified by the Third Republic's electoral laws and by the distribution of population in that era. At least half of the electoral districts for the Chamber of Deputies were predominantly rural, and many others contained a sizable minority of peasant voters. Not more than one deputy in four or five could safely ignore rural interests if he hoped to win re-election. Even more striking was the rural preponderance in the Senate, whose members were chosen by departmental electoral colleges dominated by delegates of the villages.[2] Indeed, the Senate came to be known as *la grande assemblée des ruraux*, and its members took pride in the name.

With French leaders dedicated to a kind of Jeffersonian ideal, and with the electoral system skewed in favor of the rural population, one would expect to find both the personnel and the policies of the republic dominated by farmers. In fact, however, the peasantry rarely ventured into politics directly, and the agrarian legislation of the Third Republic was so meager and unimaginative that it hardly added up to a policy at all. Many years later, an exasperated young spokesman for a new peasant generation called for an explanation of this phenomenon (which, he held, had carried over from the Third to the Fourth Republic): "It is curious indeed that our political scientists have never tried to analyze this fact in depth. . . . They would soon discover that the permanent distortion of peasant aspirations by an electoral system that appears to favor the peasants is one of the great puzzles of our political life. The whole system is paralyzed by it, and the first victims are the peasant masses."[3]

Part of the explanation certainly lay in the failure, or the inability, of the peasant masses to produce their own set of leaders, their grass-roots elite. Until the 1930's, working farmers almost never ventured into political life, even at the local level;

and they were hardly more active in organizing or leading farm syndicates or cooperatives. This passiveness doubtless sprang from a variety of sources, some beyond the peasants' control. Education arrived late in rural France, and it rarely provided more than the bare essentials; few peasants could think of competing with the more articulate and sophisticated town bourgeoisie for elective office, or with large landowners for syndical posts that might require some skill in oratory or accounting. Talent, too, had a tendency to flow away from the countryside toward the city; peasants' sons with intellectual gifts or ambition usually left the farm, leaving the less gifted to compete for village leadership. In some regions, the survival of quasi feudal relationships between the traditional leaders of society and the peasant masses served as a psychological barrier against the emergence of able youngsters. In more egalitarian provinces, a deep-rooted suspicion and jealousy of neighbor toward neighbor sometimes led to a kind of instinctive closing of ranks against potential grass-roots leadership.*

Village mayors, departmental councilors, deputies, and senators were usually large landowners rather than working farmers.[4] Electoral committees in rural areas were dominated by the so-called *notables*: the old aristocracy, the long-established bourgeoisie, and the new elite of the republican era—notaries, doctors, lawyers, teachers, shopkeepers, civil servants. The degree of solidarity between this new small-town bourgeoisie and the surrounding peasantry was probably not very great, despite

---

* See, for example, p. 189 below. This unneighborly suspicion has often marked intervillage relationships as well. The mayor of one rural commune whose population had declined from 700 to 250 between 1880 and 1950, and whose resources would no longer support necessary local services, was asked whether his constituents would consider fusion with an adjoining commune whose chief town was two miles distant. "We want nothing to do with foreigners," was his brusque reply. *Revue administrative*, III (1950), 469–70.

ritualistic assertions to the contrary. In many respects the two groups shared the same sort of existence, and they ought to have had interests in common; yet they apparently lived back to back rather than side by side.[5] The fact that most peasants asked and expected little of the state in this era made it easy for town politicians to *seem* to represent peasant interests, and to persuade both the peasants and themselves that they were doing so.

This is not to suggest that the politicians were hypocritically indifferent to the peasants' wishes. On the contrary, perhaps they were too responsive to those wishes, and too shortsighted to provide their rural constituents with some kind of enlightened leadership. The reflexes of most peasants at this time were defensive and negative; they sought to protect themselves against foreign competitors, against middlemen, against such acts of God as hail, floods, tax collectors, and draft boards. Protection of this sort, to a considerable degree at least, the politicians of the Third Republic gave them. When crops were wiped out by some quirk of nature, parliament was usually generous to a fault;* when parliament could no longer postpone the adoption of an income tax, it virtually exempted the bulk of the peasantry; whenever international tensions relaxed a bit, it shortened the period of military conscription that weighed so heavily on peasants' sons. But all this scarcely added up to a coherent and constructive agricultural policy. Indeed, if the Third Republic had an agricultural policy at all, it amounted to little more than high tariff protection on farm products, subsidies for the development of cooperatives and mutual-insurance societies, and (after 1918) the gradual electrification of the rural regions.

---

* Toward the end of the Third Republic, Senator Hennessy recalled the good old days when a farmer might write to his deputy: "I've been wiped out by hail, it's cost me a million francs, try to get me a hundred thousand." "In those days," Hennessy added, "he probably got the million and then wanted two hundred thousand more." *Journal officiel, débats du Sénat,* Dec. 26, 1939, p. 745.

The keystone of the Third Republic's agricultural legislation was the tariff law of 1892, to which Jules Méline's name has been attached. That law created Méline's reputation as the Galahad of the peasantry, and led later Ministers of Agriculture to give his portrait a permanent place of honor on the wall of the ministerial suite. There is some reason to doubt, however, that the Méline tariff was adopted in response to peasant pressures, or that it suited the real needs of French agriculture. Industrial interests—particularly the textile producers—were the principal sponsors of high tariff protection; and Méline was shrewd enough to hitch agricultural protection onto the bill in order to ensure its passage. He found support among the large cereal-growers of the northeast, who were seriously threatened after 1880 by the incursion of lower-priced American, Russian, and Australian grain. The great mass of small peasants were only marginally affected; indeed, they stood to lose as much as they gained by a tariff system that would keep consumer prices high. Still, they were attracted by the idea that agriculture ought to enjoy "equality" with industry in tariff protection, and they were sensitive to the threat that a flood of foreign farm imports might force sweeping changes—incalculable and therefore fearsome changes—in their way of life. Even the small peasants, therefore, were receptive to the legend that Méline had saved them from extinction. As for the large cereal-growers, they undoubtedly benefited from the Méline tariff, for many of them would have found it difficult or impossible to convert to other crops.

A few people at the time denounced the Méline tariff as a disastrous error, and they have been echoed by a great many others since.[6] According to these critics, the effect of the tariff was to turn France's economy toward a kind of semi-autarky, and to petrify French farming in its nineteenth-century mold— just at the moment when natural trends might have carried it toward modernization. The charge is valid, though only in part. The tariff did not condemn French agriculture to inevitable stagnation; it merely provided an easy excuse for both peasants and politicians to fall into lazy, routine habits. Some farmers resisted the temptation and turned to modern methods even without the spur of economic necessity. This happened chiefly in such regions as the large cereal-growing areas of the Paris basin and the northeast, the highly efficient small-farming area adjoining the Belgian frontier, and the newly developed region of early vegetables and fruits along the Breton coast.

The politicians, by contrast, had no trouble persuading themselves that agriculture had received its just due from the state, and that the peasants could work out their own problems under the protective umbrella of the tariff. Over the next quarter-century, no cabinet proposed a serious agricultural program. The nation's system of agricultural education remained meager and antiquated. The government's corps of agricultural experts was too thinly spread to provide much active leadership in modernizing farm techniques, or in shaping the outlook of the younger peasant generation. The state's annual appropriations for rural equipment (roads, power lines, water systems, irrigation and drainage, housing improvement) were ridiculously low. Perhaps the politicians ought not to be blamed; their rural constituents asked only to be let alone, and might well have resisted any serious program of agricultural reform. All one can say is that France's political leaders failed to offer their constituents any alternative to stagnation.

* *

Although the peasantry took little active part in politics until the Great Depression of the 1930's, the professional organization of peasants began much earlier. Parliament in 1884 passed a bill legalizing the formation of groups for "the defense of economic, industrial, commercial, and agricultural interests," and during the next three decades local or regional farmers' syndicates were established in every section of France.[7] Few of these syndicates were organized by the peasants themselves; most were organized by local crusaders from the landed aristocracy or the bourgeoisie. The most vigorous sponsors of agrarian syndicalism in the early years were large landowners who had been influenced by the Social Catholic current of the time—by the paternalistic and corporatist ideas of such doctrinaires as Frédéric Le Play and the Marquis René de la Tour du Pin. The syndicate founders were imbued with a spirit of *noblesse oblige* and a sense of the integrity of France's traditional rural society, but these considerations were mixed with less high-minded ones: notably a desire to insulate the peasantry against the inroads of republican ideology, and thus to preserve a bloc of voters committed to political and social conservatism. The syndicates thus established were open to all rural elements, from large landlords to share tenants and farm laborers; they rested on the concept of a single *classe paysanne*, of a *monde paysan* quite distinct in its values and mores from the rest of French society.

Although most of these right-wing organizers took upon themselves the task of preaching the social and moral role of agrarian syndicalism, they were quickly drawn into more mundane activities—notably the cooperative buying of fertilizers, seeds, and other essential farm supplies. Only by supplying such services could they hold the interest of the peasant members, who cared more about fertilizer prices than about social or moral preachment. Most of the syndicates thus degenerated into "fertilizer shops" (as a contemptuous later generation labeled them); and they might more appropriately have been called cooperatives, save for the fact that many peasants found the word *syndicat* less alien than the neologism *coopérative*. The right-wing syndicates were federated in 1886 as the Union Centrale des

Syndicats des Agriculteurs de France. Both the name of the organization and the location of its central offices (in the Rue d'Athènes in Paris) were significant, for the UCSAF was housed in the building owned by the wealthy landlords' league called the Société des Agriculteurs de France. Although the national headquarters exercised little central control over the local syndicates, a powerful regional structure did emerge in certain areas—notably in Brittany (with offices at Landerneau) and in the Rhône Valley (the so-called Union du Sud-Est). By 1914 several hundred thousand peasant families were affiliated with the UCSAF, either through one of its 10,000 local syndicates or through related groups such as the newer mutual-insurance associations.

In response to this *syndicalisme des ducs*, republican leaders of the center and left organized their own "Jacobin syndicalism" in the countryside. Peasant votes had helped to consolidate the Third Republic during the 1870's; the republicans were determined to expand their rural strength, if only to avert a monarchist resurgence. While parliament set out, under Jules Ferry's leadership, to provide rural France with a complete network of free lay schools (whose teachers were to be the regime's most dedicated agents), local republican activists took advantage of the 1884 law to create a network of peasant associations throughout much of the country. Here again, most of the organizers were not peasants but town-dwellers with a sense of mission. Their emphasis, unlike that of the conservatives, was frankly economic rather than social and moral (though anticlerical republicanism was their doctrinal bedrock). They preferred to call their groups cooperatives (or *mutuelles*) rather than syndicates—though in fact it became increasingly difficult to differentiate the two. These groups were further strengthened after 1890 by parliamentary subsidies to newly organized farm-credit and mutual-insurance societies; the grants were prudently doled out by the Ministry of Agriculture, which had been a republican stronghold from the start and which early became a bastion of the Radical Socialist faction.

By 1914 the membership of these various left-wing farm organizations roughly equaled that of the right-wing syndicates of the UCSAF, and they too had their federation, the Fédération Nationale de la Mutualité et de la Coopération Agricoles (FNMCA), with headquarters in the Boulevard Saint-Germain in Paris.[8] Thus two rival syndicalisms confronted one another at the national level, and often in individual villages as well. Sometimes their antagonisms erupted into open clashes (as when a Radical Minister of Agriculture in 1907 unsuccessfully tried to clip the wings of the UCSAF by outlawing commercial activities by the syndicates).[9] More often, the two factions coexisted in an uneasy neutrality.

If agrarian syndicalism before 1914 was useful both to the peasants (who got cheaper fertilizer and some protection against the hazards of nature) and to the politicians (who got some dependable voting support), it did nothing to help the peasants influence political decision-making, develop a sense of professional solidarity, or solve the fundamental economic and social problems of rural France. A few peasants gained some rudimentary experience in administering a cooperative or a mutual-aid society; but in the main, those managerial functions were left to the large landowners or to town-dwellers initiated into the mysteries of bookkeeping. Syndicate officials raised few questions about changing the country's agrarian structure as France and Europe moved into the twentieth century. Traditionalism had a powerful grip, scarcely less strong on the left than on the right. Right and left alike favored undifferentiated organizations uniting all elements of the rural population, and both proclaimed the unchallengeable virtues of smallownership (preferably combined in "harmonious" fashion with a limited degree of large farming). The Radicals' conception reflected their deep-rooted egalitarianism, which rejected the idea of economic or hierarchical differentiation; if all men were citizens of equal worth and equal rights, why separate them along lines of economic or social status? The conservatives, on the other hand, clung to the doctrine that a kind of organic relationship bound all rural elements together into a harmonious whole; that behind the appearance of diversity, there existed a single *classe paysanne*.

Both left and right thus favored the maintenance of a numerous small peasantry, by artificial methods if necessary. No doubt ulterior motives underlay this doctrine, at least to some degree. To the Radicals, committed as they were to the ferocious defense of the small independent, an independent smallowner class represented an almost inexhaustible source of votes. To the large landlords and "capitalist" farmers of the right, the existence of the small peasantry provided shelter against collectivist or Jacobin critics and a useful justification for keeping farm prices high. Privileges granted to the small farmer might easily be extended to the large one as well; and it was easier politically to plead the small farmer's case.* The small peasantry also provided a built-in supply of supplementary labor in many areas.

Toward the turn of the century, a few minority voices began to be raised in opposition to these widely shared dogmas. An occasional economist like Paul Leroy-Beaulieu rose to reassert the old Physiocratic doctrine that "the days of small individual property are numbered"; but such heresies were largely ignored.[10] More significant was the growth of Marxism in France, with its insistence that the small peasantry was doomed to be swallowed up by large capitalist agriculture, which in turn would be replaced by complete collectivization. In the 1890's, how-

---

* Agricultural orators, remarked one Frenchman ironically, have always divided French farmers into two categories—the large and the small. But when the time comes to draw the line between them, "the class of large farmers remains empty." Adolphe Javal, "L'Organisation de la profession agricole," *Journal des économistes*, CVI (1936), 74.

ever, French Socialism abandoned its Marxian orthodoxy in favor of a policy of small-peasant defense. The party program, revised in 1892, now advocated the expropriation of large property alone, and promised a series of unprecedented reforms in support of small owners and tenants. The Socialists' brilliant new recruit, Jean Jaurès, became their principal spokesman on agricultural matters. Jaurès preached a mixed rural economy in which small operation and large collective farming would co-exist. The government would relieve smallowners of their crushing load of debt and taxes, and offer them cheap credit to modernize their farms. The expropriated large properties would either be turned into collective farms run cooperatively by the landless farm laborers, or be left in the hands of small tenants who would continue to work the land at much-reduced rents.[11]

The bourgeois parties, according to Jaurès, were quite indifferent to peasant needs despite their ritualistic praise of the peasant virtues; their secret goal was a completely capitalist agriculture, and that goal was fast coming into sight as large ownership encroached on the smallowner. The Méline tariff, he contended, was a device to achieve this bourgeois end; for the large capitalist farmers alone would profit by its illusory remedy of higher farm prices. In fact, however, statistics did not lend much support to Jaurès's thesis that large farming was rapidly crowding out small agriculture. Furthermore, the Socialists' switch to defense of the small farmer had its regressive side, in that it sacrificed "the 'productive' thrust of original Marxism to a concern for justice-in-distribution characteristic of the stalemate society."[12]

Yet the new party line, as expressed by Jaurés, exposed a fundamental weakness in the dominant dogma of the time—the myth of peasant unity, of a common interest and a common way of life binding all rural elements together. By recognizing the existence of deep clefts within the rural population, and by advocating two different policies for France's two agricultures, Jaurès and the Socialists first formulated a point of view that would not prevail for another half-century. In the years before the First World War, Socialist appeals were only beginning to penetrate the countryside. The first converts were farm laborers of the northeast, and scattered clusters of marginal smallowners and tenants in the center and the southwest.

Meanwhile one other sign of a new approach to peasant problems was appearing in the remote back country of Brittany. Few parts of France had retained so much of the flavor of the *ancien régime*. Social relationships were still marked by a quasi-feudal spirit; when some Social Catholic aristocrats began to found right-wing syndicates there after 1884, they were regarded by many fellow landlords as revolutionaries, not much better than socialists. Despite the gains achieved by liming acid soil, farming in Brittany was hard. The overcrowded land barely provided a living for the tenant farmers, whose wives were far more fertile than their soil.

Into this rural backwater came, in 1897, a vigorous and iconoclastic young Breton priest. Félix Trochu, a native of Morbihan, might be described as an unfrocked Radical; he had been brought up in a fiercely anticlerical family, and he always retained the combative spirit of his parents. After his clerical training, he promptly joined the tiny new faction of Christian Democrats, whose adherents found the older Social Catholicism much too bigoted and narrow. Trochu's superiors, already irritated by his crusading zeal for urban working-class reform, lost all patience when he was so indiscreet as to cry "Vive la république!" at a public meeting. He was promptly exiled to a remote rural parish near Saint-Malo, where he soon discovered that misery and injustice were not confined to cities and towns. He set to work at once to organize local syndicates and mutual credit and insurance societies in the villages roundabout, and before long he began to encourage other country priests to follow his example.

Trochu was an impassioned exponent of what he called "peasant emancipation"; he sharply challenged the Social Catholics' idea of a single *classe paysanne*. Diversity and conflict, he believed, were genuine and deep-seated; he insisted, therefore, on the need for "parallel syndicates" that would separate landowners from cash tenants and share tenants. Such a conception outraged conservatives wherever Trochu sought to spread his gospel.

In 1899 Trochu and a few collaborators founded a Christian Democratic daily newspaper in Rennes. This paper, *L'Ouest-Eclair*, was shortly to become the most influential paper in Brittany, and for some thirty-five years Trochu was to remain (in fact though not in name) its editor. For a generation the idea of "peasant emancipation," of peasant activism at the grass-roots level, was steadfastly preached in its columns. Meanwhile the work of village organization was carried forward, against great difficulties, by a number of Trochu's friends and disciples in the clergy—particularly after 1918. The enduring consequences of this long campaign can be easily detected in the Brittany of our own day. In no other part of France is agrarian syndicalism so solidly implanted at the village level, so remarkably disciplined, so tough and effective. Nowhere else has the small peasantry been so successful in developing its own corps of leaders, dedicated to the cause for which the Abbé Trochu began to work two generations ago.[13]

* *

One important development in the decades before 1914 was a gradual easing of population pressure in many parts of the countryside, owing to the nation's declining birth rate and the drift to the towns and cities. In the early 1890's the steady increase in the number of farms operated in France—an increase that had continued unbroken since the Revolution—slowed, stopped, and was reversed. The government's agricultural survey of 1892 showed a total of 3.5 million farms—almost the same as ten years earlier. By 1929, the figure had fallen to about 2.9 million—mainly owing to the absorption of tiny farms into medium-sized ones.[14]

On the whole, large farming showed no tendency to increase, except in the Paris basin and the northeast, where concentration had begun as early as the eighteenth century. Much of the land here was operated not by owners but by prosperous tenants, who rented parcels belonging to dozens of scattered owners who had departed for the cities. In much of central and southern France, on the other hand, the rural exodus left a great deal of land unworked, especially when its agricultural value was marginal. In some parts of the south, the outflow of French peasants was partially balanced by a new inflow of Italian farmers, eager for land on any terms. The standard pattern for these newcomers was share tenantry, which enabled an immigrant blessed with no resources save a large family to take over an abandoned farm by sharing the proceeds with the absentee owner. A generation later, after much toil and scrimping, these immigrants often managed to buy a piece of land, or to move down from the relatively barren hill regions into the fertile valleys. Only in heavily overpopulated areas like Brittany, where large families remained the rule, did the rural exodus produce little effect. All it did there was to keep the intense pressure on the land within bearable limits, and to provide Parisian housewives with a constant supply of low-paid, hard-working Breton maids.

Adequate figures on farm income, or on the peasants' share of the total national income, are not available for the decades before the war. Probably the peasantry in 1914 was somewhat better off on the whole than it had been fifty years earlier; but the improvement, if any, had been neither uniform nor steady nor very great. From about 1880 to the turn of the century, French agriculture suffered from a prolonged crisis, caused by the competition of imported grain and meat, by a general economic slackness throughout western Europe, and by the disastrous impact of a vine disease called phylloxera. French wheat, which had long been an item of export, could no longer compete in foreign markets after 1880; over the next twenty years its price in France dropped by almost one-third. Phylloxera, which struck the south in 1875 and spread rapidly into other regions, destroyed about half of the nation's vineyards before it could be brought under control. The crisis speeded the drift to the cities, and buttressed the arguments of high-tariff advocates. Thanks to Méline, the wheatgrowers were able to stay in business; thanks to disease-resistant grape roots imported from the United States, the winegrowers were able to make a new start. Most vineyards now were transferred from the dry, rocky hillsides to the fertile bottom land of the Midi that had formerly nourished other crops.* These new vineyards lent themselves to large-scale production; their yield was very high, though of middling quality. Their success increased the tendency toward monoculture in a large section of the Midi, which thus became more susceptible to the fluctuations of the market.

The reconstruction of the vineyards promptly landed the winegrowers in a new crisis—the consequence of overproduction and disorderly marketing. From 1900 to 1907, wine prices lagged so badly that most growers were forced to sell at a loss. The desperate situation in the Midi led in 1907 to the most violent peasant disorders that France had known since the Revolution. Passions were whipped up by a curious agitator named Marcellin Albert, a bearded messiah who left his small vineyard to lead a taxpayers' strike, to arrange the mass resignation of mayors and town councils in several hundred communes, and to harangue crowds that (according to some estimates) reached half

---

* No substitute crop could be found for the old vineyard land on the hillsides. Traces of those vanished vineyards, like archeological relics of a dead civilization, can still be seen today in certain parts of southern France.

a million. Troops had to be called out to maintain order; there was violence, and even some bloodshed. It took Premier Clemenceau to put a final stop to Albert's activities.*

In the end, salvation came to the winegrowers not through governmental action but through a combination of market developments and self-help. In 1907 the Midi winegrowers decided to join forces to police the market against suspected fraud.[15] Their new Confédération Générale des Vignerons du Midi (CGVM) grappled effectively with the fraud problem; it soon boasted a membership of 70,000, and its example was copied by winegrowers of other regions. In 1913 these various regional groupings pooled their strength on a nation-wide basis, forming the Fédération des Associations Viticoles (FAV). Thus there emerged, as a kind of by-product of the great wine crisis, the first of the so-called "specialized associations" that were destined to gain such momentum in the interwar period.

* *

No episode in the modern era marked the French peasantry so indelibly as the First World War. Twenty years later, Premier Edouard Daladier was to justify his retreat at Munich on the ground that France must not "sacrifice another million or two million peasants"; and he added (to mixed applause and protests) that 80 per cent of the front-line soldiers in the First World War had been peasants.[16] Perhaps he exaggerated; yet it is clear that no other segment of society sacrificed so much in the war. Draft deferments, which were common for urban

---

* Albert, who came to Paris in person to present the winegrowers' grievances, succumbed to Clemenceau's blandishments and agreed to urge moderation on his disciples. Worse still, he accepted a hundred-franc bill from Clemenceau to buy his return ticket. His adherents concluded that he had been bought off by the government. The passage of time has restored Albert's halo, and has made him a kind of folk hero of the winegrowing Midi. An activist organization founded there after the Second World War adopted the name Comité Marcellin Albert.

groups, were rare exceptions in the countryside; three-fifths of all men actively engaged in agriculture were mobilized, and most of these recruits were assigned to the infantry. Farms continued to operate, thanks mainly to the efforts of old men, women, and children. When the casualty lists were totaled at the end of the war, 53 per cent of the dead or missing were peasants.[17] No one can stand before a village *monument aux morts* without being shaken by the cruel record carved there in stone.

True, there was another side to the war experience. For those peasants who remained on the farm, the period brought a degree of prosperity (or at least an appearance of prosperity) that was quite unprecedented. The desperate need for foodstuffs and raw materials drove prices upward despite governmental controls; even the small subsistence peasant was pulled into the market economy and managed to store away a small hoard of banknotes. In the postwar years, much of France's farm indebtedness could be paid off, and many peasants could expand their holdings by purchasing long-coveted strips of soil. To a considerable degree, however, these wartime profits represented a kind of enforced saving that derived from the inability to buy needed equipment and fertilizer during the war. They were also canceled in part by currency inflation.

For a time after 1918, it seemed that the over-all effect of the war had been merely, as one commentator put it, "to speed up the earlier evolution of agriculture, without changing its direction."[18] Thirty years later, the same commentator could view the war with deeper comprehension as "a turning point rather than a mere stage in the history of [French] agriculture—mainly because it profoundly altered the peasant mentality."[19] Generalizations of this sort are almost impossible to test, or even to state with much precision; yet they may be perfectly valid. The mobilization of a whole generation of young peasants, and their exposure to barracks life and trench warfare, unquestionably had a profound effect on those who experienced it. Many of these veterans could not reconcile themselves to the simple village life they had known; they preferred to look for factory or white-collar jobs. In those who remained on the farm throughout the conflict, a subtler process of change undoubtedly occurred. Contact with young men home on leave from camp or from the front must have given them a broader view of life. For almost the first time in French rural history, their lives were intimately bound up with events occurring far from the village. Their increased importance in the national economy, and their temporary prosperity, may also have given them new confidence and self-respect.

Yet the deeper effects of the wartime experience seem to have been not confidence and self-respect, but a bitter resentment, an increased hostility toward politicians and the urban world, a sense of being victimized and misunderstood. Some Frenchmen, in the years that followed, held that the war had done much to bridge the gap between town and country. More often, it seems to have widened that gap, and to have added new tensions. The peasants felt that they had earned not only the admiration and gratitude of the city-dwellers, but a fully recognized equality of status in French society. Instead, the urbanites complained of the high price of food in the immediate postwar years, and grumbled at the well-fed, grasping "peasant profiteer." A Parisian newspaper published a caustic description of a war-enriched clodhopper proudly driving a new automobile into town with a calf reposing beside him on the front seat, and the disparaging epithet *cul-terreux* came into current use. On balance, urban-rural tensions were probably heightened rather than reduced by the wartime experience; and many peasants reaped from it an increased but embittered self-consciousness.

At the time, this change of temper seems to have gone largely unnoticed. The shrewd historian-essayist Daniel Halévy did not notice it in 1920, when he made one of his periodic pilgrimages to a rural area that he knew well. It was the economic crisis a decade later that broke the crust on the peasants' long-repressed bitterness. When Halévy returned to the provinces in 1934, he found them gripped by what he described as a *sombre humeur,* in which memories of the war constituted a major ingredient. "They don't speak much about their suffering," he wrote, "but they forget nothing, and at the bottom of their embittered hearts there remains a desire for vengeance. Their rancor has slumbered for fifteen years . . . , but the crisis has torn away the veil; it has set free the old resentments and is arousing new ones."[20] Halévy's impressions were those of an outsider, Parisian and intellectual to the core; yet he was sensitive enough to see the signs of a fundamental change in rural attitudes, and to detect that the new peasant self-consciousness of the depression decade was rooted in the experience of the war.

* *

The country's policymakers, however, were occupied with continuity rather than change in the postwar decade. French statesmen, like those of other Western nations, were more concerned to return to "normalcy" than to move forward into a new era. Little effort was made to re-examine the role of agriculture in the nation's economy, or that of the peasantry in the nation's society. Although there was increased talk of "modernization" and "progress," these terms were mainly attached to plans for industrial growth. The peasants were left largely to themselves, except that the government perpetuated wartime controls on farm exports throughout most of the decade. The false prosperity of the war period ended early in the 1920's, as French and world agricultural production climbed back to normal. By the middle of the decade, French farmers (like those of most countries) were suffering from what contemporaries called "the price scissors." One natural result was a resumption of the prewar population shift from country to city, this time at a faster pace than ever before.

Neither parliament nor government offered much in the way of constructive leadership in agricultural matters. If politicians defended the peasantry against urban critics, they did so only with oratorical weapons. Annually at budget time, or in the course of interpellations on agricultural policy, a long parade of deputies and senators took the rostrum one by one to voice what they took to be their constituents' grievances. These so-called "agricultural debates" took place before an almost empty Chamber; each speaker catalogued the particular complaints of his voters, and thus got himself usefully on the record. No party spokesman sought to relate the needs of the peasantry to those of the nation as a whole.

Legislative action on farm issues was sporadic and, on the whole, meager. Just after the war ended, several promising bills were adopted: to finance the re-equipment of farms in the war-devastated areas, to encourage the regrouping of scattered land parcels, and to improve and systematize agricultural education at all levels. Only the first of these had much effect; the others lacked either teeth or adequate financing.[21] Some measures were also adopted to strengthen existing farm organizations or to create new ones. The farm cooperatives were at last given a basic statute; state agencies called *offices agricoles* were set up in each department, with the mission of furthering technical experimentation and demonstration; and the long-debated system of *chambres d'agriculture* (first proposed in 1840) was at last approved.*

---

* The *offices agricoles* were regarded by many conservatives as a Radical Socialist device to avert the establishment of elective *chambres d'agriculture*. The Chambres would presumably be controlled by the conservatives in many regions, whereas the Offices reported to the Ministry of Agriculture through its departmental agents. The Offices were abolished in 1935 as an economy measure.

The broad outlines of the original plan were followed fairly closely. The Chambers—one in each department—were designed to be the peasants' official representative organs, empowered to discuss ways of advancing agriculture's interests and to transmit the farmers' opinions to the government. Elected by the peasantry, they would enjoy an assured (though small) income from a share of the land tax. The Chambers began to function in 1924, but it soon became clear that their impact would be slight unless they could fuse the strength of their ninety departmental units. Extralegally, the presidents of the Chambers began to meet periodically in Paris and to develop a central secretariat. Left-wing cabinets frowned on this practice, but during the ministry of Pierre Laval in 1935 it was legalized by decree. The new central agency bore the clumsy title Assemblée Permanente des Présidents des Chambres d'Agriculture; it was more commonly known as the APPCA. It had barely begun to function effectively when the republic fell in 1940; and although it was dominated by conservatives, the Vichy regime promptly abolished it together with the departmental Chambers. After a long interlude, the Chambers and the APPCA were to be resurrected by the Fourth Republic.

On two occasions during the 1920's, programs of somewhat broader agrarian reform or development were presented to parliament. Both proposals failed of adoption. The first plan, in 1920, was inspired by a tract written just after the war by one of France's leading agricultural experts, Pierre Caziot.[22] France's future, according to Caziot, lay in the consolidation and further extension of peasant ownership. Economically as well as socially, the family farm was the ideal unit upon which to build a sound agriculture and a healthy nation; therefore vigorous state action was needed to regroup excessively small holdings and to partition large holdings into family-size units. The Caziot plan called for the creation of regional land societies, organized by farmers' associations and subsidized by the state, with authority to buy and restructure farm land as it might come on the market, and to sell it on easy terms to worthy tenant farmers or peasants' sons. Although the Chamber's committee on agriculture reported the bill out favorably, it failed to reach the floor of parliament. Buried for a generation, the scheme was to be resurrected in modified form some forty years later, when de Gaulle's Fifth Republic set out to experiment with structural reform.[23]

In 1927, another plan of a quite different sort was advanced by Minister of Agriculture Henri Queuille, a Radical Socialist from the hill country of central France. Queuille's scheme was designed to increase farm production and productivity by means of a program of state technical aid extending over a number of years. It proposed to appropriate a billion francs for the purpose, half of which would go to research and education, the rest to the modernization of production and marketing. Advocates of the plan hoped to provide the rural areas with a network of trained agronomists—at least one to each canton—and to subsidize such experiments as the collective purchase and use of agricultural machinery. Although everyone paid lip service to the proposal, the appropriation was cut out of the 1928 budget, for most politicians at the moment were in a cautious mood and doubted that funds could be found for so costly an investment in the future.

Such action as the state took on behalf of agriculture during the 1920's was of the modest, short-term variety, the only kind possible in view of the limited budgetary credits granted annually to the Ministry of Agriculture. But at least the long and undramatic task of bringing electricity and running water into the villages was carried steadily forward; by 1940 electricity was available in 96 per cent of the communes, and one commune out of three was supplied with water. Other problems, such as the grave deficiencies of rural housing, went almost untouched and even unmentioned.* Perhaps the most representative state action of this decade of "normalcy" was the much-publicized scheme of Minister of Agriculture Henri Chéron to decorate peasants whose ancestors had worked the same land, in unbroken succession, for at least five hundred years.[24] For the politicians, the past still seemed to hold a greater charm than the future.

* *

The postwar decade brought a new drive for more effective professional organization of the farmers—though there was still little grass-roots activity. In 1919 a group of prewar agrarian syndicalist leaders created the Confédération Nationale des Associations Agricoles (CNAA)—the first serious effort at organized peasant unity. The CNAA was designed not to replace the existing syndical and cooperative organizations, but to serve as a coordinating body or capstone; its board of directors was made up of representatives of the older groups. Some CNAA enthusiasts hoped that it might gradually come to speak for a united peasantry, but they were quickly disappointed. As one veteran syndicalist put it, "The CNAA is a table around which we can talk; it must have no other pretension."[25] Political rivalries combined with professional jealousies to hamper the CNAA's further development; it never managed to move beyond its limited coordinating function.

The older syndical and cooperative movements continued to operate much as they had done in prewar days. Occasionally

* According to the census of 1946, the average age of rural houses was 120 years. An official survey in the 1950's showed that although 90 per cent of all peasant homes had electricity, only 34 per cent had running water, only 10 per cent had inside toilet facilities, and only 4 per cent had a bath or shower. The number of rural homes classed as *taudis* (slum dwellings) was 750,000—a proportion as high as that of urban areas (*Paysans*, nos. 18 and 20, June–July and Oct.–Nov. 1959, pp. 73–75 and 66–67). In Brittany as late as 1950, a large proportion of peasant homes consisted of a single room with a dirt floor.

they went beyond mere technical and commercial activities to engage in educational programs or in some mild lobbying. But neither right-wing nor left-wing syndicalism showed much vigor; the same old leaders remained in control, unchallenged by any new elite. What organizing energy there was went into another type of organization—the so-called "specialized association," speaking for the growers of a particular crop. The winegrowers, it will be recalled, had pioneered in this kind of enterprise before the war with the creation of the CGVM; during the 1920's similar organizations were set up for almost every important product. The most influential ones, owing to sheer numbers or to vigorous leadership and solidarity, were the CGVM, the wheatgrowers' Association Générale des Producteurs de Blé (AGPB), and the beetgrowers' Confédération Générale des Betteraviers (CGB).

By 1930 it was clear that the specialized association was the most effective formula yet devised for attracting peasant support and for lobbying in parliament. Its advantage over the syndicates was obvious: its principle of action was based on a common material interest. Each association knew exactly what it wanted, and could devote its full effort to formulating a precise set of demands. Unfortunately, this concentration on matters of special interest rarely served the general interest—whether of the peasantry as a whole, or of the nation. The growing influence of the new associations, the pressures they could bring to bear on parliament, threatened to introduce an increased fragmentation into the government's agricultural policy.

On at least two occasions rival associations—the winegrowers and the beetgrowers—negotiated with each other almost like sovereign powers, reconciled their differences in a kind of treaty, and persuaded parliament to enact that treaty into law. After the First World War, a sharp rivalry developed between the winegrowers and the beetgrowers over the right to distill their respective crops into alcohol. Spokesmen for the two groups met at Béziers in 1922 and worked out an agreement to share the market and to link the prices of beet and wine alcohol. The agreement depended on the government's willingness to buy excess production for distillation, and to mix the resulting alcohol with gasoline to form what was euphemistically called a *carburant national*. This the government agreed to do in 1923. When the arrangement was threatened during the economic crisis of the 1930's, the beetgrowers and winegrowers met again (at Narbonne in 1935) and successfully revised their "treaty." Again the government accepted their terms.[26]

From the outset, control of the specialized associations fell to the big producers, who possessed the resources, the time, and the technical training to establish and run such organizations. Furthermore, the large growers stood to gain the most if a favorable price or tariff or tax deduction could be secured. For obvious reasons, however, they sought to enlist as many small-peasant members as possible, and claimed to speak for large and small growers alike. Both shrewd calculation and sincere conviction doubtless entered into their thinking. Politicians were more likely to heed an organization that spoke of defending the small peasant; but, in addition, the large growers often genuinely shared the peasantist views of the politicians. Many small peasants did join one or more specialized associations, even though their polycultural farms produced only minute quantities for the market. Whether the small grower really benefited from membership in these organizations is a complex issue, one that was debated at length after the Second World War.

Only in Brittany were there any significant signs during the 1920's of a grass-roots movement designed to awaken the small peasantry to active self-defense and self-help. After 1918 the pioneering efforts of the Abbé Trochu and his adherents began to show important results. A young priest, the Abbé Mancel, became the new apostle of "peasant emancipation," and began to organize syndicates open only to what he called *cultivateurs cultivants*. Thanks to the powerful support of Trochu's journal,

L'Ouest-Eclair, the movement prospered. In 1920 these local syndicates were grouped into a new organization, the *Fédération des Syndicats Paysans de l'Ouest;* in 1921 a periodical called *Progrès rural* began to appear; in 1926 a peasant youth group —the first important one in modern France—was formed, and became an affiliate of the Fédération. By the end of the decade the Fédération had syndicates and youth affiliates in two hundred Breton communes, and was beginning to spread southward into the Vendée as well. In 1927, a regional congress of Mancel's Fédération and youth-group organization drew more than 1,200 participants; a similar congress of the old-line right-wing syndical movement attracted only 300. With its own network of mutual credit and insurance facilities, and with the dynamism provided by its young activists, the Fédération seemed to be emerging as a serious rival to the conservative Landerneau syndical group, whose aristocratic leaders had long regarded Brit-tany as their fief.

The Cardinal-Archbishop of Rennes, Alexis Charost, viewed Mancel's movement as potentially "more dangerous even than the workers' syndicalism of the cities."[27] Breton conservatives were already fuming at Trochu's journalistic crusade in support of the new Christian Democratic party (the Popular Democrats), and at his attacks on the neo-monarchist Action Française (which had wide support in Brittany, notably in the Catholic hierarchy). Every bishop in the region publicly warned his flock to shun Mancel's syndicates. "Beware of these peasant leagues," cried Charost, "that . . . seek to entangle your syndicates in a serpent's coils. The Church's doctrine is that of Jesus Christ, who recommends the union of classes."[28] The conservatives denounced Mancel as a demagogue, a destroyer of rural unity, and a traducer of young Catholics, whom he was encouraging to associate with anti-clericals and unbelievers. They quoted a Breton Socialist leader who had written, somewhat incautiously: "The Abbés Mancel and

Trochu are working for us. On the day of Socialism's triumph
. . . we will have to thank these Sillonist abbés, who, by awaken-
ing the peasants to new ideas, are hastening the hour when the
army of peasants, laborers, and intellectual workers will carry
out the social revolution."[29]

For a time Mancel and Trochu managed to resist, thanks to
the Vatican's silent support. But in 1930, Charost finally succeeded in forcing Trochu's withdrawal from the staff of *L'Ouest-
Eclair*. The simultaneous impact of the depression soon completed the destruction of Mancel's syndicates; their credit system
collapsed, and their desperate appeals for financial aid from their
old rival, the Landerneau group, were ignored. Some of Mancel's young activists were soon to find a new messiah in the agrarian demagogue Henri Dorgères; others sank into disillusioned
silence; still others retired to await the day when a small-peasant
movement grounded on democratic ideals might be able to survive and prosper in France.*

---

* A much feebler attempt at grass-roots activism developed in the southwest during the 1920's. The organizer of this Entente Paysanne (1925)
was a Cahors journalist and agronomist named Edmond Jacquet. His movement made some converts in the southern Massif and the southwest, but it
quickly collapsed when the depression destroyed its Peasant Bank. A number of its militants then joined the new Parti Agraire (see below, Chapter 3).

3

The End of Lethargy: The Great
Depression

FROM time to time something happens to stir up the sluggish stream of rural life, and perhaps even to make it change its course. In France, one of these crucial episodes was the Great Depression. "This epoch," writes a young peasant leader of our own day, "marked the beginning of a new stage for the peasant world, the full development of which would not take place until after the Second World War. That stage can be described as the arrival of the peasant mass at an awareness of its collective needs—an awareness whose slow maturation is occurring before our eyes."[1]

It is debatable whether the depression really initiated a rural revolution, or merely speeded one that was already in the making. Very possibly the impact of the Great War and the tensions of the postwar decade had already prepared the peasantry for a fundamental change of temper, so that the depression merely provided the culminating shock. At any rate, the depression years constitute a kind of watershed. Before the depression, the peasantry was for the most part passive, inarticulate, atomized. Since the depression, the peasantry has become increasingly active, vocal, organized. The transition was not an immediate one; indeed, it is still in process today.

That the depression should have had so great an impact may seem paradoxical, for the peasants were not its only victims, perhaps not even its principal victims. Most economists contend that industrial prices dropped more sharply than agricultural prices, so that the price scissors of the 1920's were temporarily reversed in favor of agriculture.[2] Besides, the very backwardness of many marginal small farms gave them a peculiar advantage in a period of crisis. A raft may be slower than a speedboat, but it is a good deal more stable in heavy weather. The precapitalist small farmer, largely self-sufficient even in normal times, was only indirectly affected by the collapse of world trade. From 1930 to 1936, the century-old rural exodus seems to have slowed considerably; indeed, it was partially offset by a reverse current, unemployed city workers returning to the family farm to ride out the depression.[3]

Yet even though the peasants were shielded against certain effects of the crisis, they too could feel its impact, and their pent-up discontent began to break through the surface. Agricultural prices dropped by about 50 per cent between 1930 and 1935; but world prices dropped even more drastically, and there was widespread alarm lest the world glut of wheat and wine might suddenly be dumped on the French market. The peasants' total buying power, which, according to the most widely quoted statistician of the period, had finally regained the 1913 level (1913 = 100) in 1928–29, fell to approximately 90 in 1930, fluctuated between 87 and 85 during the next three years, then fell again to 77 in 1934 and to 72 in 1935.[4] Further evidence of the farm crisis was provided by tax statistics. In 1929, the number of farmers subject to the so-called surtax on agricultural profits was 633,471; by 1935 it had fallen to 92,233.[5]

Agitators and organizers began to find willing listeners in the countryside. In Chartres in March 1933, a mass meeting called by the newly formed Parti Agraire attracted a huge crowd (some carrying the symbolic pitchfork); before the day was out, the prefect had been attacked, and a number of demonstrators and policemen had been injured in violent street clashes. In 1934, for the first time in modern French history, an angry crowd of peasants converged on Paris to demonstrate on the Champs-Elysées, and the dairymen of the Paris region staged France's first successful producers' strike.[6] No wonder Halévy spoke of a *sombre humeur*. Silent and docile in the old days, the typical peasant (according to Halévy) had grown "disillusioned and bitter"; he was "saddened by the justifiable reflection that he had been abandoned in the solitude of his fields, and that his labors were viewed with contempt."[7] Some dedicated apostles of the peasantry were appalled at the change in mood. Thanks to the corrupting influence of demagogic politicians, wrote Michel Augé-Laribé toward the end of the decade, the peasants had learned to demand and protest, to direct incessant appeals to the state. "The peasant soul," he mourned, "has deteriorated in quality. . . . One may properly ask whether the agricultural population of this country still possesses that solidity that has caused it to be regarded as the foundation of the nation."[8]

* *

Neither the parties nor the individual politicians could ignore the signs of distress and resentment in the countryside; willingly or not, they were forced to grapple with rural problems. Tariff protection, flood relief, and electrification were no longer adequate palliatives; the state was drawn steadily deeper into a policy of intervention in agriculture—a policy which, once begun, could never really be reversed. Although state action during the depression years was piecemeal and somewhat incoherent, its general character was consistently Malthusian; it sought to check the fall in farm prices by adapting output to the shrunken level of domestic consumption. Such reductions in output, however, proved difficult to achieve.

The first steps were taken by André Tardieu, the brilliant

but arrogant Parisian deputy who astonished his colleagues by volunteering for the post of Minister of Agriculture in 1931. Although no one in political life could have had less in common with the peasantry, Tardieu flung himself with his customary energy into devising a program for the crisis. Perhaps his purpose was to build a nation-wide political clientele rather than to save the peasantry. In any case, his remedies were more drastic than those of any Minister of Agriculture for a generation. They included a scheme to orient production by subsidizing certain items in short supply; a system of quota restrictions to reinforce the tariff barrier against foreign farm products; and an attempt to regulate the production and marketing of wine. Tardieu's wine statute was designed to limit the planting of new vineyards, to impose a steeply progressive tax on large producers, and to authorize the government to block the marketing of part of the harvest. Despite sharp attacks from many quarters, the project (considerably modified) became law in 1931. Some conservatives saw it as an ominous precedent that might lead to more state control over agriculture. They were not entirely wrong, but their hands-off alternative might have led even more rapidly to the same result.

Tardieu's reforms, striking though they were, proved to be quite inadequate, and his successors did no better. Their efforts focused mainly on wheat and wine—the "electoral crops" par excellence, for wheat was produced by 1.9 million farmers and wine by 1.6 million. Almost every imaginable scheme was tried to buttress the price of wheat: a minimum price law, controls on acreage, state purchase of the surplus crop, the establishment of an "interprofessional" committee on marketing, even a brief and disastrous return to complete marketing freedom. During one eighteen-month period, parliament debated five successive schemes of widely varying character. Despite all these efforts, the price of wheat stubbornly continued to drop from year to year, until in 1935 it allegedly reached the lowest point since the French Revolution.[9] Only toward the end of 1935 did an upturn come; and although the Laval cabinet claimed credit for this triumph, many observers traced it to a simpler cause—the persistent rains that destroyed most of that year's wheat harvest.

A solution to the wine problem proved to be almost as difficult. Tardieu's wine statute of 1931 contained too many loopholes to be effective, as one bumper crop succeeded another both in France and in Algeria. In 1933 parliament plugged some of these loopholes; sharper controls on new planting were instituted, and the state was given increased authority to block the marketing of part of the harvest. A huge crop in 1934 promptly wrecked this law; parliament once again tightened the restrictions on planting and marketing, and ordered the compulsory distillation of part of the crop by the state's Service des Alcools for use as fuel. Still the price drop continued. Midway through 1935, the Laval cabinet again reinforced the restrictions, this time by decree-law. Blockage and compulsory distillation were extended; so was the special tax on production, which would henceforth be paid by middle-sized as well as large winegrowers. The decree-law also provided subsidies for the uprooting of vineyards, and warned that this practice might have to be made compulsory. Once again, however, the weather came to the aid of the hard-pressed politicians; short crops in 1936 and 1937 brought an end to the glut, at least for the time being. The much-amended wine statute remained on the books as the cornerstone of the state's wine policy, even though its effectiveness had been dubious. Its meager success depended largely on the provisions for compulsory distillation, which required the Service des Alcools to buy an annual share of the crop at a fixed price. Since the resulting product was sold at a loss to industrial firms or mixed with gasoline to form high-cost motor fuel, the cost of this operation had to be borne by French taxpayers and motorists. If this was a solution of sorts, it was hardly a sensible one.[10]

Although wheat and wine together produced less than 30 per cent of the nation's farm income,[11] the growers of other crops —beetgrowers excepted—were too scattered or too poorly organized to make their influence felt very strongly. The beetgrowers, small in numbers and tightly organized, managed to limit production by imposing their own acreage controls. In addition, they used diplomacy and pressure to keep a share of the lucrative alcohol market. Part of their crop, like that of the winegrowers, continued to be bought by the Service des Alcools at a fixed price, thus ensuring them a steady income at the taxpayers' expense.

The haphazard character of the state's agricultural policy in the depression years strengthened the appeal of certain systematizers who claimed to have sure solutions for the country's agricultural problems. Foremost in this category was the Socialist Party, which for some years had been advocating the creation of *offices*—i.e., governmental regulatory and marketing agencies— for various major crops.* After 1930 the Socialists repeatedly introduced bills to establish a Wheat Office and a Wine Office; and on one occasion (shortly after the 1932 elections brought a swing to the left) they persuaded the Chamber of Deputies to approve the Wheat Office. The bill was blocked by the Senate, however; and four subsequent tries in the Chamber proved futile. Many rightists and Radicals believed (or professed to believe) that organizations of this sort would pave the way to complete state control of agriculture, and eventually to outright socialization. Nevertheless, the idea of permanent market regulation began to make some converts outside Socialist ranks—notably in

---

* These were different from the *offices agricoles* mentioned on p. 32.

the new Parti Agraire. But the Agrarians' aim was to create agencies that would be run by the profession rather than by the state; it thus reflected their vaguely corporatist outlook.

* *

The depression aroused at least a few Frenchmen to go beyond the short-term problem of farm prices and reflect on the larger problems of agrarian structure. Neither the peasants nor the politicians led the way in this doctrinal discussion; for the time being, the issue drew the attention only of agricultural specialists and urban intellectuals.

According to one school of thought, French agriculture should be radically reorganized for maximum productivity. To these "neo-physiocrats" or "industrializers," the test of success was a simple one: the highest possible production at the lowest possible cost. To that end, marginal land ought to be taken out of cultivation, uneconomic crops ought to be abandoned, the disappearance of microfundia (excessively small farms) ought to be hastened, and emphasis ought to be placed on specialized education and technical aid. Some exponents of this thesis relied on natural evolution within a laissez-faire system to do the job; others held that the state would have to intervene to speed the process. As one impatient reformer put it, "If the small farmer chooses to vegetate at home, that's his own business; but if the whole country suffers the consequences, that's something else again. . . . We don't need peasants to have sound agriculture."[12]

Conservatives disagreed. Predictably, they saw the problem as fundamentally social rather than economic. Their favorite slogan was borrowed from the Swiss novelist C.-F. Ramuz: "Being a peasant is not a job, but a way of life." The preservation or restoration of peasant farming, they asserted, is well worth some sacrifice in technical efficiency. "The peasant world today presents . . . a last great island not yet inundated by mass society."[13] To men of this persuasion, the rural exodus of the past century was a tragic betrayal of France's true heritage, and the central aim of a proper agrarian policy should be to root the smallowner on the soil. Most politicians shared this view, in some degree at least. Parliament's legislation on wheat and wine during the depression era always embodied special privileges or exemptions for the small grower, whose interests were warmly defended by speakers from every party. Even the Socialists came out for the family farmer, a category redefined to include those who hired a little help in the busy season.[14]

Peasantist doctrine had an old pedigree in France. What was new in the depression era was the discovery, or rediscovery, of corporative theory by some of the peasantists, who seized upon it as the cure to all the nation's ills. A few of the new converts found their inspiration in Fascist Italy; Roger Grand, president of the UCSAF, was received by Mussolini in 1933 and came away singing the praises of this "most illustrious of present-day reformers," this historic figure who, like Charlemagne, had grasped the trend of an age.[15] Some others, like the younger syndical official Rémy Goussault, were more impressed by the German example, and eagerly accepted invitations to visit the Third Reich for a firsthand look at the *Blut und Boden* experiments of Hitler and Walther Darré. But most French corporatists shied away from statism in favor of a pluralist and professional corporate organization entrusted with broad powers to shape its own destiny within the state.[16] Their doctrine did not imply that part of the state's legitimate powers should be transferred to the organized professions. Rather, the state must be stripped of powers that it had allegedly usurped from certain "organic collectivities." A weak state and a strong society built on hierarchical and organic principles—this was their goal.

In the depression years, a small group of young intellectuals and bureaucrats (most of them employed in the central offices of various agrarian syndicates and cooperatives) began to meet informally at luncheon to discuss the corporatist idea. Some of these young doctrinaires were sons of prosperous landowners; most had attended one of the advanced agricultural schools (notably the Catholic Ecole d'Agriculture at Angers). Action promptly followed talk; in 1934 they gained control of France's largest syndical organization, the right-wing UCSAF. They promptly overhauled its administrative machinery, increased the degree of central control over regional and local units, and renamed the organization the Union Nationale des Syndicats Agricoles (UNSA). As a further mark of independence, its headquarters were soon transferred from the building of the conservative landlords' league in the Rue d'Athènes to a location in the Rue des Pyramides. The old UCSAF, declared the new leaders, had chosen to remain decentralized, and had sought only to organize the farmers. Its successors intended to stress the principle of national peasant unity, and meant not merely to organize the farmers, but to speak for them as well.[17]

Alongside the resurgent doctrines of the neo-physiocrats and the corporatists, a third conception of agrarian structure began to emerge in the depression decade. A number of agronomists and agricultural economists in French universities and advanced agricultural schools saw the Danish and Dutch systems as possible models for France.[18] Like the corporatists, these men wanted to keep a large population of small farmers on the soil. But like the neo-physiocrats, they contended that efficiency and productivity were of central importance—that to preserve a mass of marginal, subsistence-type peasants would merely guarantee an increase in social conflict and a corresponding decline in national solidarity. Their goal was a sharp expansion of government aid, educational facilities, and cooperative organizations, all with a view to transforming the small peasantry into efficient producers. The success of such a program, however, would depend on a long process of indoctrination aimed at both the peasants and the politicians; and neither the leaders of farm organizations nor the most influential members of parliament were yet prepared to take the lead in a campaign of this kind. The older agrarian elite was still too stubbornly traditionalist, the younger syndical leaders too enamored of their new corporatist gospel. As for the politicians, accustomed as they were to concentrating on short-range problems and easily diverted by other issues that seemed more pressing, most of the talk about structures seemed to them academic and irrelevant.

* *

While politicians improvised and doctrinaires pontificated, activists were at work finding practical ways to crystallize the discontent of the countryside. On the left, the Communists and the Socialists founded new peasant syndicates, in 1929 and 1933, respectively. On the right, the Parti Agraire, established in 1927 but almost unnoticed at first, began after 1930 to attract a following. Already, however, it was confronted by two right-wing rivals: the corporatist UNSA and the Comités de Défense Paysanne, created in 1928 by a curious rural demagogue named Henri Dorgères.

The Agrarian Party was the brainchild of an eccentric crusader, Gabriel Fleurant, who preferred to call himself Fleurant Agricola. A onetime lycée professor, he had abandoned the classroom in 1906 to become a full-time organizer of farm cooperatives. After the war he was attracted by the rise of peasant parties in the new nations of eastern Europe, and attended a congress of the "Green International" at Prague. Inspired by the experience, he managed to round up a few sympathizers and a financial angel (Jacques Casanova, attorney for a large milk-processing corporation), and launched his new party at Aurillac in 1927.

For several years its impact was slight; it was confined to the hill country of central France, and seemed unlikely to develop a national following. Part of the trouble was that the party's doctrine lacked clarity; its spokesmen sometimes urged a united "rural class" to oppose its urban enemies, sometimes called on the small peasantry to defend itself against the large landowners, and sometimes appealed for an alliance between the peasant owners and the urban middle class. These inconsistencies, and the fact that most of the party's spokesmen were urban intellectuals, lent some color to the charge that its founders were merely ambitious politicians seeking a vehicle on which to ride into parliament.

No one took the Agrarian Party seriously until the depression suddenly offered it new opportunities for demagoguery. In 1932 it managed to elect its first deputy (from the Puy-de-Dôme, in the Massif Central). By 1934 it was spreading outward from its original base in the massif, and could claim organized support in about one-third of the departments of France. Some of its leaders began to develop delusions of grandeur; they talked enthusiastically of entering three hundred candidates in the next elections, and of becoming the official political arm of a united peasantry by means of an organizational agreement with the various farm syndicates, cooperatives, and specialized associations.[19]

Meanwhile, however, the Agrarians had to face some dangerous new competitors for peasant support. The most spectacular of these was the movement headed by Dorgères, whose name was to become a symbol of barnyard demagoguery for a whole generation. Born in 1897 in a town near the Belgian border, the son of a butcher named d'Halluin, Dorgères moved to Brittany in 1923 to work on a newspaper of Action Française views. Finding his real name difficult for Bretons to pronounce, he adopted the pseudonym by which he was shortly to become notorious.[20] In 1927 he took over a moribund agricultural weekly journal in Rennes, and set out to make himself the peasants' tribune. When parliament in 1928 adopted a system of compulsory social insurance for farm laborers, Dorgères brought together some thirty outraged peasants of the region and founded the first of his Peasant Defense Committees.

The moment was propitious for Dorgères's brand of rabid protest.[21] As the atmosphere of economic crisis spread, many peasants were receptive to a voice that blamed all their difficulties on the corrupt politicians and the decadent town-dwellers. Dorgères profited, too, by the disintegration of the Abbé Mancel's Christian Democratic peasant syndicates in Brittany; some of Mancel's most vigorous young activists went over to Dorgerism.* More important, however, was the support he began to attract from certain influential right-wing figures like Jacques Le Roy Ladurie of the UNSA, Adolphe Pointier of the Wheatgrowers' Association, and Jacques Lemaigre-Dubreuil, founder of the Taxpayers' League. By 1935 Dorgères could claim a following of 35,000 (mainly concentrated in the west and north), and had enough financial support to establish a weekly and a monthly, both with nation-wide circulation. Also in 1935, he formed a youth group called the Jeunesses Paysannes, which, with its green-shirt uniform, its motto ("Believe, Obey, Serve"), and its symbol (a crossed pitchfork and sickle), gave Dorgerism a quasi-fascist tinge. His rising fame brought him an invitation to speak in the most exclusive lecture series in Paris; fashionable ladies applauded as he called the peasantry "the only sound force in the nation, undefiled by orgies, cocktails, or night-club balls."[22] Despite his freely expressed contempt for parliamentarism, he tried his luck at running for deputy; in a by-election at Blois in

---

* The most loyal convert was Jean Bohuon, a smallowner near Rennes, who became Dorgères's chief lieutenant in the Ille-et-Vilaine. In 1956 both Bohuon and Dorgères finally won election to the Chamber of Deputies, but they lost their seats when the Fourth Republic fell.

1935, he outdistanced all rivals in the first round of voting, and was barely beaten in the run-off by a coalition of all parties.

Dorgères's real talent, however, was demagogic rather than organizational or political. When critics disparaged him as "barren of ideas but expert in bellowing," he cheerfully replied: "So I'm only an agitator? All right then, I'll agitate!" Journalists reported that this unimpressive little man was somehow "transfigured" when he appeared before a rural mass meeting to whip up peasant passions, to call for a nation-wide tax strike, or to threaten that a host of pitchfork-armed peasants might soon descend on Paris to cleanse the Augean stables of parliament. Clashes with the police often accompanied his demonstrations, especially when peasant crowds were convoked to block sheriff's sales. A touch of barnyard humor won the hearts of many farmers. "We are the ones who represent reality! We are the ones who represent beefsteak!" On one occasion a heckling deputy was seized by Dorgères's Greenshirts and locked up in a pigcart until police arrived to rescue him—whereupon the Dorgerists ceremoniously sprayed the cart with disinfectant to make it fit for pigs again.[23]

All this agitation in the hitherto quiescent countryside aroused urban fears of a real jacquerie, with Dorgères emerging as a bucolic version of Mussolini or Hitler. But Dorgères, like the corporatists, rejected statism and sought to reduce the state to the role of mere arbiter among the organized professions. *"Vive la république corporative et familiale!"* was the slogan of his electoral campaign in 1935.

For a time, it seemed that the various right-wing currents in the countryside might flow together to form a powerful torrent. In July 1934, on the initiative of the Agrarian Party leaders, a Front Paysan was formed; its constituent units were the Agrarians, Dorgères's Committees, the UNSA, and several of the major specialized associations. This action was precipitated by a press announcement that a Socialist-Communist united front was in the making. Fleurant Agricola was named chairman of the Peasant Front's executive committee, and Dorgères secretary-general. The Front's manifesto was a curious blend of high-flown and demagogic phrases: it denounced the Marxists "and their protectors, the international bankers," and called for the establishment of a cleansed and "human" republic, based on the family and the farm.[24]

For a time, it seemed that the Peasant Front might catch on as the only force in France capable of challenging the emergent Popular Front in the 1936 elections. But by 1935, personal jealousies and doctrinal conflicts were causing cracks in the Peasant Front's impressive façade. The Agrarians' efforts to speak for organized agriculture as a whole were opposed by the Dorgerists and certain syndical leaders. Moderate elements in the Agrarian Party (and in the UNSA as well) deplored Dorgères's demagoguery, especially to the extent that it seemed to threaten the forcible overthrow of the government. Finally, the Agrarian Party was reluctant to endorse the corporative doctrine, which was central to both the UNSA program and the preaching of Dorgères. Late in 1935, the Peasant Front's activities were cut short; its executive committee announced that the Peasant Front label might not be used by any candidate for the Chamber. The Agrarians' dream of peasant political unity had been shattered.

Indeed, the Agrarian Party's own unity was in serious jeopardy. Some of its leaders were dedicated peasantists whose central goal was the defense of the small family farm, and these men were increasingly irritated at the invasion of the party by new and alien elements. Among these "immigrants" were several large landowners with political ambitions; worse yet, there were lawyers and other nonagrarians who (as the purists put it) "had never cultivated anything except chicanery." Some were doubtful republicans, having ties with Dorgères and with such groups as the authoritarian Croix de Feu and the quasi-fascist Solidarité Française.

Late in 1935 a faction of old party members led by Henri Noilhan, the Agrarians' secretary-general, and Louis Guillon, their only deputy, concluded that the party's leader, Fleurant Agricola, had secretly permitted the new elements to buy control of the party organ, *La Voix de la terre*. The Noilhan group challenged Agricola at the party congress of February 1936, but were met by evasion and denunciation. Outvoted, the Noilhan group walked out of the congress and established a rival party, the Parti Social-Agraire.[25] A vituperative feud followed, with the journals of the two factions denouncing each other with sectarian fervor. This schism, accompanied by much washing of dirty linen, gravely compromised the Agrarians' electoral chances, for it occurred just as the campaign was about to open. Agricola's party ran seventy-two candidates for the Chamber, but elected only nine; Noilhan's new group ran seven candidates and elected only one (who was promptly invalidated). Thereafter, both groups sank into relative obscurity; almost no one noticed when the schism was quietly healed in 1939—just in time for the party to be split once more by the fall of the Third Republic.*

* *

While these rightist whirlwinds swept erratically through the countryside, left-wing organizers were finding the peasantry more resistant to conversion. The Communists' peasant spokes-

---

* The reconciliation of 1939 was made easier by the death of Agricola in 1936. Most of the Agrarian Party leaders rallied to Pétain in 1940, and what was left of the movement formally merged with Dorgères's Peasant Defense movement in 1941 (*Le Cri du sol*, nos. 73 and 75, May 24 and June 7, 1941). A few rebels like Paul Antier, deputy for the Haute-Loire, chose instead to join the anti-German resistance, and emerged after the war with a claim to republican purity. For the later history of the Agrarian Party's successor, the Parti Paysan, see below, pp. 116–17.

man, Renaud Jean, had founded a Confédération Générale des Paysans Travailleurs (CGPT) in 1929, just in time to profit from the economic crisis; but despite the unrest produced by the depression, the results were disappointing. Addressing itself frankly to the underprivileged rural groups—marginal small-owners, small farmers and share tenants, and landless laborers —the CGPT took hold only in limited areas of the Massif Central and the southwest, where rural leftism was a long-standing tradition. Its weekly organ, *La Voix paysanne*, limped along with a circulation that never enabled Jean to break even financially. He made some tentative efforts to draw other small-owner movements into a common front—first the Parti Agraire, then the Socialist Confédération Nationale Paysanne (CNP)— but they rejected his advances. Many years later, Jean wrote off his prewar effort to organize the peasantry with the blunt phrase "C'était un échec."[26] The Communists nonetheless made enough rural gains in the 1936 elections to warrant replacing Jean's struggling weekly by an officially sponsored, subsidized party organ, *La Terre*.[27]

The Socialist-oriented CNP fared better. Its founder, Henri Calvayrac, was a young white-collar employee whose forebears had been peasants in the southwest. Perturbed by the rural exodus that had been draining the countryside of its ablest young men, he had decided after the First World War to return to the soil, and had taken up a small farm near the Spanish frontier. According to a fellow-worker in the CNP, the decisive influence in Calvayrac's life was a boyhood meeting with Jean Jaurès, who from then on became his "new Christ."[28] In 1933 Calvayrac and several of his Socialist friends met at Limoges to found the CNP and to create a peasant weekly, *La Volonté paysanne*. Although the leaders of the CNP denied any organic connection with the Socialist Party, the personal link was close, and after Léon Blum took power in 1936 the CNP was to emerge much more openly as an agency of the party. It appealed primarily to the smallholding regions of central and southwestern France, and its adherents never exceeded 10,000.

At times the CNP advocated rather harebrained schemes of grass-roots activism, as when it called for the creation of village "peasant councils," to be modeled on the urban workers' factory councils and entrusted with such multifarious and ill-defined tasks as fighting fascism, revising land rents, leading demonstrations, and opposing war.[29] But the CNP's doctrines also had a remarkably constructive and farsighted side. Indeed, some of Calvayrac's editorials on the basic problems of French agriculture anticipated the views of the post-1945 generation of agrarian reformers, and were almost unique in the prewar era. Calvayrac stressed the need for technical progress, for expanded production, for increased exports of farm products; he rejected Malthusian autarky and the hoary illusion that high tariffs constituted an agrarian cure-all.[30] Such views were far ahead of their time in the 1930's, and they found little echo either among the peasantry or among the politicians. Although the CNP was to enjoy a brief spell of artificial prosperity during the Blum period, it promptly slipped back into obscurity when the Popular Front disintegrated.[31]

Of all the new peasant organizations of the depression era, only one was destined to endure and to put its mark on rural France; yet that particular movement drew the least attention at the time. This was the Catholic youth group called the Jeunesse Agricole Chrétienne (JAC), founded in 1929 with an initial membership of twenty-seven young peasants.* Its organizers

---

* Thirty years later, the JAC's organ described this act as "the beginning of the most formidable revolution yet experienced by the agricultural profession of France—and perhaps of the world" (*Jeunes Forces rurales*, no. 334, June 1, 1960). Father Foreau, the first national chaplain of the JAC, is commonly regarded as its founder, though in fact he was chosen by his superiors to coordinate a number of local groups already set up by

were not peasants but priests; its purpose was not to awaken the peasantry but merely to check the encroachment of unbelief in the villages, many of which seemed to be imitating the cities in their flight from the faith. The activities of the JAC (and its feminine counterpart, the JACF, created in 1935) were innocuous enough in these early years; they consisted of little more than devotional exercises and social fellowship.

By the end of the depression decade, a national rally of the JAC could attract 18,000 participants; but the movement was confined almost entirely to the fervently Catholic regions (the extreme east, the extreme west, and parts of the southern Massif). If anyone had ventured to predict that within a generation the JAC would be a major social and economic force in rural France, he would have been dismissed as a lunatic. Leadership for the countryside, as everyone knew, had to come from the cities and towns; and if young peasants showed unusual talent, their proper path to social advancement was emigration to the cities. Even the peasants themselves were not yet conscious that the Great War and the depression had shaken the foundations of the old rural society, and had prepared the way for the emergence of a new rural elite.

---

various parish priests. Father Foreau was a Jesuit of rural origin, who had taught for some years at the Catholic Ecole d'Agriculture in Angers. He served as chaplain of the JAC for about twenty years, and he died in 1956 (*Cahiers du clergé rural*, no. 185, Feb. 1957, pp. 79–80). Foreau successfully insisted that the movement be run by laymen, advised and aided by priests but not dominated by them.

4

Abortive New Deal: The Popular Front

EIGHT months after the Popular Front took power in 1936, an Agrarian Party deputy won brief notoriety, and loud applause on the right, by a dramatic speech in the Chamber: "Every society, they say, needs slaves so that the rest may be wealthy. The Popular Front, too, has chosen its slaves—the peasants!"[1]

Joseph Cadic's impassioned attack reflected a widespread belief that the Popular Front government would sacrifice peasant interests on the altar of the proletarian consumer. The Popular Front was seen as "an essentially urban phenomenon,"[2] and with some justice, since the legislative elections confirmed a tendency already revealed in the municipal elections of 1935: namely, an urban trend toward the left and a rural trend toward the right.[3] Yet Cadic's rhetoric was rhetoric only. Rural France, as always, had scattered its votes from right to left; regions that were historically oriented toward the left clung to their old habits, or moved even further to the left.[4] So it was that the Socialists made notable gains in the rural southwest, largely at the expense of the Radicals; and so it was that the Communists, for the first time, made serious inroads into a few strictly agricultural regions, mainly in the Massif Central and the southwest.* True, rural rightists were moving further to

* The most notable Communist gains were in Lot-et-Garonne, Corrèze, Dordogne, and Haute-Vienne—all regions of smallownership and/or share tenantry. The Socialists' gains were more widely generalized throughout much of the smallowning center and south, though they lost ground to the

the right, and they outnumbered the leftists by as much as two to one. Still, enough Popular Front deputies owed their seats to rural voters to ensure against a frankly anti-peasant policy in the new Chamber.[5]

Indeed, few left-wing politicians in 1936 could have been termed anti-peasant in spirit. Most Radical deputies, and many Socialist deputies, were good peasantists; and even the Communists' farm platform in 1936 offered doctrinaire peasantists no grounds for alarm.[6] The Popular Front's farm platform (as distinguished from the programs of its component parties) was devoted largely to emergency relief measures rather than to basic reforms:

Higher produce prices [*révalorisation des produits agricoles*], combined with a campaign against speculation and the high cost of living, in order to reduce the gap between wholesale and retail prices.

The creation of a national interprofessional Cereals Office, in order to end speculators' gouging of both producers and consumers.

Aid to agricultural cooperatives, the delivery of fertilizers at cost price by the national nitrate and potash offices, the control and price-fixing of superphosphates and other fertilizers, the expansion of agricultural credit, and the reduction of farm rents.

The suspension of property seizures, and assistance to debtors.[7]

Except for the proposed Cereals Office, there was nothing here to offend any political faction; certainly no anti-peasant attitude, but rather sufficient caution to suit the most single-minded peas-

Communists in a few of their old rural bastions. The statistics reveal no clear correlation between landowning status and voting behavior, though regions where cash tenantry predominated were most often inclined toward the right, and regions of share tenantry toward the left. Smallowning departments varied widely, from right to extreme left. Far more decisive than landowning status was local or regional tradition, in which attitudes toward the Church constituted a major factor. François Goguel, *Initiation aux recherches de géographie électorale* (Paris, 1949), pp. 43–44.

antist. Once in power, however, the new coalition was to prove itself much more daring than its pre-election promises had suggested. Its improvised New Deal, which aroused the wrath of many rightists, went well beyond any previous governmental program of agrarian reform. Yet in the end, most of its reforms were to prove totally abortive.

* *

As Minister of Agriculture, Premier Léon Blum chose his Socialist colleague Georges Monnet, one of the rising stars of the party and widely regarded as Blum's heir apparent. Although Monnet came from a well-to-do bourgeois family, he had tried his hand at farming after 1918, when his father bought him a large farm in the war-devastated Aisne department. (His enemies on the right alleged that he had been a dismal failure as a farmer, even though his farm lay in the heart of France's best wheat-growing region.) He had soon turned to politics, and he entered the Chamber as a Socialist deputy in 1928. The appointment of so prominent a politician to the Ministry of Agriculture suggested that Blum meant to act vigorously in that sphere.

To no one's surprise, Monnet gave top priority to the Socialists' often proposed scheme for a national Wheat Office. Although the price of wheat had risen after 1935, it remained low and the prospects for market stability were uncertain. Virtually all politicians and wheatgrowers were convinced that some kind of market regulation had to be tried; but opinions varied about the degree of regulation and the locus of control. Right-wingers who accepted the idea of an Office—a regulatory agency empowered to buy, store, price, and market wheat—insisted that it be controlled by the profession and not by the state.

Monnet's bill, introduced as soon as parliament convened, drew immediate criticism, for it proposed to vest control of the Wheat Office in a central council that would include representatives of the consumers and the government as well as the growers, and that would require unanimity when fixing the annual price. The government would thus be in a position to veto the wishes of the growers on the crucial issue of price. The bill also required the marketing of all wheat through cooperatives, and thereby threatened the vested interest of many small grain dealers with friends in parliament. It proposed to institute a graduated tax on wheat deliveries, assessed primarily against the large producers, with the proceeds to be used for financing the operations of the Office.

When the bill reached the floor of the Chamber early in July 1936, it met a sharp barrage of fire from spokesmen for the center and right. Their hope was to split the Popular Front by frightening most of the Radical deputies into rejecting or watering down the bill. The Office, they warned, would outrage peasant opinion, which disliked every kind of regimentation and *paperasserie*; France was still the country where, *Dieu merci,* "we laugh when we see Guignol whack the gendarme." Furthermore, the system would penalize the most efficient growers through its graduated tax arrangement; it would destroy the private grain dealer and the small miller; it would vest too much power in the state. Monnet, sure of his majority, waited out the barrage and refused virtually every proposed amendment. At the end of a marathon session lasting twenty-six hours, the weary deputies approved the measure by a large margin.[8]

But a more severe test still lay ahead, for the Senate's composition had not been altered by the Popular Front surge of 1936. The upper house was still dominated by the Radicals of conservative orientation, with powerful support from the right. Late in July the bill reached the Senate floor, where it was bombarded for four full days by angry critics. The Wheat Office scheme, they said, was "far more drastic and disturbing than the forty-hour week law"; it would be "the handsomest Marxist monument known to legislation anywhere"; it would mean "the certainty of serfdom for the French peasantry." Its real purpose, they alleged, was to hold down wheat prices in order to ensure cheap bread; it would give the tax authorities new weapons for harassing the peasantry; it would destroy the grain dealers, part of that great middle class "which is the true rampart of democracy." New arguments, too, were introduced. Some senators urged that piecemeal measures be replaced by corporative controls over all farm production; others pleaded for a system of differential prices that would enable the small grower to compensate for his higher unit costs of production. But the crucial issue, as the debate moved on, was the locus of price-fixing power. A senatorial amendment provided for price-fixing by majority vote, rather than unanimity, in the central council. Since the growers' representatives were to hold 29 of the 51 seats on the council, the Senate's purpose was to vest complete price-fixing power in the wheatgrowers themselves. After inserting this key amendment (together with several others), the Senate adopted the bill by a two-to-one majority.[9]

A complete deadlock ensued. For two weeks, the bill shuttled back and forth between Chamber and Senate, while its managers sought to find phraseology that would satisfy both houses. Five times the Chamber voted to reaffirm its original text, with mild changes to please the Senate; five times the senators stood stubbornly on their revised version. All else gave way before the price-fixing issue. The senators insisted that the growers could be trusted to act unselfishly, without losing sight of the national interest; Monnet and his supporters insisted that no special-interest group could be given such authority, and argued that the state's representatives could be trusted to look out for the growers' interests. At last, losing patience, Monnet warned that rather than retreat on this point, he would prefer to jettison the entire bill. This threat of a return to an unregulated market shook many senators, who foresaw both economic and political disaster. Reluctantly, they agreed to a compromise that would authorize the central council to fix prices by a three-fourths vote. Since the growers could scarcely hope to control that proportion of the council, the compromise in effect entrusted final authority to the state. On the seventh weary round, this altered version of the Wheat Office bill was accepted by both houses.[10]

High hopes and grave fears had been inspired in the countryside by the Wheat Office controversy. Neither hopes nor fears were to be fully confirmed by the functioning of the new agency over the next few years. Both in 1936 and in 1937, relatively poor harvests eased the problem of oversupply, but of course brought a natural tendency toward a rise in price. The Wheat Office checked this tendency, despite angry pressure from the growers and the Senate. These critics declared that their predictions had been confirmed: the Office was simply a state mechanism to ensure low food prices. Worse still, they added, the government had packed the Office's central council with its henchmen; instead of permitting the most representative farm organizations (notably the UNSA) to select the growers' delegates, it had used the excuse of time pressure to appoint the leaders of the tiny Socialist-controlled CNP. On one occasion, the two CNP delegates had enabled the government to block a price increase by a one-vote margin in the central council.[11]

By the time the Popular Front disintegrated in 1938, the Wheat Office was being confronted with a quite different problem; and this one it solved less effectively. Bumper harvests in both 1938 and 1939 made it clear that the Monnet law contained no adequate provision to deal with the threat of oversupply. Although the Office managed to buy up the entire 1938 harvest, thus averting a possible price collapse, it faced a worse crisis in 1939, since it entered the new harvest season with bulging granaries and depleted resources. Deputies from smallowning regions blamed the large growers for the glut, and called for production controls. Other voices were raised in favor of subsidized dumping abroad. The government took neither path, but struck out in a third direction. By a decree-law of April 1939, the Office was given a sizable treasury advance to tide things over until it could somehow dispose of the surplus; in July, a further decree stripped the growers of even their nominal voice in price-fixing, and vested that power squarely in the government. The Office was instructed henceforth to receive excess wheat (beyond the year's consumption needs) without payment, and to recompense growers for that excess only if and when the Office could dispose of it. Right-wing critics could not restrain their joy at "the downfall of that ridiculous idol the Wheat Office, demonstrating the failure of a mystique."[12] The greatest experiment of the Popular Front era, the proudest achievement of Blum's agrarian New Deal, had apparently shown its futility within three short years.

But the rightists' cries of triumph proved to be somewhat premature. Although it is possible that the Wheat Office was really on the verge of collapse in 1939, and that it was saved only by the fortuitous outbreak of war (which made some kind of control machinery necessary), the fact is that the Office did survive, to become a permanent feature of the French government's agricultural policy. Vichy was to change its name slightly (to Cereals Office, or ONIC), and some Vichy elements were to try unsuccessfully to convert it into a truly corporative agency. Since the restoration of the republic, its utility has never been seriously disputed.

A broader and deeper question—the impact of the Wheat Office on peasant attitudes—is much more difficult to analyze. At the outset, peasant opinion appears to have been either neutral, skeptical, or hostile;* but it did not remain so for long.

---

* According to Fauvet and Mendras, *Les Paysans et la politique*, p. 106, "the creation of the National Cereals Office provoked a general outcry among the peasantry." Perhaps so, yet there is no easy way to test the assertion. Farm journals and syndical organs did not necessarily reflect the views of their readers.

Late in 1937, the Wheatgrowers' Association interrupted its furious polemics against the Office to warn its members not to carry their criticism too far lest the government decree a return to the free market. Most peasants could remember what the free market had meant in 1934–35; by contrast, even state "dictation" was popular.[13] It appears that the Office, combined with the wine-marketing control machinery established in 1931–33, succeeded in persuading many peasants that violent price fluctuations could be controlled, and that governmental action might correct the failings of the law of supply and demand. Furthermore, the Office surely strengthened the idea of professional organization; for all wheatgrowers had to market their crops through storage cooperatives, which many peasants joined for the first time. The Office thus helped to weaken the grip of the intense individualism that had marked the traditional peasant outlook, and that had been the despair of organizers and reformers alike.[14]

* *

Some critics of the Wheat Office had complained that the real need was for dealing, not just with wheat prices, but with farm problems as a whole. In a sense, Monnet shared this opinion; he publicly declared his intention to add other Offices for all major crops.[15] Yet no other Office was ever established; indeed, none was even proposed during Monnet's tenure as Minister. Perhaps time was too short, or other matters more pressing.

Among those matters was the issue of relief for hard-pressed and underprivileged rural groups: farm laborers, small tenants, marginal smallowners. The Popular Front program had hinted at aid for such groups; many left-wing deputies had promised rural relief in their campaign speeches; and extensive social reforms had been granted to the urban workers immediately after Blum took office. Monnet's program was ambitious. By cabinet decree, the system of family allowances was extended to farm laborers; and early in 1937 the Chamber approved bills legalizing collective bargaining for farm workers and granting them a modified version of the eight-hour day. The Chamber also passed bills providing for a revision of farm rentals, relief for farm debtors, the extension of the family-allowance system to share tenants, and the protection of cash tenants against unjust practices by landlords.[16] Without exception, these measures were buried in that "graveyard of laws," the Senate. During the next three years, interested deputies repeatedly tried to prod the Senate into action, but without effect; each time a measure was reported out for debate, the senators promptly sent it back to committee for further study. The Popular Front's program of agrarian social reform thus produced only meager results.

The same fate befell another hotly debated government proposal—this one in the field of marketing. Early in 1937 Monnet introduced a bill to legalize collective marketing agreements by the producers of specific crops. On the initiative of a majority of producers, such agreements would become compulsory for all growers of that crop. Why Monnet abandoned his plan for a series of Offices in favor of the collective marketing scheme is something of a puzzle. No such proposal had been advanced in the Popular Front's electoral program, or by either the Socialists or the Communists in the past. Indeed, the bill's chief sponsor was the milk producers' association, supported by the influential beetgrowers' lobby.[17]

Considering these auspices, the bill had an extraordinary reception in the Chamber. The Communist Renaud Jean (the newly elected chairman of the Chamber's committee on agriculture) described it as the most important agricultural measure ever to come before the French parliament. At the other extreme, right-wing deputies, together with some Radicals, charged the government with seeking to install "a veritable dictatorship over agriculture's economic life, over conditions of sale and prices"; one Agrarian leader even spoke of the sovietizing of French agriculture. Other deputies assailed the bill as an effort by the big agricultural and industrial interests to crush the small farmer and the small middleman. Each peasant, they argued, should remain free to work out his own marketing arrangements without state interference, in accordance with "the ancestral rules of our economic life."[18]

Monnet professed complete bewilderment at these attacks; his bill, he declared, was designed only to help farmers pool their strength against rapacious commercial and industrial interests. Milk producers who sought joint action in dealing with middlemen had often been frustrated by a shortsighted minority of their colleagues. The government's bill would enable the majority to enforce its will, and would thus contribute to the long-range goal of strengthened peasant organization and unity. After all, he added dryly, the measure was much less drastic than Britain's Milk Marketing Act—put through by the Conservative party.[19] With amendments (notably making the collective agreements regional rather than nation-wide, and requiring a two-thirds majority of growers' representatives to make agreements effective), the bill was adopted by the Chamber. But the great experiment got no further; the Senate buried it. Twenty-five years later, the de Gaulle republic, prompted by pressure from a new generation of young peasants, revived the collective marketing scheme in a slightly different form.

* *

Not all the activity of the Popular Front era was confined to parliament. The factory sit-down strikes of June 1936 had some repercussions in the large-farming areas, where a few agricultural workers tried similar tactics. Whether these strikes were spontaneous is not entirely clear; angry rightists charged that urban agitators mounted on bicycles had invaded the region to stir up trouble, and that left-wing politicians had rushed in to fan the blaze of social unrest. In any case, the strikes produced a kind of small-scale repetition of the Great Fear of 1789: smallowners in many villages gathered in the public square and swore to resist any workers who sought to occupy their farms. There were occasional street brawls between town workers and farm owners, with the shopkeepers pitching in on the farmers' side.[20] The agitation soon died down, though it resulted in a few collective labor contracts on a local scale, and in the adoption by the Chamber of a bill to legalize such collective bargaining. The most striking consequence was the sudden burgeoning of trade union activity among the farm workers. The agricultural labor branch of the Confédération Générale du Travail, a division that had scarcely existed except on paper, leaped from a membership of 7,000 in early 1936 to almost 200,000 early in 1937. The Catholic Confédération Française des Travailleurs Chrétiens (CFTC) also began for the first time to organize a farm labor branch.[21]

Labor organizers, encouraged by this flood of new adherents, decided to strike hard in 1937. As the harvest season approached, they demanded that a nation-wide collective wage agreement be negotiated with the government, even though the bill legalizing such agreements was stalled in the Senate. In the Paris basin and the northeast, a large number of farm workers laid down their tools, threatening the loss of the entire crop. Dorgères sprang to action in defense of the farm owners; the "red belt" around Paris, he announced, must be surrounded by a "green belt" that would check the spread of the revolutionary virus. Dorgères recruited squads of his Greenshirts and of urban volunteers to act as strikebreakers; the strikers retaliated by chasing many of these volunteers into farm buildings and besieging them there. Eventually Monnet had to ask that the Garde Mobile be sent in to avert serious violence. In the end, the strike movement disintegrated; the farm owners stood firm, preferring to risk the loss of their crop rather than retreat, and a majority of the workers refused to join the strike.[22] The up-heaval produced no result save to exacerbate social tensions; the farm workers remained, on the whole, the most underprivileged segment of the French working class.*

Meanwhile, another important change was occurring in the countryside: the drift to the cities, which had slowed down during the depression years, suddenly took on the proportions of a population hemorrhage, thanks largely to the adoption of the forty-hour week for urban labor and the nationalization of the railway system. The shortened work week suddenly forced the state railway agency to recruit 85,000 new employees; and it was immediately deluged with some 300,000 applications, most of them from rural districts.† Right-wing politicians and agrarian leaders complained that the countryside was being drained of all its vigorous young men by this "suction pump"; and they were not entirely wrong. Railway jobs were not the only lure. The forty-hour week, with extensive leisure for the many diversions of urban life, had a powerful appeal to young peasants accustomed to a seventy-hour week and no diversions at all. During the three years that followed the accession of the Popular Front, almost 300,000 peasants (male and female, mostly below the age of thirty) deserted the farm.

The flight to the city seemed to many conservatives to support their contention that the Popular Front's reforms had been paid for by the peasantry. If things were getting better in the

---

* There were approximately 1.2 million permanent farm laborers in the late 1930's, not including family labor. Wages varied widely, but were much lower than those in urban areas; protective legislation was not strictly enforced; housing conditions were often submarginal. The agricultural survey of 1929 indicated that 250,000 workers were still housed in sheds or barns (*Journal officiel, documents de la Chambre des députés*, 1939, annex no. 5725). Left-wing deputies frequently complained that the Popular Front's social reforms (family allowances, paid vacations) were generally evaded.

† Paul Pouzin, *Problèmes agricoles d'un temps difficile et de toujours* (Paris, 1950), p. 52. If the age ceiling had not been set at thirty, Pouzin added, there might have been almost a million applicants.

countryside, they asked, why should so many young peasants want to leave? In fact, they argued, agricultural buying power had not been raised at all, and the gap between urban and rural living standards had been widened. Their favorite statistician, Jean Dessirier, supplied monthly figures purporting to prove that total agricultural buying power had dropped from 80 to 70 during Blum's first year (1913 = 100), and managed only a limping recovery to 80 in 1938–39.[23]

Postwar studies indicate that the peasants fared about as well as other segments of society after 1936. On the whole, their living standard was about the same as in 1913.[24] To be sure, this was rather a grim standard. The average net income of French farmers in 1938 and 1939 provided them with no more than a minimal return on the value of their land, plus a minimal wage for themselves and working members of their families; there was little or no profit margin. Since some farmers did operate at a good profit, the great majority must have scraped along at a bare subsistence level, with an income roughly equal to that of a landless farm laborer.[25] If Dessirier was unjust in claiming that "the whole so-called Popular Front policy has only consolidated the retrogression of French agriculture," it is clear that the Popular Front period saw no effective measures taken to solve France's peasant problems.

* *

Any violent swing in politics is likely to produce an equally sharp counterswing. For a time, the Popular Front's electoral victory in 1936 shocked much of the right into embittered silence; but within a few months, dedicated rightists were hard at work trying to recover the initiative. As usual, however, the rival factions competing for peasant support found it hard to reconcile their differences.

Dorgères remained active despite the fiasco of the Peasant

Front and the defeat of most of his disciples at the polls. His demagogic performances still drew large crowds, and the membership of his Peasant Defense movement apparently continued to grow.[26] But there was good reason to believe that Dorgerism had passed its peak as an effective political and social force. Dorgères's enemies denounced him as a hireling of wealthy schemers; politicians who had once feared him now scoffed at him or ignored him completely. His former allies of the Agrarian Party were better off, with a dozen deputies in parliament. Yet they, too, failed to maintain their momentum; the party schism of 1936 hurt them badly, and after Agricola's death they lacked imaginative and charismatic leadership.

In these circumstances, the conduct of right-wing activism fell chiefly to the UNSA, with its energetic spokesmen and systematic doctrine, its support from wealthy sympathizers, and its solid, long-established organizational base in such regions as Brittany and the Rhône Valley. In May 1937 the UNSA staged a peasant congress at Caen that attracted an unprecedented amount of public notice. All the leading corporatist spokesmen were there to assert the importance of the peasantry for the nation's health, to lament the drift to the cities, to denounce the disastrous policies of the Popular Front, and to call for a complete reorganization of the nation's social and political structure. The rural population, they claimed, had never really been represented in parliament, despite what politicians said. In fact, politics always corrupted these self-styled rural representatives; only a new system of professional representation in a national corporative body could restore the peasantry to its proper place and induce a return to the soil. Short of such reforms, France faced the disappearance of its peasant base—which would mean, in effect, national suicide.[27]

In the wake of the Caen congress (intended as the opening barrage in a campaign of psychological warfare), the UNSA founded its new weekly journal, *Syndicats paysans*. Unlike most farm journals, which were filled with a combination of complaints about farm prices and advice on how to avoid mildew, *Syndicats paysans* devoted itself to theoretical questions. At the same time the UNSA embarked on an organizational drive that carried it into parts of the country hitherto immune to its appeal. Its greatest success was in the nature of a windfall. Traditionally, the southwest and large parts of the Massif Central had been strongholds of the left. In 1937 an aristocrat of the Albi region, Count Alain de Chantérac, set out to challenge this left-wing dominance by founding a regional movement with the remarkably eclectic name Fédération des Syndicats Agricoles Corporatifs d'Action et de Défense Paysanne. For a time Chantérac flirted with Dorgères, who believed that the new movement would swell the ranks of his own Peasant Defense. But after using some of Dorgères's activists during the organizational phase, Chantérac broke with the Greenshirt leader and threw in his lot with the UNSA instead.[28] His movement prospered so mightily that by 1939 his weekly organ, *L'Effort paysan*, claimed 150,000 readers, and his delegates at a UNSA congress outnumbered those of any other regional group.[29] Chantérac's professed purpose, like that of the UNSA's leaders, was to give agricultural syndicalism a doctrine, a mystique. Fertilizer shops were not enough; it was the mission of syndicalism to renew the nation's strength and restore the natural unity of the rural world. A simple choice faced the peasantry: corporatism or sovietization.

The disintegration of the Popular Front in 1938 seemed to reduce the internal threat of "sovietization," but UNSA leaders had already detected what they took to be an even graver external threat—a general war, stirred up by French ideologues in the service of an alien doctrine. Beginning with the Austrian crisis in February 1938, every UNSA organ crusaded vigorously against the warmongers. French leaders, declared Le Roy

Ladurie in *Syndicats paysans,* ought to talk less about the German soldier and more about the German peasant and German
land reforms.* Under the scarehead LES PAYSANS AUX TRAN-
CHÉES, LES NÈGRES À LA FERME, *L'Effort paysan* soberly reported that the Minister of Agriculture had prepared secret
plans to import gangs of farm laborers from North Africa and
the colonies, who would replace mobilized peasants in case of
war.[30] The Czech crisis in September brought the campaign to
an almost hysterical climax. *L'Effort paysan* described the Czech
affair as "nothing more than a pretext to satisfy certain ideo-
logical passions and esoteric hatreds"; national, regional, and
local officials of the UNSA bombarded the government with
thousands of telegrams demanding peace. When the Munich
settlement suddenly dissipated the nightmare, UNSA leaders
claimed a large part of the credit, and strongly implied that
peasant pressure had shaped the government's decisions.[31] Cen-
tainly no other interest group in France outdid the UNSA in
its year-long campaign for peace at any price.

The vigorous growth of the UNSA suggested to right-wing
leaders that the tide of rural opinion was now running strongly
in their favor. Further evidence seemed to be provided by the
senatorial elections shortly after the Munich crisis. Center and
right gains in rural areas exceeded those of the left; a number
of Radicals who had been too loyal to the Popular Front were
defeated. With the Senate's conservative tendencies reinforced,
it became certain that none of the long-pending Popular Front
reforms would ever emerge from committee.

The shift to the right did not mean an end to agrarian reform, however; it opened the way to reform of a different kind.
In July 1939 the center cabinet suddenly issued a set of decree-

---

* It ought to be noted, however, that the appeasement campaign in
the UNSA press rarely revealed any hint of pro-Germanism or of admiration for the Nazi system. Nor were there any overt signs of the anti-
Semitism that recurred frequently in the organ of the Parti Agraire (e.g.,
during Blum's second government in 1938).

laws that were greeted enthusiastically by the right-wing press
and the UNSA. Collectively labeled the Code de la Famille,
these decrees embodied the peasantist doctrine cherished by all
French conservatives (and even by many leftists). Their purpose
was to protect the small family farm, to encourage rural families to produce more children and to stay on the land. The system of family allowances, previously confined to urban and rural
wage-earners, was extended to farm operators as well, with
the state to pay most of the cost. Young rural couples about to
embark on a career of farming were made eligible for state loans,
most of which would be written off if the couple had five children. The civil code's provision for equal inheritance was modified in an effort to keep family farms intact; when only one of
several sons remained on the farm, he would henceforth be
given credit for each year of farm work when the time came
to buy off his co-heirs.

This was the kind of reform that had long been preached by
right-wing groups. The UNSA claimed full credit for the government's action, though it warned that the new family allow-
ance system was more statist than corporatist in structure. The
next step, according to the UNSA, must be to give the profession control of its own affairs.[32] Curiously, the Family Code also
won the approval of the Communists; La Terre informed its
readers that the party's tireless activities in defense of the small
peasantry had driven the government to act.[33] The Code was
in fact no more than a palliative, but no politician dared to challenge legislation designed to improve the lot of the small farmer,
and it passed without debate. Barely a month after its promulgation, however, France was at war; and before the decrees could
be put into operation, the republic had collapsed.

5

Unity and Reform from the Right:
The Vichy Period

THE VICHY PERIOD is often viewed as an anomalous and largely meaningless interlude in the development of modern France—as a time when one small faction of aggrieved reactionaries around Pétain set out to repeal the nineteenth and twentieth centuries, while a rival faction of right-wing radicals in occupied Paris sought to rebuild France on the fascist model. The reactionaries' goal was patently impossible, while the fascists' hopes depended on an Axis victory; therefore (so runs the common thesis) the Vichy phase was doomed to futility, to be swept away (as it was in 1944) leaving scarcely a trace behind.

This simplistic view of Vichy as a dead-end detour in French history was easier to accept in the immediate post-liberation years than it is today. In longer perspective, the Vichy episode seems a great deal more complex; indeed, it can be seen as a link (though a somewhat twisted link) in a chain of development that extends unbroken through the past three or four decades. Nowhere is this clearer than in agriculture. Vichy's policy toward the peasantry embodied—in part, at least—the program that had been advocated in prewar days by one of the most aggressive groups of agrarian activists. Furthermore, many of Vichy's agricultural reforms were to outlast the regime, while most of Vichy's peasant elite soon returned to positions of influence in the postwar syndicalist movement.

Vichy lost no time in asserting peasantism as its official creed. Pétain himself led the way, delivering frequent homilies in a Virgilian vein. "I hate the lies that have done us so much harm. As for the soil, it does not lie. It is the motherland itself. A field that goes out of cultivation is a bit of France that dies. A field restored to cultivation is a bit of France reborn." Or again: "From this miracle, repeated each day, comes France—a nation that is industrious, frugal, devoted to liberty. It is the peasant, with his heroic patience, that has created France. It is the peasant that ensures our economic and spiritual stability."[1] Vichy propagandists made much of the fact that Pétain came from a peasant family; Henri Dorgères took to calling him *le maréchal paysan*, and claimed that Pétain relished the title.* The myth of peasant unity, of a *classe paysanne*, was vigorously promulgated; and this "class," constituting about a third of the whole population, was repeatedly told that its values and virtues would inspire the new and purified France. For the first time in history, wrote Michel Augé-Laribé, a national revolution was destined to begin on the soil.[2]

Although peasantism coincided with German policy toward defeated France, the Vichy line was almost certainly not dictated by the victors. Perhaps some ultra-collaborationist Vichy leaders were out to curry favor with the Germans by saying what Berlin wanted to hear, but most Vichyites genuinely desired to restore the "healthier" France of pre-industrial days. As Marc Bloch

---

* Dorgères, *La révolution paysanne*, p. 123. Dorgères's veneration of Pétain verged on the bathetic. "The Pétain miracle," he declared, "is, at five centuries' distance, the equivalent of the Joan of Arc miracle." "The Head of the State deserves our total faith, our blind faith. It is by following him without argument, without scheming, without grumbling, that one best serves the cause of France" (*Le Cri du sol*, nos. 49 and 53, Dec. 7, 1940, and Jan. 4, 1941). Dorgères was appointed to a high post in the Corporation (delegate-general for propaganda), and to Vichy's Conseil national (a kind of substitute for parliament). Eventually, however, his enthusiasm for Vichy cooled, and he even took some part in the resistance movement.

noted in his private journal, the men around Pétain had "never ceased to regret the disappearance of the old docility that they believed to be an innate quality of all simple peasant societies." Yet Bloch was honest enough to add that the Vichy doctrinaires were inspired by something more than sheer bigotry. Even in the twentieth century, he reflected, a nation can gain much by having its life rooted in the soil; for this peasant base not only gives it economic stability, but maintains a reserve of human vitality. The real danger, in Bloch's opinion, was that Vichy might try to turn France into a mere historical museum.[3]

There were certainly some Vichyites whose ideal was a historical museum; indeed, Pétain probably headed the list. But this was not the dominant view. On the contrary, most of the leading men in agriculture during the Vichy era were proponents of change, advance, reform—even if their ideas were of a rather peculiar sort. Only a few belonged to Pétain's generation of old-fashioned paternalistic landlords, bent on preserving property rights and quasi-feudal owner-tenant relationships. The majority belonged to the new generation of agrarian conservatives that had come into prominence after 1930: men who operated large or middle-sized farms, or the sons of such men; men who had attended one of the higher schools of agriculture (usually Catholic); men who were active in agrarian syndicalism. Men of this kind had tended to cluster in the UNSA, the most dynamic and vocal farm syndicate in the 1930's; and it was the UNSA that provided Vichy with both its doctrine and much of its personnel in the sphere of agrarian action.

* *

In September 1940, only two months after the Pétain government was established, a group of UNSA leaders presented a draft law for the creation of a corporative structure in agriculture, the Corporation Paysanne. The UNSA had been agitating for such a reform for a decade, and although some of its leaders hesitated now on the ground that the corporatist ideal might be fatally flawed by its association with the German victory, the majority pushed on without hesitation. Foremost among them was Louis Salleron, the UNSA's semiofficial theorist—a man whose passionate temperament brooked no delay. Salleron was the principal author of the draft law of September 1940.[4]

The corporatists found many willing listeners in Vichy. Pétain himself, at the very outset, had publicly proclaimed his intention to end "liberal disorder" by developing a set of corporative institutions for the whole economy. But his Minister of Agriculture, Pierre Caziot, was somewhat more skeptical. As will be recalled, Caziot, whose plan for strengthening and extending family farming had been considered by parliament in 1920, was a dedicated peasantist. He was also the nation's leading expert on land values, having spent most of his long career as a high official of the Crédit Foncier (the government land bank founded by Napoleon III). Called to office by Pétain in July 1940, he had at first hesitated to accept, for he was profoundly anti-German in the old conservative-nationalist tradition.* But his sense of public service, and no doubt the lure of high office, had quickly overcome his scruples.

Caziot favored a unified peasant organization, but he demurred at the word "corporation" and preferred some more

* Caziot's appointment as Minister came as a complete surprise to him. The news was brought by a neighboring farmer who had picked up a radio broadcast from Vichy (Hoover Institution, *France During the German Occupation 1940–1944*, Stanford, 1957, p. 251). Caziot, described by an acquaintance as "a crafty [*rusé*] peasant type," was shrewd enough to insist that responsibility for food supply be placed in a separate ministry. After the liberation, Caziot was found guilty of collaboration, and was condemned to "national degradation" for life, with confiscation of half his property. He was eventually pardoned when search of the German archives disclosed a telegram from the German Ambassador, Otto Abetz, urging Caziot's arrest as a "noncollaborator" (*Le Monde*, Jan. 6, 1953).

innocuous label such as "National Agricultural Confederation." Pétain's insistence led him to give way, much to his later regret; for he came to believe that many of the Peasant Corporation's difficulties might have been avoided if a more neutral title had been used.[5] In his negotiations with the Corporation's sponsors, Caziot proved to be much more stubborn; for several weeks the UNSA's draft shuttled back and forth between them, with side trips to various legal authorities, technicians, and spokesmen for farm organizations. The text was rewritten some twenty times, and in the end it differed considerably from the original Salleron draft. Next, the approval of the German authorities had to be secured, in order to make the law operative in the occupied zone. Here, too, lengthy negotiations were required; the Germans were suspicious and tried to persuade Caziot to pattern the Corporation after their own agricultural organization, the Reichsnährstand. Again Caziot proved stubborn, and in the end the Germans reluctantly gave their approval.[6] The law—which its UNSA sponsors proudly called the Peasant Charter—was promulgated at last on December 2, 1940.

Outwardly, the character of the Peasant Corporation seemed clear enough; it would be (as its chief official later put it) "a decentralized organization possessing disciplinary powers," and it would institutionalize the concept of peasant unity. The old rural divisions and rivalries, both political and social, would be rubbed out; in each commune there would be a single "corporative syndicate" comprising all peasant families, whether landowners, tenants, share tenants, farm workers, or rural artisans. These local syndicates would be grouped into regional units called "corporative unions" (normally one for each department, as it turned out); and representatives of these unions would assemble at intervals to form a National Corporative Council. Alongside this symmetrical hierarchy, and subordinated to it, would be a series of unified professional groups with strictly economic or social functions—cooperatives, mutual-insurance or credit funds, and "specialized groups" representing the major farm products.[7]

Yet the appearance of symmetry and simplicity concealed a whole series of grave ambiguities. Would all peasants be required to join the Corporation? Would its local and regional officials—respectively known as "syndics" and "regional delegates" (later "regional syndics")—be elected from below or designated from above? Would the Corporation be truly autonomous, with its own regulatory and disciplinary powers, or would it be subject to the supervision and even the dictation of the Minister of Agriculture? All these uncertainties clouded the Corporation's future from the outset, and produced tensions that hampered its operation throughout the Vichy years. Some of the main questions were still unanswered when Vichy disintegrated in 1944.

The issue of compulsory versus voluntary membership, which produced a good deal of puzzled debate during the first year or so, was eventually sidestepped rather than settled. Corporation officials concluded lamely that membership was voluntary, but that all peasants were bound by the Corporation's regulatory actions and must contribute to its financial support.[8] The chief source of the ambiguity lay in Article 9 of the law, which declared that "adherence to the various professional agricultural organizations [cooperatives, mutual-aid groups, and so on] implies affiliation with an agricultural corporative syndicate." Since almost all peasants belonged to some sort of cooperative or mutual-aid group, the idea of voluntary membership in the Corporation became almost meaningless. In practice, however, many cooperatives and mutual groups never got around to transmitting their membership lists to the local corporative syndicates; and those that did transmit them usually left it up to the syndicates to try to collect dues from their members.[9]

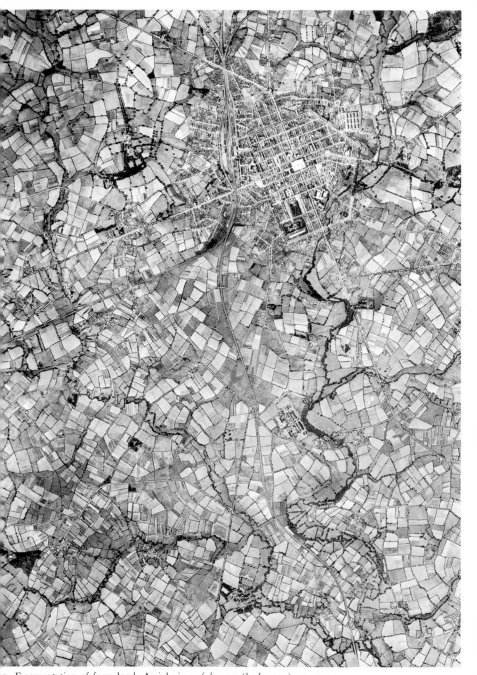

1. Fragmentation of farm land: Aerial view of *bocage* (hedgerow) country in the Charente region of southwestern France.

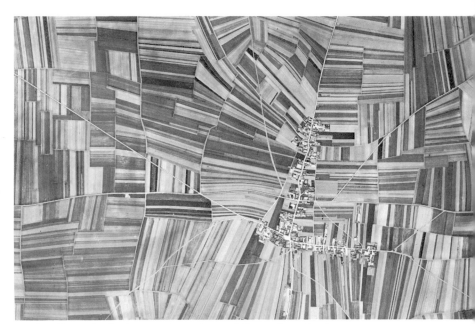

2 and 3. Contrasting land patterns in north-central France: Large-farming area in the Paris Basin, extreme parcelization in the Loiret department.

4. Renaud Jean

5. Henri Dorgères

René Blondelle

7. Michel Debatisse

Some representative leaders of farm organizations.

8. Two generations in agrarian syndicalism: Joseph Courau (FNSEA President 1956–63) and Marcel Bruel (FNSEA Secretary-General 1961–   ).

9. JAC leaders in conference, 1943 (Secretary-General René Colson speaking).

10. René Colson at a JAC congress in 1950, shortly before his death.

11 and 12. Old and new in rural housing: Traditional farmhouse in central France, modern farmhouse in the southwest.

13 and 14. New and old in farm techniques: Two present-day harvesting
scenes in north-central France.

Peasant protest, peaceful style: Tractor roadblock in Brittany, 1963.

16. Peasant protest, violent style: Demonstrating farmers clash with armed police at Amiens, February 1960.

Whether officials were to be elected or appointed was a more serious issue, for its resolution would determine the future character of the Corporation. Corporative systems in other countries functioned as agencies of the state. Moreover, Pétain and his circle believed that elections inevitably led to division and demagoguery. Thus there was no provision for the election of officials in the law of December 1940; local syndics were to be appointed by the next higher echelon of the Corporation, the regional union, and regional delegates were to be appointed by the Minister of Agriculture. The law did provide, however, that each local syndicate and regional union might "propose" nominees for these posts as syndics, and Louis Salleron, chief doctrinaire of the corporatists, promptly interpreted this clause to mean the free choice of "real natural leaders" by their fellows in each commune. He added: "It may be hoped . . . that as soon as normal conditions can be restored, election pure and simple will be substituted for election with ratification."[10] A set of temporary syndics was appointed in 1941 to serve during the organizational period, but in 1942 Vichy specifically authorized the choice of local and regional nominees for the post of syndic by election—and, what is more, by secret ballot.[11] Although these nominees still had to be formally appointed by the next higher echelon in the Corporation, they were almost always accepted.* *De facto* rather than *de jure,* the Corporation ratified the free choice of syndical officials from below.

Of all the ambiguities surrounding the Corporation, the most crucial concerned its relationship to the state—or, more precisely, to the Ministry of Agriculture. The doctrinaires of corporatism were determined to avoid the kind of state control that marked the Italian and German systems; indeed, they viewed corpora-

* F.-M. Jacq, who served as a regional syndic in Brittany, later recalled that he had rejected only one of approximately six hundred nominees proposed by local syndicates. In that exceptional case, two candidates had been separated by only one vote (interview with M. Jacq, June 1951).

tism not as a special variety of statism, but as its polar opposite. They demanded a broad and genuine autonomy for each of the organized professions, with the state confined to the limited role of coordination. Such a relationship would have been difficult to work out even if Vichy had immediately reorganized the entire French economy on a corporative basis. But with agriculture alone possessing its corporation, the problem became almost insoluble.

From the very outset, the corporatists found themselves engaged in a partly open, partly concealed struggle with the defenders of the state's authority—notably the career civil servants of the Ministry of Agriculture. This struggle had begun during the drafting of the basic law of 1940. In the UNSA's original project, the Corporation was made virtually independent of ministerial control, and was drastically decentralized in structure—indeed, it would have possessed no national apparatus whatsoever. This draft was sharply altered by Caziot and his advisers; they added a National Corporative Council as capstone of the organization, and assigned the Minister of Agriculture an active (though still somewhat ambiguous) supervisory role.[12] The Minister was authorized to name representatives (called *commissaires du gouvernement*) to speak for him at both the national and regional levels—though the nature of the relationship between *commissaires* and Corporation officials was not made clear.

The next four years brought sporadic tugs-of-war between Ministry and Corporation, with the corporatists constantly on the defensive. The Ministry's advantage stemmed in part from the Corporation's dependence on state subsidies.[13] In addition, the Corporation's leaders were outmaneuvered by successive ministers and professional bureaucrats; and they were further handicapped by the peculiar pressures of the period—notably the increasing exactions of the Germans in the sphere of food supply.

To start with, the government had seemed inclined to let the corporatists organize and run their own institution. Several UNSA leaders were appointed to key posts during the organizational period: Salleron became delegate-general for economic and social questions, Rémy Goussault for syndical organization, and Charles du Fretay for specialized groups. Similarly, most of the regional delegates appointed in 1941 were men who had been active in the UNSA or in affiliated groups. Under their guidance, the task of organizing thirty thousand local syndicates and coordinating the old cooperatives and mutual-aid societies was largely completed by the end of 1942.

Yet all was not well among the corporatists. For one thing, they enjoyed only precarious control of the National Corporative Commission, a temporary organization of thirty members whose function was to supervise the erection of the Corporation's permanent structure, after which it would give way to the National Corporative Council. The membership of this Commission (appointed by the Minister of Agriculture) represented a rough balance between corporatists and former officials of the old Boulevard Saint-Germain group, the Radical-oriented FNMCA.[14] Furthermore, the Ministry of Agriculture was whittling away at the Corporation's autonomy by a series of supplementary laws that buttressed the authority of the *commissaires du gouvernement*.

Moreover, the Ministry was proceeding with its own program of agricultural reforms without much reference to the Corporation's opinions. The National Corporative Commission was rarely consulted before these reforms were promulgated, and when the Commission sought to take the initiative by addressing resolutions to the government, its proposals were usually ignored.[15] By the end of the Corporation's first year, some outspoken corporatists were complaining vigorously. According to Salleron, "The struggle is . . . open between the old cadres and the new principles. The truth forces us to say that the first year's experience of the Peasant Corporation marks a clear-cut success for statism. The Corporation is practically without financial resources, and, in its every move, it is kept on leading strings by the administration. This grave fact must be brought to the attention of the peasant world. If, in fact, the Corporation does not become the peasants' instrument of liberation, it will be the most perfect instrument of oppression one can imagine."[16]

Salleron's challenge was not ignored; late in 1941 he was dismissed from his high post in the Corporation, and shortly afterward his weekly journal, *Syndicats paysans*, ceased publication.[17] True, a few weeks later Caziot was replaced as Minister of Agriculture by Jacques Le Roy Ladurie, a leading corporatist, but this change of personnel—one of Pierre Laval's first acts on his return to power in April 1942—produced no fundamental change of policy. Le Roy Ladurie promptly clashed with Laval over German demands for foodstuffs and labor draftees, and managed to find an early excuse to resign.* The Ministry of Agriculture passed into the hands of Max Bonnafous, a close friend of Laval with more interest in using the Corporation as a tool than in endowing it with antonomous authority.[18]

Late in 1942, the government announced that it was time to convert the Corporation's temporary organs into permanent ones. But two years of experience, it added, had revealed a number of flaws in the 1940 law; and these alleged flaws were corrected by a new law of December 16, 1942. The general effect of the reform was to increase the degree of centralization

---

* Interviews with Jacques Le Roy Ladurie (July 1960), the Count de Chantérac (March 1951), and Louis Salleron (1951). Chantérac, a close friend and warm admirer of Le Roy Ladurie, held a high post in the Ministry during the latter's brief tenure. He was also regional syndic in the Tarn and a member of Pétain's Conseil National. Le Roy Ladurie became active in the resistance movement toward the end of the Vichy period, and was elected to the National Assembly shortly after the republic was restored.

in the Corporation's structure, and to reduce still further the Corporation's autonomy. The Minister of Agriculture was made ex officio president of the National Corporative Council, and was vested with power to appoint (and dismiss) most of the Corporation's national and regional officials. The Corporation would henceforth be headed by a National Syndic, to be named by Pétain himself from a list of five nominees proposed by the National Corporative Council. The exact role and powers of the National Syndic, however, were left obscure. Furthermore, no remedy was offered for the Corporation's lack of financial independence.[19]

The 1942 law also embodied a painful challenge to the corporatists' cherished myth of peasant unity. The original law had lumped together the whole agricultural population, from absentee landlords to farm laborers, in undifferentiated syndicates. Two years of experience had proved that this kind of rural solidarity, however desirable, simply did not exist. "The unity of the farming profession," declared a high Corporation official in a remarkable bit of double talk, "is the product of interests that are too diverse and too complex to be faithfully represented by a single organism."[20] Most notably, farm laborers, small tenants, and share tenants had shown virtually no interest in joining the corporative syndicates. The 1942 law recognized this rural diversity by creating syndical subdivisions called *sections sociales* at the regional level, plus a new Chambre Syndicale at the national level, in an effort to ensure direct representation for each agrarian category. In addition, a somewhat more elaborate organizational structure was provided for the various farm groups that were affiliated with syndicalism—the specialized groups, the cooperatives, and the mutual-aid and farm-credit associations. If peasant unity remained the goal of corporatist leaders, it was clearly to be a heterogeneous rather than a homogeneous kind of unity.

In its last two years the Corporation achieved next to nothing. Its national leaders spent most of their time battling the state bureaucracy and the German occupation authorities. Most of the agrarian reforms inaugurated by Vichy were conceived and drafted in the Ministry of Agriculture rather than in the offices of the Corporation. On the regional and local levels, the Corporation was equally ineffective. In regions with solid pre-war farm organizations, the officials and technicians of prewar days continued to provide the same services as in the past; they simply carried on under the new corporative label. In regions where agrarian syndicalism had been weak or nonexistent, or where it had been dominated by the left, the Corporation's local units proved to be little more than a façade.[21]

Yet the Corporation had its constructive side: it helped to instill in peasant minds the idea of uniting with other peasants to improve the conditions of rural life. The enormous amount of talk, official and unofficial, about the need for organization and the concept of unity, left a permanent mark in many rural areas. In a great many villages where two rival syndicates or cooperatives had confronted each other before 1940—both of them too weak to achieve very much—the enforced merger under Vichy proved to be permanent.[22] Like the myth of workers' unity among French proletarians, the myth of peasant unity contained an emotional force that partially counterbalanced the divisive factors in the countryside. When the Corporation was swept away in 1944, the idea of unity survived in the new Con-fédération Générale d'Agriculture that replaced it.

The Vichy experience also speeded the emergence of a peas-ant elite. No other segment of French society—not even the urban workers—had been so slow in producing leaders. Most of the old farm syndicates and cooperatives had been established and run by men from the landed aristocracy or the urban bourgeoisie; most of the politicians who represented the countryside had like-wise been of nonpeasant origin. Not until the crisis decade of

the 1930's had an indigenous peasant elite begun to emerge;
even then the process had been slow and limited, and most of
the leading activists were outsiders. As we have seen, able young
peasants usually got ahead by leaving the land, rather than by
staying on it and becoming local leaders.

The Vichy era temporarily slowed this flow of the rural elite
toward the cities. In addition, Vichy proclaimed the official principle that every commune and every region must have its peasant syndicate "to promote and to manage the common interests
of peasant families in the moral, social, and economic domains."[23]
Suddenly the Corporation had to turn up more than thirty thousand local or regional syndics capable of assuming this unaccus-
tomed task of leadership. Most of these officials were chosen
by a procedure resembling election, and virtually all of them
(as required by the law of December 1942) were active farmers.
Thus the syndics were men with genuine roots in the local farming community, men who in most cases enjoyed the respect and
support of their neighbors. Some had attained local status before
1940 by participating in the management of cooperatives or
mutual-aid societies. Yet even these men acquired new prestige
as official spokesmen for their peasant community—the kind of
prestige that deputies and departmental councilors had traditionally enjoyed in the countryside. By 1944, therefore, France possessed an identifiable corps of peasant leaders.

To be sure, this new elite did not represent a perfect cross
section of rural society. For one thing, more than a million farmers were languishing in German prisoner-of-war camps; and
many others, too young for army service in 1939, became subject to the Germans' forced-labor draft after 1942, and departed
for Germany or for the *maquis*. The age structure of the rural
population during these years was therefore skewed upward,
and its choice of leaders reflected this fact. Furthermore, many
peasants of deeply republican or left-wing sympathies rejected

Vichy and all its works, and refused to participate in syndical affairs. By force of circumstance, therefore, the syndics chosen were usually middle-aged men of substantial property and conservative inclinations. Yet even under normal conditions men of this stripe would probably have been chosen, for they were the ones whose affluence, social position, ambition, or talent had enabled them to emerge from the ruck before 1940—to attend one of the advanced agricultural schools, or to devote some spare time to a farm syndicate or cooperative. In other words, they had been marked out as potential rural leaders even before Vichy thrust them to the fore.

In some respects it was unfortunate that France's peasant elite should have emerged at such a moment, for everyone who served the instruments of Vichy risked being cast into the discard after Vichy fell. The syndics, in particular, were placed in an equivocal position by the functions they had to perform on behalf of the Corporation. Their most onerous task was to oversee collection and delivery of the food supplies exacted by the Germans—a task that the Corporation had reluctantly taken on in the hope of serving as a buffer between the occupation authorities and the peasantry. To some degree it probably did serve that function; according to a statement made by a high German official late in 1943, the Corporation had "played a large part in creating the present tension and spirit of resistance among the farm population," and might even have to be dissolved.[24] Many peasants, however, viewed the Corporation as an agency of oppression rather than of defense. By 1944, a number of local syndics had become "the most dishonored men in the countryside,"[25] and some never were restored to honor. But on balance, the Corporation proved beneficial as a training ground; for every syndic whose usefulness was permanently impaired, two or three others emerged as natural spokesmen of the peasantry and went on to prominent positions in the agrarian syndical movement of the postwar era.*

One serious fault of the Corporation was the tendency of its spokesmen to focus narrowly on the social role of the peasantry as a unique category distinct from the rest of the nation, and to ignore the material problems of French agriculture. Louis Salleron, in his zeal to denounce what he called "the liberalo-Marxist error," had once gone so far as to advocate "the wholesale preservation of the present structure of the peasantry, which demographically, economically, socially, and morally amounts to near-perfection." And he had added blithely in 1941 that France might easily double or treble its existing peasant population.[26] Such views were advanced against a background of paternalistic moral preaching from some of the Corporation's Catholic sponsors, who urged the peasants to return to their ancient mores, to resist the temptations of easy living in the cities, even to abandon the use of corrupting *argot*.[27]

Yet in the end the Corporation's leaders did begin to develop some awareness of the kind of reforms that were needed. By 1944, Salleron was drafting proposals for postwar agricultural planning, large-scale technical aid to lower production costs, and

---

* The Corporation's National Syndic, Adolphe Pointier (formerly president of the Wheatgrowers' Association), went into retirement after Vichy fell; but the Assistant Syndic, Camille Laurens, was soon elected to the National Assembly, and served as Minister of Agriculture for a time in the 1950's. Laurens, a small stockbreeder from the southern Massif Central, had first emerged to peasant leadership in Chantérac's prewar syndical movement.

A rough check of the Corporation's high personnel shows that of approximately 150 men who served as regional syndics or assistant regional syndics, almost one-third regained positions of national prominence in the postwar syndical movement or in politics. At a session of the APPCA in January 1959, 26 of the delegates in attendance had been regional syndics or assistant syndics of the Corporation. According to Michel Cépède (*Agriculture et alimentation*, p. 75), "almost all" local syndics remained in local syndical leadership positions after the war.

the cooperative use of farm machinery.[28] The National Corporative Council, at its last two sessions in 1944, devoted itself to a discussion of postwar modernization and protective legislation for tenants and farm laborers.[29] And a circular to all syndics from the National Syndic, Adolphe Pointier, called on them to resist every pressure for a return to the old routines after the war. "We intend," he wrote, "to combine the preservation of peasant ways with the utmost modernization of our farms"; France's aim must be "to lead all nations toward an agriculture of the most up-to-date kind."[30] The Corporation had moved a long way—in doctrine, if not in material accomplishments—from the bucolic pastorales of the Pétainists in 1940.

* *

In the realm of positive reform, more credit must go to the Vichy Ministry of Agriculture than to the Corporation. Pierre Caziot was especially active during his two years as Minister. He offered subsidies to encourage peasants who had moved to the cities to return to the soil, and to put unused land back into cultivation; he provided easy government credit to permit the modernization of rural housing; he drafted a broad new law on agricultural education, designed not only to train more agronomists but to provide all peasant children with the rudiments of technical knowledge; and, finally, he and his aides tackled the serious problem of fragmented farm holdings. Their solution was in two parts: (1) a law to simplify and speed the process of *remembrement* (the regrouping of scattered parcels of land), and (2) a further relaxation of the civil code's provisions on equal inheritance, in order to check the break-up of family farms. After Caziot's dismissal, only one significant reform measure was taken: a farm-rents statute promulgated in 1943 to protect the rights of cash tenants. This statute was one of the few reforms of the Vichy era that originated in the offices of the Peasant Corporation.[31]

Although Vichy's reforms compared favorably in scope with the accomplishments of any four-year period during the Third Republic, they hardly constituted a real revolution from above. The changes introduced were both piecemeal and superficial; they sought not to alter France's traditional agrarian system, but to protect it against erosion. True, the Vichy legislation offered some promise of improving rural conditions, and thus perhaps reconciling the peasantry to its role as social ballast. But for a regime that put so much emphasis on its central concern for agriculture, Vichy's agricultural measures showed little imagination or daring.

Partly because Vichy's life was so short, the practical impact of its reforms was slight. Only about a thousand ex-peasants took advantage of state subsidies to return to the soil.[32] *Remembrement*, which could now be initiated by the government as well as by the landowners, was given a new stimulus, but it was hardly under way by 1944.* The law protecting tenants' rights, though it corrected a few long-standing abuses, did not alter the landowner-tenant relationship in any fundamental way.† The educational reform, for lack of adequate financing and controls, had disappointing results. Although it called for compulsory post-elementary-school courses under specially trained instructors, only 7 per cent of all eligible peasant boys and girls were enrolled

---

* The Vichy law on *remembrement*, though slightly strengthened since the war, remains the basic legislation on this topic.

† The statute gave tenants some security against eviction, and required owners to compensate tenants for improvements. It also set up joint commissions to handle owner-tenant disputes. Landlords, however, were given a special advantage by a clause pegging rents to the 1939 value of certain farm products; they were thus protected against inflation. In 1945, the republic perpetuated some aspects of the Vichy law in its statute of rural leases, but made the terms more favorable to tenants.

in such courses five years later.* Of all the Vichy legislation, the most effective was the provision of government loans to improve rural housing; by 1944, some 230,000 applications for such aid were on file, and more than 100,000 home improvements had been completed.[33] This and several others of Vichy's agrarian measures were quietly perpetuated by the postwar republic, either in their original form or in a modified version. Twenty years later, such schemes as the *remembrement* program were producing significant results in some rural areas.[34]

* *

It is not easy to reconstruct what was going on in the villages during the Vichy years. Agrarian leaders and ministerial bureaucrats leave a mark on history; rural life meanwhile tends to flow on without apparent incident. Even before 1940 the peasantry possessed no institutionalized means of expression save the ballot; and now that elections were suspended, they could speak only indirectly through the still inchoate Corporation.

Urban Frenchmen at the time were inclined to view the peasantry with unconcealed resentment and jealousy, and to believe that most farmers were profiting by the era of scarcity to gouge city consumers. One of the commonest legends of the war and liberation periods concerned the *lessiveuses*—the laundry baskets that were allegedly used by black-marketing peasants to store up their accumulated hoards of currency. Indeed, de Gaulle's hesitation to carry out a drastic currency exchange in 1944–45 was widely attributed to his fear of an angry explosion among

---

* Pierre Drouin, in *Le Monde*, April 30, 1949. The Vichy law did, however, encourage the growth of *maisons familiales*, which the Catholics had begun to develop after 1935. These institutions enrolled children who had completed elementary school, and provided them with several weeks of technical and moral training. Only a handful of *maisons familiales* existed before 1940, but by the mid-1950's there were about 300, with an enrollment of 14,000 students.

the peasants, whom the measure would despoil of their ill-gotten profits. The legend contains a little truth and much exaggeration. Black-marketing came to be a common practice—indeed, one that was recognized and built into the system by Frenchmen and Germans alike. Some peasants undoubtedly accumulated paper fortunes, and a great many emerged from the war with larger cash reserves than they had ever before possessed.[35] For the first time in many generations, the rural standard of living probably approached that of the cities—and even exceeded it in the realm of food consumption.[36] But if this last advantage was real enough (and keenly felt by the urban population), much of the peasants' apparent wealth was factitious. They stored up money because there was little or nothing for them to buy; much of their hoard would eventually have to be reinvested in farm equipment, fertilizer, and household items (at inflated prices) as soon as the market returned to normal after the war. On the whole, therefore, Serge Mallet's phrase "an illusory Golden Age" is an appropriate one for this period, so far as the peasantry was concerned.

Some urban critics also denounced the peasants for their alleged political apathy or neutralism. It is true that most anti-German resistance leaders came from the cities, yet there is every reason to believe that the rural population provided its due proportion of rank-and-file resistance sympathizers and activists. No other group could so effectively hide refugees or aid escaping airmen who had been shot down over France. Many peasants furnished information to the espionage networks whose task it was to transmit military intelligence to London. And the *maquis* forces in the hill country were almost entirely dependent for subsistence on the good will of the nearby peasantry. The sociology of the resistance movement has not been adequately studied, but all the evidence suggests that the peasantry contributed its full share both of activists and of victims.[37] To some degree at least, this experience counterbalanced the new urban-rural tensions produced by wartime food shortages, and tended to erode the old psychological barriers between peasants and town-dwellers. Here and there, common action in the resistance could be prolonged into common postwar action in the syndicates or in politics.

6
Unity and Reform from the Left:
The Liberation Epoch

AS EARLY as 1941, a handful of ex-militants of the old left-wing agrarian organizations had begun to meet secretly and to plan for the future. Most of them had been active in the Socialist-oriented Confédération Nationale Paysanne; a few had been officials in the predominantly Radical FNMCA of the Boulevard Saint-Germain. Although the idea of resurrecting the prewar organizations had some appeal, most of the conspirators preferred a single peasant organization roughly equivalent to labor's CGT. Late in 1943, therefore, they set up the clandestine Confédération Générale d'Agriculture (CGA), and set out to recruit members by means of an underground newspaper called *La Résistance paysanne*.[1]

The driving force in the new organization was Pierre Tanguy-Prigent, a young Breton peasant leader and politician of the prewar decade. Tanguy's home village on the Channel coast lay in the heart of a prosperous early-vegetable region—a region whose leftist and anticlerical spirit stood in sharp contrast to the rest of strongly Catholic Brittany. Tanguy, after a sketchy elementary education, had won local fame by organizing a peasants' cooperative in opposition to the powerful Landerneau syndicate; a combative and articulate youngster, he had developed a reputation as a kind of peasant Robin Hood. In 1936, running on the

Socialist ticket, he had been swept into the Chamber of Deputies on the Popular Front wave. At twenty-six, he had been France's youngest deputy.

Despite Tanguy's energetic efforts, his new CGA made little headway during the underground period. Much of the nation's peasant elite was committed to the Corporation; and of those who were anti-Vichy, many had their own ideas about the future. Certain ex-officials of the Boulevard Saint-Germain hoped for a revival of the prewar organizations, with the old FNMCA at their head. At one point, their friends in Algiers even persuaded de Gaulle's provisional government to adopt this plan.[2] On the other wing, the Communists had begun late in 1943 to organize their own network of activist groups—the so-called Committees of Peasant Defense and Action (CDAP)—throughout large areas in the center and the southwest. These Committees built on the foundations laid by Renaud Jean before the war; most of their organizers had been active in Jean's old CGPT. Their leaders emphasized the need to liberate French soil before giving any thought to postwar planning,* but their minds were on the future.

Meanwhile the National Resistance Council (the capstone of the federated underground movements, allied with de Gaulle's government in exile) had begun to take some tentative steps toward postwar agricultural planning. In 1944 it set up a five-man agricultural committee representing various political viewpoints, with a former CNP official named Roger Dusseaulx as its secretary. The committee accomplished little, but on de Gaulle's return to Paris in August it was asked to recommend a suitable Minister of Agriculture for the new provisional government. The

---

* We find this theme even in the last underground issue of *La Terre* (July 1944): "All that counts at the moment is *un tableau de chasse abondamment pourvu de gibier nazi.*" In a few villages in the Massif, the Communist-sponsored peasant committees had even managed to put up candidates for the post of local syndic in the Corporation, and to get them appointed by Vichy (*La Terre*, Limoges, August 1944).

committee suggested Tanguy-Prigent; and de Gaulle (whose interest in agricultural problems was marginal at best) agreed without much hesitation.[3] Tanguy held the post for the next three years—a record of unbroken tenure exceeded by only one other Minister of Agriculture in modern French history. His opportunities were great; the opposition was in temporary eclipse, and most of his backers asked only that he rally all factions to the task of reconstruction. Time was to show that they had misjudged their man; for if Tanguy was a reformer, he was also a rigidly sectarian politician.

It is true that he faced no easy task. He was surrounded by a variety of conflicting demands, and he was hampered by the disastrous state of the nation's food supply. Farm production had fallen to about half the prewar level; and so long as the war continued, little could be done to improve the situation. It was not a propitious moment for embarking on drastic long-range reforms, even if the cabinet and de Gaulle could have been persuaded to adopt such a program. Some reform proposals were ready at hand; several individual planners had been at work during the last months of the occupation, and were prepared to offer Tanguy constructive advice. But although certain of these proposals were well conceived, they tended to be strongly technocratic or "neo-physiocratic" in tone.* To carry them out would

---

* The most qualified of these planners was Professor René Dumont of the Institut National Agronomique, who began early in 1943 to think and write about postwar agrarian reform. During the liberation era, however, he was shunted aside by the men around Tanguy—notably Michel Cépède and Gérard Vée, both old-line Socialists. His ideas soon found a hearing in the Planning Commission set up in 1946; they were elaborated in his book *Le Problème agricole français* (Paris, 1946). Other wartime planners were André Philip and Pierre Lefaucheux (see below, p. 112n), the demographer Louis Chevalier (whose book *Les Paysans*, strongly "peasantist" in tone, was written in anticipation of the liberation), and a group of Dominican priests headed by L. J. Lebret, who in 1942 founded a remarkable monthly called *Economie et humanisme* as a vehicle for the group's "doctrine communautaire."

have required either rigorous authoritarian controls, or a carefully planned campaign of psychological preparation and education in the countryside.

In a general way, Tanguy shared the ideas of these reformers; his goal was a planned, modernized, efficient agriculture in place of the heterogeneous agrarian structure inherited from the past. He had envisioned a single unified peasant organization as the agency through which basic changes could be accomplished. But the politician's concerns were never far from his mind; he was also determined to put the peasant organization into the hands of good Socialists, who would use it to root Socialist influence in the countryside.

Tanguy's CGA had emerged from the underground period as little more than an idea; his task now was to transform it into an institution. Of his three potential sources of opposition, the right was silent and the Radical center—the advocates of a return to the pluralistic syndical pattern of prewar days—was not really dangerous; the urge for reorganization and reform was too strong at the moment. More serious was the threat from the left; for the Communist CDAP had developed real grass-roots strength in the Massif and the south, and had seized control of many Corporation offices and local farm newspapers when Vichy collapsed. More than two thousand village committees had been established during the last months of Vichy; and with the liberation, party agents redoubled their activities. Every peasant, declared the CDAP, was welcome to join: "There must be no more talk of Whites and Reds, of Catholics, Protestants, and atheists. There is no longer any place for such terms as large, or middle-sized, or small, or proletarian; there can only be French peasants, joined together in fruitful union."[4] Communist leaders announced that a national CDAP congress would be held at Toulouse in November, with a view to creating a permanent national organization. Alongside the CDAP army, Tanguy-Prigent's CGA appeared to be little more than a lonely headquarters unit.

Luckily for Tanguy, however, the Communists adopted a strategy of integration: they chose to enter, and to work within, existing labor and peasant organizations, as well as within de Gaulle's government itself. Evidently they felt they had a good chance of swaying these organizations to Communist ends, or perhaps even taking them over. At any rate, CDAP leaders agreed to take part in a meeting of 42 old and new peasant organizations (syndicates, cooperatives, mutual-aid and credit associations) on October 20–21, 1944, and committed themselves to participation in the new CGA.[5] The much advertised Toulouse congress of the CDAP a few weeks later thus lost its meaning, and the Peasant Action Committees disappeared there in an orgy of speechmaking.

Meanwhile, Tanguy's plans were rapidly taking shape. By an ordinance issued on October 12, the government had formally dissolved the Corporation (which Tanguy described as "a criminal enterprise in the service of Germany, modeled on the Hitlerite and especially the Italian corporative systems"). At the same time, the principle of peasant unity was proclaimed; henceforth new farmers' organizations could be established only with the government's consent. The ordinance authorized Tanguy to appoint a National Committee for Agricultural Action, together with a series of local committees for each department, to supervise the establishment of the CGA.[6] The National Committee, hand-picked by Tanguy, was remarkable for its high proportion of dedicated Socialists and Communists. Its key figure, Anthelme Lyonnet, was not a peasant at all, but a bureaucratic official in the millers' and bakers' cooperative movement.[7] Tanguy later justified this choice of personnel by pointing out that these were the men who had helped him found the CGA in the underground era. "How could I disown friends who shared with me the risks of the resistance?" he asked at the CGA's founding congress in March 1945.[8]

A number of knotty problems confronted Tanguy's Committee. Although the Corporation had cleared the way for a unified peasant organization, it had never fully resolved various structural problems. One of these was the relationship between syndicalism proper and such "service" operations as the farm cooperatives and mutual-aid societies. In the prewar era, there had been no clear-cut distinction between them; the syndicates, like the service organizations, had customarily engaged in commercial activities instead of confining themselves to political and educational work. Vichy had attempted to separate the two functions, and had sought to place the syndicates at the apex of the Corporation, with the "services" attached to them in a somewhat subordinate capacity. Some anti-Vichyites accepted this arrangement as suitable for the new CGA; others, however, saw the "services" as the heart of any peasant professional organization, and wanted to make them completely autonomous. Some extremists even viewed agrarian syndicalism as a kind of hors d'œuvre, and argued that it might disappear altogether once the peasants were provided with a full array of cooperatives and mutual-aid associations.[9]

In the end, Tanguy's advisers settled on a compromise arrangement that appeared to favor the "services" over the syndicates. Within the CGA (a confederation, as its name indicated), syndicalism proper would constitute only one of seven component segments or "federations." This syndicalist component would be called the Fédération Nationale des Syndicats d'Exploitants Agricoles (FNSEA), and would be open to all active farm operators—owners, cash tenants, and share tenants.* Alongside the FNSEA there would be three federations representing the "services": the cooperatives, the mutual-aid societies, and the farm-

---

* Absentee landlords, who were excluded from the FNSEA, promptly organized their own special-interest group outside the CGA. This Fédération Nationale de la Propriété Agricole set up its headquarters, appropriately enough, in the building of the old Société des Agriculteurs de France (Rue d'Athènes).

credit associations. Three other federations would represent special segments of the rural population: the agricultural technicians, the Catholic farm laborers, and the non-Catholic farm laborers. Although the FNSEA would have the largest representation in central CGA councils, there was some reason to doubt that it could outvote the other six federations. Yet it was the FNSEA that seemed likely to become the peasants' real "trade union"; for it would be composed of and run by working farmers, whereas the "services" would in most cases be represented by technicians or bureaucrats rather than farmers. Furthermore, many of these technicians had traditionally been left-wing in their political sympathies.

Tanguy was understandably accused of trying to turn the CGA into a Socialist political machine, and perhaps he was, but he had another motive as well. He and his advisers believed that an agricultural revolution could not be achieved by the peasants themselves, but would have to be organized by the government; and governmental action meant working through the technicians with the more or less willing consent of the peasants. They saw the CGA as the main agency of rural change; therefore the balance of power within it would have to favor the technicians and bureaucrats in agriculture rather than the mass of peasants. The argument had some weight; still, the organizational structure of the CGA made it inevitable that an internal struggle for power would ensue before long.

The CGA's planners moved rapidly from the blueprint to the construction stage. In a sense, they chose to build from the top down; they set up the CGA before establishing its most important constituent federation, the FNSEA. Late in 1944, under the guidance of the departmental committees appointed by Tanguy, peasants met in villages throughout France to form local CGA units and to elect their officers (usually by show of hands). In many parts of the south, this process was simple: the Com-

munists' Peasant Action Committees simply converted themselves into CGA units, and kept the same officers. The problem
was more complex in regions where most of the potential peasant
leaders had served the Corporation. Tanguy's agents permitted
some of these men to stand for election; others they ruled in-
eligible for syndical office for a five-year period, although it was
not always easy to find popular substitutes. By March 1945
the local and departmental structure was complete, and delegates could be sent off to Paris for the CGA's founding congress
(March 16–18).[10]

Superficially, at least, the congress was a triumph for Tanguy
and his collaborators. Lyonnet's report on past achievements
and future plans was approved almost without debate, and a
ready-made list of nominees to the 49-member Bureau Confé-
déral was accepted without alteration. Yet signs of dissension were
appearing before the session was over. One Catholic delegate
got the floor to protest against enforced syndical unity, and to
call for a return to pluralism. (He was promptly howled down,
for the mystique of unity was strong.) There was wider protest
over the undemocratic manner of electing the Bureau. A number
of delegates (especially from the Midi) voted against the list,
or refused to vote at all;[11] and Tanguy was driven to promise
that more democratic procedures would be used at the next congress. Some weeks later, under continuing Catholic pressure, he
promised that syndical pluralism would eventually be restored,
though not while there was any chance that selfish political rivalries might wreck the hope of peasant unity. It was not until 1946
that the CGA's temporary monopoly was finally removed.

The last step in building the CGA was the establishment of
its syndical component, the FNSEA. All the other federations,
as well as their CGA capstone, were in place and functioning by
mid-1945. But the FNSEA, if it were to have any real vitality,
could not be set up by decree from above; it required free elections at the village level—the first real test of peasant opinion

since the CGA planners had begun their work.[12] Early in January 1946 the peasants were summoned to the polls. There had been much controversy in Paris over eligibility to vote; according to some estimates, only about one-third of the nation's farmers had formally adhered to the CGA.[13] It was finally ruled that all farmers might vote, and that the act of voting would automatically make them members of the FNSEA.

How many peasants turned out on election day remains a matter of debate. CGA officials announced triumphantly that about 70 per cent had responded, thus proving the peasantry's passionate attachment to syndical action and syndical unity. Hostile observers placed the figure at about one-third; but since no official statistics were ever published, an accurate estimate is impossible.[14] Far more important was the character of the vote cast; and here CGA leaders had no reason to rejoice. Indeed, something like 80 per cent of those elected had hitherto refused to take any part in the CGA. There was clearly a strong trend away from the left, except in central and southern France, where the Socialists and Communists enjoyed their greatest rural strength. Tanguy-Prigent's native department of Finistère sent only three Socialist delegates to the subsequent national FNSEA congress (as compared with twelve delegates from the new Christian Democratic party, the Mouvement Républicain Populaire); and the Communists also suffered some severe disappointments.*

---

* Interview with Roger Dusseaulx, 1946. The Communists had hoped to run their peasant leader, Waldeck Rochet, for the presidency of the FNSEA, but thought better of it when Rochet could not even win the departmental presidency in the Saône-et-Loire. Rochet was a cobbler's son from the Saône-et-Loire; he had joined the party in 1923, at the age of eighteen. After brief experience as a truck farmer, he entered the party bureaucracy as a full-time official, and was sent to Moscow for advanced training at the Marx-Lenin Institute. He became director of the party's agrarian section in 1934, won election to the Chamber in 1936, and was named editor of *La Terre* in 1937. Arrested along with the other Communist deputies in 1939, he was imprisoned in North Africa until the Allied forces freed him to join de Gaulle's Free French.

In retrospect, some leftists bitterly regretted that all farmers had been allowed to vote in 1946, rather than active CGA adherents alone.[15]

To a certain degree, the FNSEA elections represented the peasants' conscious reaction against the organizers of the CGA, whose interests struck many of them as urban and political rather than rural and professional. Much more clearly, however, it represented the natural tendency of village communities to choose tried and trusted local spokesmen: the same men who had been active in the prewar peasant movement and, often, in the Vichy Corporation. France's rural elite was still both small and new; the liberation did not magically produce a new set of potential leaders. Except in regions of leftist orientation, conservatives or Christian Democrats were swept into office. Similarly, when the FNSEA held its founding congress in March 1946, conservatives and Christian Democrats filled the posts of command. Eugène Forget, a Christian Democratic smallowner from the Angers region in western France, became president; and the still more important post of secretary-general went to a thoroughgoing conservative—René Blondelle, operator of a large modern farm in the northeast. Both men had held positions in the Corporation: Forget as an assistant regional syndic, and Blondelle as both a regional syndic and a member of the National Corporative Council. Clearly, a new phase in CGA history was about to begin: a phase of sporadic but severe internal conflict over the structure and spirit of agrarian syndicalism.

Three major factions were competing in this cold war: the leftists, the rightists, and the Christian Democrats. The leftists (mainly Socialists, with a minority Communist wing) still clung to control of the CGA's confederal organs, and sought to keep the locus of power there. Their chief spokesman was Philippe Lamour, who had been named secretary-general of the CGA in 1945. Lamour had had a curiously erratic career: a brilliant young lawyer in prewar Paris, a prolific novelist and world traveler by avocation, he had abandoned his legal practice for somewhat obscure reasons and, during the Vichy era, had settled down to operate a large vineyard in the Midi. Lamour's political record was equally bizarre. He had played a prominent role in Georges Valois's ephemeral Faisceau movement in the 1920's, had run for the Chamber as a Radical Socialist in 1936, had once served as defense counsel for the Rumanian Communist leader Ana Pauker, had allegedly gone through a brief Pétainist stage in 1940, and had emerged after the liberation as an unaffiliated leftist. Although some right-wing critics scoffed at Lamour as "a comic-opera peasant," his enormous energy, his gifts as an orator, and his remarkable intelligence and personal charm brought him to the top almost at once, and kept him there long after the leftists had lost their grip on the CGA.*

The rightist faction found its natural center of gravity in the FNSEA; its aim, therefore, was to shift power from the CGA to its separate federations, and to make the FNSEA fully autonomous. The ablest spokesman for this viewpoint was René Blondelle, whose vigor and persistence balanced the brilliance of Lamour. Before the war, Blondelle had headed the regional branch of the UNSA in his home department of the Aisne, where he operated a 600-acre rented farm. His corporatist opinions and his social conservatism had led him to cooperate in the 1930's

---

* Lamour ("séducteur par excellence," an admiring acquaintance calls him) is the kind of man around whom legends tend to collect. I am indebted to a number of informants for colorful (though often contradictory) accounts of his career both before and during the CGA era. One story, certainly distorted and probably apocryphal, is that Lamour ran for the Chamber on the Socialist ticket in 1936, campaigned in favor of his more successful Communist rival at the runoff ballot, and married the daughter of the Radical candidate three weeks later.

In recent years, much of Lamour's energy has gone into a remarkably successful project of regional planning and reclamation in the lower Rhône valley.

with both the Dorgerists and the Agrarian Party, and had brought him to posts of national leadership in the Vichy Corporation. In 1946 the farmers of the Aisne had reaffirmed their confidence in him by electing him head of their departmental branch of the FNSEA.*

Midway between these two factions, the Christian Democrats held the balance of power during the early postwar years, and sought to find some compromise that would preserve peasant unity. Eugène Forget, their chief agrarian spokesman at the time, was one of the most remarkable members of this newly emerging Catholic rural elite. A sincere and selfless man, with a purely local reputation before 1946, Forget was elevated to national prominence mainly because the better-known Catholic farm leaders had been too deeply involved in the Corporation to stand for high office so soon after the liberation. During his three years as president of the FNSEA, Forget worked unceasingly to mediate between factions, and to establish the peasant's claim to attention not only as a producer, but as a human being. In his few spare moments, he managed to commute to his forty-acre farm, and to keep it a model of efficiency and modern methods. Cynics regarded him as naïve and "soft," useful only as a temporary buffer during a period of internal stress. But to those who

---

* Although Blondelle has probably been the most important figure in French agrarian syndicalism since the war, his qualities of character are not easy to assess—even for those who have worked closely with him. Some acquaintances are struck by what they call his harsh and somewhat imperious nature; others describe him as "able and sincere, but flexible and devious." Among agrarian leaders, says one parliamentary official, he stands out as "the *grand seigneur* type." His effectiveness both in large syndical meetings and in smoke-filled committee rooms cannot be doubted. Since the beginning of his career in the 1930's, he has never been defeated in any campaign for syndical or political office. Yet in 1962 an acquaintance could describe him as "a politician who has failed"—as a man who might have risen to the very top in political life had he not crossed swords repeatedly with just those men who might have furthered his career.

knew him well, he stood as a symbol of personal integrity and dedication to the welfare of rural France.*

Blondelle's right-wing group lost no time in mounting an attack. At the FNSEA's second national congress late in 1947, Blondelle charged that agrarian syndicalism was hamstrung by the confusion of authority between the CGA and the FNSEA. Housed in the same building (the old headquarters of the Corporation, just behind the Opéra in Paris), sharing the same secretarial services, the officials of the two organizations were continually clashing over the locus of authority. The solution, he argued, was to reduce the CGA to a coordinating agency and transfer its essential services to the FNSEA. Such a reform, he declared, would drive politics out of agrarian syndicalism, and would leave professional interests supreme.[16]

Blondelle's blunt assault stirred up a bitter dispute; and although the congress adopted his general report by a large majority, its thornier issues were referred to a committee for further study. Most members still wanted to avoid any action that might permanently split peasant syndicalism into two hostile organizations; the façade of unity was therefore maintained. Over the next two years, the internal tensions increased, but it was clear that the Blondelle faction was steadily consolidating its hold. One factor that strengthened the rightists was the revival of the prewar specialized associations, and their partial absorption into the FNSEA. Several of these groups were wealthy, powerful, and aggressively led; they posed a potential threat to the CGA whether inside or outside it. In 1947 they were finally brought into the FNSEA as semi-autonomous units, with direct repre-

* It was typical of Forget that, although eligible for a high priority to buy a new car, he insisted on waiting two years for his turn on the ration list. During an official tour of the United States with other farm officials, Forget left the party at Kansas City and flew home in order to meet a prior commitment for a whistle-stop speech.

sentation on the FNSEA's governing bodies.* Their most militant spokesmen shared Blondelle's views, and exercised an influence far out of proportion to their numbers.

Meanwhile, leftist influence in the CGA was dwindling rapidly. One setback was the fall of Tanguy-Prigent, who was replaced in 1947 as Minister of Agriculture by the Christian Democrat Pierre Pflimlin. Another adverse factor was a split in the cooperative movement; soon after organizational freedom was restored, some of the largest and oldest cooperatives seceded from the Central Union of Agricultural Cooperatives (founded under CGA sponsorship after the liberation), and created a rival organization run by rightists. Still another problem was an attempt by the Communists to organize the 700,000 small cash tenants and share tenants into a new Cash Tenants' and Share Tenants' Association, conceived of as a completely autonomous unit within the FNSEA. (This maneuver was blocked by non-Communist elements, who joined the new organization, installed a non-Communist as president, and voted to make it merely a "section" of the FNSEA rather than an autonomous "association."[17])

By 1950, the rightists were ready to strike for outright control of the syndical movement. President Forget, who had almost been defeated for re-election in 1949, foresaw the trend of events, and at the FNSEA congress in 1950 he regretfully announced his resignation. Neither the politicians nor his fellow syndicalists, he remarked, had responded to his reliance on persuasion or his efforts at mediation.[18] Blondelle was promptly moved up into the presidency, while another ex-syndic of the Vichy era, 300-pound Jean Laborbe of the Rhône valley region, squeezed into

---

* The specialized associations were assigned 76 delegates to FNSEA congresses (total membership about 400), and 11 delegates on the FNSEA national council (total about 120). They often formed a bloc with the representatives of the large-farming departments.

the secretary-general's chair. The last remaining Communists, and most of the Socialists as well, were pushed out of the FN-SEA's Bureau. Some leftists clung to their high positions in the CGA and the "service" federations; but the CGA was reduced to an increasingly shadowy role, while the FNSEA leaders emerged as chief spokesmen for the agricultural profession.*

* *

The building of a unified CGA had not been the only goal of France's agrarian leaders immediately after the liberation. Tanguy-Prigent and his colleagues also intended to undertake the modernization of agriculture: rapid mechanization, a speed-up in *remembrement*, and the rational planning of crops on a nation-wide basis. All this, however, they proposed to achieve without destroying France's small-peasant base.[19] Mechanization, there-fore, would have to be carried out not on Soviet or capitalist lines, but by the cooperative use of machinery; and market organization would also require a further expansion of cooperatives (combined with the establishment of additional state marketing agencies on the model of the Cereals Office). In addition, special steps would be necessary to protect the small peasantry—particularly the small tenants and share tenants, who were least able to protect them-selves. The technocratic and the peasantist doctrines were thus combined to form a somewhat unstable compound.[20]

For some of these goals, Vichy legislation had already pointed the way; and though in principle all Vichy laws were declared null and void, in practice (as we have seen) a number of Vichy's agrarian reforms were quietly kept on the books. In some cases, Vichy's acts were amended or reinforced—as, for example, in the realm of tenants' rights. In 1945, parts of the Vichy farm-rents statute were incorporated into a more sweeping statute of rural

---

* For the subsequent conflict between CGA and FNSEA, see below, pp. 124–25.

leases, designed to protect both cash tenants and share tenants against unjust expulsion and other forms of landlord exploitation. The statute also sought to encourage the conversion of share tenantry into cash tenantry, on the ground that share tenantry represented a kind of feudal survival in the modern era.* The number of share tenants fell sharply at first, but the decline soon leveled off.[21]

Some reforms of the liberation era had no Vichy ancestry, but originated with Tanguy and his advisers in the Ministry of Agriculture. Among them was a device to encourage the collective purchase and use of tractors and other farm machinery by groups of small peasants. Such groups were authorized to form Coopératives pour l'utilisation des machines agricoles (CUMA), and to receive top priority for the purchase of expensive and scarce equipment. CUMAs sprouted at once like mushrooms after a rain; by 1948, more than 12,000 of them had been organized. During the next two or three years, however, many CUMAs disappeared, and it became clear that the movement had been partly artificial in character. While tractors were severely rationed and CUMAs enjoyed a purchase priority, well-to-do farmers had organized false CUMAs in order to get a machine without delay. The façade fell away as soon as rationing ended. Some genuine CUMAs did survive, however, in spite of the tensions they often generated among the co-owners; and by the mid-

---

* This statute of rural leases (slightly revised in 1946) set the rental period at nine years and ensured renewal at the option of the tenant, unless the owner should decide to operate the farm himself or turn it over to a close relative. It ensured a purchase priority to the tenant if the land were put up for sale. Share tenantry was henceforth to be based on a two-to-one division of the product in favor of the tenant; and share tenants who wished to become cash tenants were authorized to carry out this conversion by simple request. In subsequent years, a restrictive interpretation of the statute by the Conseil d'Etat somewhat limited its effects. Although the statute has often been criticized, either for infringing property rights or for rendering rural property relationships insufficiently flexible, it is now quite generally accepted as a useful reform.

1950's, their number began to mount steadily once more.[22] Here was one reform of the liberation era that left an enduring mark on the countryside.

Somewhat less successful was Tanguy's experiment with village youth centers called *foyers ruraux*. Before the war, opportunities for recreation in rural France had been virtually nil. As a result, the young fled to the cities if they could, and most of those who remained behind lived closed and isolated lives, separated even from their village neighbors. This social atomization was, of course, partly the product of long tradition, of mental habits deeply ingrained. Yet the young, at least, wanted some sort of recreation, and this the government now proposed to provide. A special fund was established to construct or acquire buildings for these *foyers ruraux*, and over the next few years several hundred *foyers* were established. But the scheme was not particularly successful, and the impact of the *foyers* seems to have been slight. Part of the trouble was lack of local leadership— the village schoolmaster did not always make an effective master of ceremonies. Equally serious was the hostility of both the Catholic hierarchy and the Catholic youth movement, the JAC, which by this time had rooted itself over large areas of rural France.[23] Efforts to fuse the energies of these rival enterprises failed; and in the end the JAC rather than the *foyers ruraux* was to take the lead in rejuvenating rural France.

Two other reform projects of a much more basic nature were advanced by the Tanguy group in 1944, but they encountered such violent opposition that they had to be abandoned. One of these was a plan for establishing a National Land Office (*office national foncier*); the other was designed to encourage *coopératives de culture*—i.e., voluntary mergers of several adjoining family farms for purposes of joint operation (though not joint ownership). Both schemes aroused a storm of protest against the "sorcerers' apprentices" who were allegedly "preparing the way for a kolkhoz system."[24] Tanguy's critics, whether honestly or maliciously, confused his plans with certain highly technocratic proposals for agrarian reform that had been put forward in Algiers just before the liberation, or that had been concocted by certain doctrinaire reformers in the underground.* Since at least one reformer had brutally asserted that no concessions must be made to "the peasant mentality," and that the ultimate goal must be the collectivization of all the land, the fears aroused in the countryside were understandable. Moreover, the scope and character of the proposed Land Office were ambiguously stated at the outset, and Tanguy's later efforts to soft-pedal or water down the plan only increased the suspicion and confusion that surrounded it.

The earliest description of the Land Office appeared in the Socialist pamphlet *La Rénovation paysanne*; it was remarkably opaque on a number of points, but asserted the need to modify the traditional concept of property rights and to establish alongside it the principle of *propriété culturale* (i.e., the farm operator's stake in a farm, as distinct from that of the landowner). Although the pamphlet disclaimed any intention to dispossess some

---

* The most uninhibited of these technocratic reformers was Pierre Lefaucheux, an engineer who became director of the nationalized Renault plant after the liberation. His underground essay "Passage au socialisme" was published early in 1945 in *Les Cahiers politiques* (March and April issues, pp. 37–53 and 37–48); it appeared just at the right moment to reinforce the rightists' alarm. Lefaucheux declared that pending the arrival of complete collectivism, the small peasant should be forced to increase production by threatening him with the fate of the Soviet kulaks. A less hair-raising memorandum written at Algiers in July 1944 by one of de Gaulle's provisional ministers, the Socialist André Philip, caused even more agitation —perhaps because it remained unpublished, so that wildly distorted versions of it circulated by hearsay (interview with Pierre Tanguy-Prigent, 1951). Philip was denounced by right-wingers as Tanguy's evil genius, whose "Algiers plan" was designed to open the floodgates of revolution by shifting a large part of the peasant population to the cities. Worse still, they added, "le lunatique André Philip . . . voulait faire boire aux français deux litres de lait par jour." Claude Morgat, "La crise agricole," *Ecrits de Paris*, Nov. 1950, pp. 105–6.

farmers in favor of others, it added that "an equitable distribution of that means of production, the land" was in the national interest, and it proposed to begin by handing over to the Office the confiscated farms of Corporation officials and black marketeers. The outcry that followed led Tanguy into a series of explanations, denials, and retreats. Late in 1944 he directed the editor of *La Libération paysanne* to cancel a series of articles on *coopératives de culture,* and a year or so later he issued a pamphlet asserting that his plans had been completely misunderstood. He had never intended, he said, to set up a powerful central agency, but only a series of departmental agencies; he had never intended to let them take title to property, or break up large farms, or substitute cooperative farming for family farming. He even expressed regret that the name "Office" had been used, since the label was an irritant suggesting state control. His model, he declared, was the rural structure of the Dutch or the Danes.[25]

Very likely even an abler man than Tanguy would have failed to win support for such daring reforms in the confused and complex liberation era; it may be that the right moment in history had not yet arrived. So we are told, at any rate, by one of Tanguy's admirers, the journalist Serge Mallet. "History," Mallet writes, "will view Tanguy-Prigent's failure at the Ministry of Agriculture as the result of a contradiction between the general political climate (in the liberation era everyone in the cities was 'socialist') and the mood of the peasantry."[26] There is much to be said for this view, despite its strong flavor of Marxian orthodoxy. Yet the time was ripe for leadership, and one may still ask whether abler and more perceptive leadership than Tanguy's might not have made an effective start toward altering peasant attitudes and clarifying peasant needs. At least the problem might have been stated, and given serious attention. The relative failure of the liberation-era reformers left many basic agrarian issues obscure, and postponed any serious public discussion of them for a decade.

7

Syndicalists and Politicians: The Fourth Republic

BY THE END of the 1940's France seemed to be settling back to normal. The liberation epoch, with its mingled hopes and fears of sweeping reform, was giving way to a more prosaic age. Politically, the Fourth Republic was taking on at least the outward appearance of the Third; economically and socially, the traditional structures had been modified but not fundamentally transformed. Although the old elites had been partially displaced, they occupied enough key positions to ensure the dominance of continuity over change.

In this persistence of old patterns the peasantry seemed to share. By 1950, leaders of prewar or Vichy vintage had replaced the left-wing reformers at the head of the new agrarian syndicalism, and collectivism was everywhere yielding ground. Membership in the FNSEA, which had stood somewhere between 1.5 and 2 million in 1946–49, dropped rapidly during the next four years and eventually leveled off at about 700,000.[1] The postwar surge into farm-machinery cooperatives suddenly subsided, and more than half of the existing CUMAs disintegrated. More significant still, departures for the city increased dramatically, and soon exceeded the prewar rate. After 1945, the agricultural population dropped by between 1 and 2 per cent annually: by the end of the Fourth Republic, the proportion of the active population engaged in agriculture had declined from

35 to 23 per cent, and the number of farms had fallen from
2.5 million to about 2.2 million.[2]

These trends reflected, in considerable part at least, the end
of the war-born era of chronic shortages. The transition began
in 1948, when the government discontinued many wartime controls over distribution and prices. For the first time in years,
farmers were confronted by the almost forgotten problem of
crop surpluses, and found the price scissors working to their dis-
advantage. The price ratio still favored agriculture at the beginning of 1948; by the end of the year it had been reversed,
and thereafter the gap widened, until by 1950 the disparity in
favor of industrial products was approximately 22 to 15.[3] Agriculture's share of the national income skidded from a postwar
high of 25.4 per cent in 1947 to 14.3 per cent in 1951; and
thereafter fluctuated between 11 and 14 per cent.[4]

True, the decline in farm population partially caused this
drop in agriculture's share of the national income, and there was
no serious reduction in peasant living standards. Per capita agricultural income in 1958 was reliably estimated at 25 per cent
higher than in 1938. But the nonagricultural population was
meanwhile enjoying a per capita increase of between 60 and 70
per cent; and this disparity was keenly felt by the peasantry.[5]
Besides, the 25 per cent increase was an average figure; as late
as 1958, at least half of the nation's peasants were still living a
barely marginal existence.[6] The natural consequence was a revival of the agrarian discontent of the 1930's, with buyers' strikes
and delivery strikes, mass demonstrations (featuring a new device, the tractor roadblock), and a heightened receptiveness to
the appeals of agrarian demagogues.

The first wave of this peasant disaffection was directed not
only against the government, but to some degree against the
leaders of agrarian syndicalism as well. The decline in FNSEA
membership after 1949 was especially marked in the under-

developed small-farming regions of the center and south, where some departmental units virtually disappeared.[7] Sheer poverty played some part in this flight from syndicalism, and so did political antagonisms; areas of leftist tradition were especially resentful at the conquest of the FNSEA by ex-Vichyites. But some small peasants also suspected that their interests would be poorly served by syndical leaders who came from the large modernized wheat- and beet-growing regions of the north.

The FNSEA strategists responded by renewed appeals to peasant unity, and by a fresh scheme of direct intervention in politics. Some FNSEA leaders believed that the peasants ought to have their own agrarian party, patterned after those in Scandinavia or in prewar eastern Europe. The nucleus for such a party already existed in the tiny Parti Paysan, headed by Paul Antier, a prewar member of Fleurant Agricola's old Agrarian Party. Although Antier owned a farm or two in his natal region of the southern Massif Central, he had never been a practicing farmer himself. A former court clerk, he had stood successfully for parliament in 1936 on a nonparty ticket, and had joined the Agrarian group after taking his seat in the Chamber. In 1941, after some wavering, he had joined de Gaulle's Free French movement in exile, and he had emerged from the Vichy period with a clean record. Sensing the country's need for change, he had substituted the label Parti Paysan for Parti Agraire, on the theory that a new package might attract new customers.* The contents of the package, however, had not changed very much;

---

* Antier spontaneously offered this explanation during an interview in January 1951. In response to a question about urban deputies representing a peasant party, he said that a real peasant in parliament would be as much out of place as a university professor on the farm, and he insisted that his voters accepted this argument. Antier's party attracted a curious mixture of politicians: his parliamentary group came to include Jacques Le Roy Ladurie, Jacques Isorni (one of Pétain's lawyers in 1945), and a Tahitian deputy named Oopa.

Antier still preached that peculiarly narrow variety of peasant-ist doctrine that glorified peasant individualism and the virtues of smallness above all else. His party won only a handful of seats in the National Assembly in 1946, but his parliamentary group grew by process of accretion, attracting enough strays from other conservative parties to give him twenty-odd follow-ers in the National Assembly by 1951. The Peasant Party's main strength, like that of its prewar predecessor, lay in the underdeveloped and politically conservative sections of the Mas-sif Central and the Cévennes; but it was putting out tentacles into other small-farming areas as well.

Antier, whose ambition was equaled only by his opportun-ism, was naturally eager for an alliance with the FNSEA that would make his party the official political arm of the peasantry. But Blondelle and most of the FNSEA leaders preferred to develop a kind of multiparty farm bloc in parliament. Under Blondelle's so-called "civic action" scheme, the FNSEA would give its seal of approval to any candidate prepared to commit himself to defend agricultural interests as defined by the syndi-cate. In addition, syndical officials would be permitted to stand for political office, and would thus be clearly identified as agrar-ian spokesmen. In the words of one enthusiastic advocate of this scheme, "Blondelle wants to settle scores with the deputies who have betrayed us . . . ; he also wants hostages in parlia-ment, men of our own whom we can control and who will vote our way."[8]

Although the "civic action" scheme appeared to keep the FNSEA free of party ties, in practice it opened the way to a tacit FNSEA alliance with the parties of the liberal-conservative right, whose outlook coincided with that of the Blondelle group. FNSEA support went to most of the Peasant Party's candidates and to many Republican Independents (a predominantly urban middle-class party that had formed an electoral alliance with the Peasant group). In addition, the syndicate backed a considerable number of local or national FNSEA officials who stood for office on ambiguously labeled tickets with a right-wing slant.[9]

When the electoral dust settled in June 1951, Blondelle could claim a notable victory. Not since the nineteenth century had so many farmers been elected to parliament; and two-thirds of these had enjoyed the FNSEA's official backing.[10] Most of the "civic action" deputies joined either the Peasant group or the Republican Independents in the Assembly; and the two groups chose to prolong their electoral association by organizing a common bloc in parliament. With a total of almost a hundred deputies (a figure that increased to 130 by the end of the session), the Independent-Peasant bloc was one of the most powerful groups in the Assembly. From 1951 to 1956, every Minister of Agriculture came from this group.

Blondelle moved at once to consolidate his victory. At his suggestion, the farm bloc in parliament was given structural form; the friends of agriculture in both houses (and in the Economic Council as well) organized an "intergroup" called the Amicale Parlementaire Agricole (APA), drawn from all parties of the center and right but dominated by the Independent-Peasant bloc.* During the next five years, FNSEA spokesmen appeared regularly at APA meetings to lecture the politicians on agriculture's needs. No other interest group in France enjoyed this kind of direct entree to parliament—as the press was quick to point out. According to the popular weekly *Paris-Match*, "six unknown leaders" of the FNSEA now commanded "an army of 1,200,000 men, whose secret tribunal makes and unmakes ministries, while a frown from M. Blondelle throws the two

---

* The Communists refused to participate in the APA, and the Socialists also refrained until 1958. There were about a hundred members during the Fourth Republic. At one point, ex-premier Edgar Faure was elected to the presidency of the APA—an action that outraged many agrarians, for Faure was a lawyer of strictly urban background.

assemblies into a panic." And the Parisian daily *Combat* sourly proposed that the constitution be amended to give parliament its right name—the National Peasant Assembly.[11] FNSEA leaders congratulated themselves. "Thanks to your presence in parliament," Blondelle told the members of the APA in 1952, "we have seen a change in the behavior of this country's parliamentary assemblies." Indeed, he added, the nation itself had at last begun to "think agriculturally" (*penser agricole*).[12]

Already, however, the fruits of "civic action" were turning bitter. Directly after the elections, Paul Antier was named Minister of Agriculture—a triumph of unprecedented proportions for a self-styled peasant spokesman. But Antier's glory proved to be fleeting; he quickly fell out with both his premier, René Pleven, and his own chief lieutenant in the Peasant Party, Camille Laurens. Success evidently went to Antier's head; he began to think of himself as France's next premier, and to intrigue behind Pleven's back. Pleven promptly requested his resignation, and Antier was doubly outraged when Laurens accepted appointment as his successor. The squabble culminated in a party split, which, though patched up intermittently over the next few years, eventually ended (in 1957) in permanent schism.

Tensions also developed between the Peasant group and the Republican Independents; for despite their tactical alliance, they represented quite different interests. Most of the Independents spoke for liberal-conservative business elements in the urban areas, or for the large modernized farmers of the northeast; most of the Peasant deputies came from relatively backward small-farming districts south of the Loire.[13] Although the two parties managed to maintain their alliance, it was not easy for them to agree on the major agrarian issues. Small wonder that they preferred to obscure some of those issues, or to deny their existence.

Such issues were, nevertheless, both real and chronic. The

postwar years of agricultural recovery had actually widened the gap between the modernized and the underdeveloped farm regions, between what people were beginning to call "France's two agricultures";[14] and the anomalies of France's marketing system operated to the same effect. Growers of products in the "free sector" (meat, milk, fruits, and vegetables) were exposed to all the hazards of a fluctuating market, while the growers of cereals and sugar beets basked in the protective shadow of state-regulated marketing devices. Between the two, the winegrowers enjoyed a qualified measure of state protection. Most of the cereals and beets were grown by the large modernized producers of the Paris basin and the northeast—i.e., by just those producers who had assumed the dominant role in the FNSEA. As the gap between the "two agricultures" widened, many small peasants began to suspect that they were being victimized not only by their urban enemies but by their syndical leaders as well.

FNSEA leaders denied that the syndicate was a tool of the large farmers. Several key officials of the FNSEA, they pointed out, were themselves small or middle farmers and understood the problems of the small peasantry. Furthermore, although the large farming areas provided most of the syndicate's financial support, the small-farming regions controlled a majority of the seats in the National Council—indeed, they were given favored treatment, for despite the membership decline in these areas after 1950, they were allowed to keep their full representation in the FNSEA's central organs.[15] As for the FNSEA's action program and lobbying activities, how could any peasant doubt that the key to the agrarian problem, for small and large farmers alike, was higher farm prices?

Critics of the FNSEA replied that a powerful minority had learned how to dominate the organization for its own ends. One of this minority's instruments was the Fédération du Nord et du Bassin Parisien, a regional organization of a dozen or so large-farming departments with headquarters in Paris, where FNSEA representatives from the affiliated departments met to concert strategy prior to FNSEA Council sessions or annual congresses.[16] The large growers were much better financed, and had been able to develop tougher and shrewder leadership, than the more dispersed small peasantry. Furthermore, said the critics, their leaders were adept at dividing the small peasantry against itself, notably by persuading delegates from the Catholic and conservative west to oppose delegates from the more leftist central and southern departments in the name of faith, property, and the social order. Indeed, on occasion these western small-peasant delegates actually proposed, argued for, and voted through the large farmers' program. Finally, the handful of small farmers in high syndical posts were "pawns" appointed by the large growers to ward off criticism.*

The arguments of the FNSEA's critics are perhaps more convincing than those of its defenders. Whether by conscious manipulation or not, the large-farming group did keep a powerful grip on the syndical machinery by teaming up with socially conservative elements from the small-farming west and from scattered areas in the center and southeast. Whether for selfish reasons or not, the FNSEA leaders focused their main lobbying efforts on goals that would benefit the large growers more directly than

* The most important of the small-farmer officials were Secretary-General Albert Génin (who operated a 25-acre polycultural farm in the Isère), Assistant Secretary-General Lucien Biset (40 acres in the Savoie), and Assistant Secretary-General Louis Bidau (15 acres in the Basses-Pyrénées). Several instances of collaboration between the syndical leaders and delegates of the small-farming west were described to me by young syndicalist leaders during a series of interviews in 1960. At one FNSEA session where the large wheatgrowers were attempting to end certain special privileges for small growers, six speakers took the floor in support of the change—all of them from the small-farming west. When the FNSEA's national council was elected in 1960, syndical leaders managed to defeat certain young-peasant candidates from the south by persuading western delegates that these candidates were dangerous leftists.

the small peasants. Nothing was likely to change this state of affairs so long as profound differences of outlook continued to divide the small peasantry against itself and to outweigh such common interests as it possessed. The kind of agrarian unity sponsored by the FNSEA spokesmen rested, ironically enough, on the perpetuation of these differences within the small-peasant group.

* *

Meanwhile, rising peasant discontent gave the left-wing leaders of the old CGA a chance to challenge the Blondelle group, and to threaten an open schism in agrarian syndicalism. The crisis developed in 1953, when serious price and marketing problems hit both the winegrowers of the south and the cattle- and hog-raisers of central France. Wine prices had already been sagging since production returned to the prewar level in 1950; with bumper harvests, the compulsory distillation of surplus wine no longer sufficed to ensure a balance between supply and demand. All through 1952, parliament wrangled inconclusively over rival plans for disposing of the surplus. By 1953, wine prices were down by 50 per cent, and the winegrowers, with a new harvest ripening in the fields, found their storage vats still half-filled with the last year's yield. Their discontent erupted into action; in July and August, the Midi experienced the most violent demonstrations since the days of Marcellin Albert. Old techniques —the mass resignation of rural mayors—were combined with a new one, the use of tractor roadblocks. Soon the agitation spread to central France, where declining meat prices had aroused the small peasantry.

In September 1953, delegates from FNSEA units in eighteen departments of the Massif Central and the Vendée-Poitou region met at Guéret to discuss joint action. The dominant figure at the session was Roland Viel, a former lieutenant of Tanguy-Prigent in the postwar CGA, and now a farm operator and syndical leader in the Clermont-Ferrand region. The so-called Guéret Committee (which was henceforth to enjoy a permanent though somewhat intermittent existence) summoned the peasantry of the region to a mass demonstration, complete with roadblocks, on October 12.[17]

Although the FNSEA national headquarters publicly assured the demonstrators of its moral support, its leaders can hardly have welcomed an upheaval of such proportions. Their successes in the 1951 elections had left them in rather a dilemma. Before the elections, they had been free to blame all the farmers' difficulties on the politicians; after the elections, they *were* the politicians—with their own beachhead in parliament and their political friends in the Ministry of Agriculture. The proposed demonstration was against a government in which the FNSEA in effect participated. Here was the unanticipated cost of "civic action," which had given the farmers' syndicate direct access to the centers of decision-making at the cost of committing it to a particular political faction. The FNSEA's leaders could have no real enthusiasm for activism aimed against its own political allies.*

The cabinet, prodded by FNSEA warnings, attempted to appease the Guéret Committee by a series of emergency measures. On September 30 it issued a set of decrees intended to regularize and stabilize the marketing of farm products; the new system was based on the principle of collaboration between the government and the farm organizations. One of these decrees was designed to pacify the winegrowers; new mechanisms were established to liquidate surpluses and (in the longer run) to reduce acreage and production.[18] A week later, in response to the

---

* The FNSEA attempted to evade this dilemma by focusing its criticism on the Minister of Finance (the traditional devil of French agrarians), or by accusing that vague and hostile entity "the administration" of frustrating the will of parliamentarians and peasants alike. It also sought to channel rural discontent by organizing its own safe-and-sane demonstrations; e.g., a mass meeting of 20,000 peasants in the largest hall in Paris, in July 1953.

Guéret Committee's activity, the government promised immediate price support measures for beef and milk products. All these decisions were taken after consultation with the farm organizations; indeed, the FNSEA later boasted that it had helped to draft the marketing decrees of September 30.[19] The specialized associations representing the wine, wheat, and milk producers found the decrees satisfactory; they recommended that the protest movement be abandoned, and many of their adherents followed that counsel. The Guéret Committee, however, insisted on proceeding with its roadblock plans, and the FNSEA hesitated to veto the action for fear of losing peasant support. An agent dispatched by the FNSEA attempted privately to dissuade the agitators, but without success; on October 12, hundreds of roadblocks were thrown up throughout the Massif Central, and the Guéret Committee could claim that it had successfully demonstrated the small peasants' determination to defend their own interests by direct action.[20]

The roadblock rebellion led directly to agrarian syndicalism's most severe internal crisis: an open conflict between the FNSEA and the CGA. The top CGA posts, for what they were worth, continued to be held by leftists: Pierre Martin (a prominent cooperative official) was president, and Philippe Lamour was still secretary-general. At a session of the CGA Bureau in 1951, Lamour and his friends had tried to outmaneuver the FNSEA leaders by proposing to convert the CGA from a coordinating body into a real farmers' syndicate (to be renamed the Confédération Générale des Agriculteurs), intended to rival or even replace the FNSEA. Blondelle's friends in the CGA Bureau sidetracked this proposal without difficulty.[21] The leftists then switched to another tactic; they set out to build up the three "technical" federations (cooperatives, mutual-aid associations, and farm-credit groups) as a possible rival to the FNSEA. The technical federations pooled their strength in a single syndicate, the

Confédération Nationale de la Mutualité, de la Coopération, et du Crédit Agricole (CNMCCA), which in 1953 adopted a program of broad agrarian action that went considerably beyond the narrow service functions.[22] But this maneuver also failed. Lamour and his colleagues in the CGA did not really control the technical federations, which remained in the grip of a prewar generation of cooperative and mutual-aid officials—men whose leftist sympathies had been muted by the passage of time, and whose Radical or Socialist heritage survived only in the form of a stubborn and anachronistic anticlericalism. Such men were not likely to challenge the FNSEA for control of the syndical movement; indeed, many of them preferred Blondelle's views to Lamour's.

The tensions between FNSEA and CGA were brought to a breaking point by the peasant agitation in central and southern France. Three days after the roadblock demonstrations, the Guéret Committee met again (this time with Lamour himself in the chair) to weigh the results. Delegate after delegate angrily accused the FNSEA leaders of duplicity during the operation, and of chronic indifference to the problems of the small peasant. The FNSEA had grown accustomed to "counting in tons rather than in human beings," and Blondelle's "civic action" program was simply a piece of political chicanery. The delegates issued a call for a series of regional groupings on the lines of the Guéret Committee, dedicated to the defense of small-peasant interests within the FNSEA.[23]

Blondelle responded by pushing through the Bureau of the CGA a change of statutes that amounted to self-liquidation. The CGA henceforth would be restricted to the vaguest sort of coordinating role; its only function would be to provide a meeting place for occasional joint sessions of various farm organizations. Lamour's post as secretary-general was abolished; the CGA's separate budget was suppressed; and the staff was reduced to a single secretary.[24]

In reply, Lamour and Roland Viel announced the formation of a nation-wide Comité Général d'Action Paysanne, with Lamour as president. Viel announced that the new Committee would shortly call a national congress in Paris to create a permanent organization of small and middle farmers, either within the FNSEA or outside it, but within the CGA in any case.[25] An exchange of personal attacks followed, with Viel accusing Blondelle of "betrayal" and "dictatorship," while Blondelle called Viel a troublemaker and an ambitious incompetent.[26]

But the Viel-Lamour Committee proved to be a damp squib. When its supporters convened in Paris in January 1954, only thirty-one of the ninety departments were represented, and most of the delegates came from the relatively poor and strongly leftist regions of the center and south. Viel admitted that he had been unable to drum up enough financial backing to permit even minimum activity by an independent small farmers' association.[27] The Committee settled for a role as a special-interest group within the FNSEA; and even in this limited sphere it failed to muster nation-wide small peasant support. For a few weeks it drew fleeting notice in the press, after which its name was heard no more. For a time, a number of departments south of the Loire boycotted the FNSEA by refusing to pay dues or to send delegates to sessions of the National Council; but even this form of passive resistance was soon abandoned. If the small peasantry lacked enthusiasm for its syndical leaders, only a minority viewed the old CGA general staff as a satisfactory substitute. A quite different kind of leadership would be required, either to crystallize the discontent of all the small peasants or to commit them to some new kind of peasant action.

* *

With rural resentment spreading, the time seemed ripe for demagoguery. So it appeared, at least, to Henri Dorgères, the Greenshirt apostle of prewar days. For nearly a decade after the war, Dorgères had been an isolated and almost forgotten figure. The liberation government had jailed him in 1944 on collaboration charges, but when his case finally came to trial, witnesses testified convincingly to his resistance activities, and the court gave him a suspended sentence.[28] His early attempts to resurrect his prewar movement had been entirely futile, but he had gotten hold of a moribund agricultural weekly, had scraped together barely enough funds to publish it, and had persuaded a few of his old lieutenants to rejoin the cause.[29] Now, as peasant discontent grew, he began once more to attract crowds of curious or angry listeners.

Meanwhile, a younger and equally flamboyant rival was also bidding for peasant support. Pierre Poujade, whose anti-tax crusade in defense of artisans and shopkeepers had rapidly won him notoriety after 1953, decided to convert his organization into a political movement that might batten on the discontents of urban and rural groups alike. In 1955 he set up a peasant auxiliary called the Union de Défense des Paysans, recruited a few new agitators with some experience in peasant demagoguery, and set out to pour oil on the rural embers. Poujade got a widely varying reception in the countryside; many peasants considered him a kind of itinerant entertainer, or an alien petty bourgeois with no real understanding of agricultural problems. Yet his appeals found an echo in certain small-farming regions, and offered still another outlet for the mounting discontent.[30]

On the extreme left as well, hopes were rekindled by the resurgence of rural unrest. The Communists' organizational activity among the peasants had stagnated badly since the failure of the party's post-liberation bid for power. Each year, the number of rural party cells had declined; from 12,060 in 1946 it dropped to 5,924 in 1954. Despite party urgings, peasant Communists abandoned the FNSEA in droves; in 1955, a high party official reported that 60 per cent of the farmers holding party cards were no longer affiliated with the syndicate.[31] Partly because of this exodus, the Communists lost control of all but four departmental units of the FNSEA, and even in those departments the Blondelle group managed to set up rival units that partially neutralized the party's local influence.* The tenants' branch of the syndicate (SNPBR), in which the Communists retained several high posts, barely managed to limp along; efforts to organize farm laborers were virtually abandoned in many regions, and only a minority of farm workers remained in the CGT.[32] More and more often, Waldeck Rochet complained, party comrades were heard to remark: "What's the good of defending the small peasants, since capitalism condemns them to disappear anyway? All we need to do is let nature take its course. When they've been proletarianized, it will be easier to win them over to socialism."[33]

When the Viel-Lamour Committee made its attempt to create a syndicate of small and middle peasants in 1953–54, Communist leaders attacked the enterprise as a selfish political maneuver. Admittedly, the Blondelle leadership ought to be opposed, Waldeck Rochet declared, but this oppositionist activity should be conducted from within the FNSEA and not from outside it; division of the peasantry would inevitably bring a weakening of peasant action.[34] The party did sponsor the creation of a series of regional winegrowers' leagues and peasant defense movements claiming to speak for the small farmers; but it viewed

---

* Communist-controlled syndical units survived in the departments of Charente, Corrèze, Haute-Garonne, and Landes; but they were excluded from the FNSEA in favor of rival non-Communist units. They have continued to operate (and still do in 1963) as wildcat unions. Those in Charente and Corrèze are largely artificial entities, kept afloat by party subsidies (though the Charente unit has a vigorous leader in Raymond Mineau). The Landes unit is more solidly based; its main strength is drawn from the share tenants of the region, and derives from their long struggle against genuine injustice. The Haute-Garonne unit subsists as a kind of fluke; it is run by a wealthy and influential cooperative official of the region. The Communists have retained some influence in a few other FNSEA units also: e.g., Lot-et-Garonne, Gers, and Allier.

these organizations as a supplement, not an alternative, to syndical action.[35]

Through these "front" movements, and through *La Terre* (which continued to be the most widely read farm journal in France), the Communists crusaded tirelessly for special favors to the small peasant: easy credit, low-cost health insurance, increased old-age pensions, tax exemptions, differential wheat prices. They also campaigned against virtually every governmental or syndical experiment in mild constructive reform: the *remembrement* policy, the rural migrations movement, the program of vineyard-uprooting, the state's attempts to fight alcoholism. They violently denounced reform plans of a more fundamental nature—for example, the so-called "green pool" scheme to integrate western European agriculture, and proposals to speed the consolidation of dwarf holdings into viable family farms. "As for us," *La Terre* declared self-righteously, "we are for preserving *all* family farms."[36] At intervals (either in response to critics, or in an effort to keep their own followers straight) they admitted openly that the smallest farms could not possibly be adapted to the demands of modern production.[37] But, they argued, it was better for the small peasant to remain a small peasant than to be proletarianized by the big agrarian capitalists. Someday the peasantry would realize that its only means of escape from this painful dilemma was "voluntary" socialism of the Soviet-bloc type.

The party line of the 1950's reflected not only the generally pessimistic mood of the period, but also the doctrinaire Marxist conviction that no real change could ever occur within the capitalist framework except at the dictation of (and for the benefit of) a tiny exploiting minority. In effect, the Communists chose to stand for the status quo, plus a few palliatives. This line undoubtedly had wide appeal at the time, particularly to the marginal and submarginal peasants who still made up so large a segment of the rural population; in both 1951 and 1956, the party's rural vote held up remarkably well despite its organizational torpor. Time ultimately exposed the weakness of the Communists' position: by betting against the possibility of constructive agrarian reform through democratic processes, they left the field wide open to more pragmatic rivals. But in the generally gloomy and skeptical mood of the early 1950's, the Communists' wager seemed safe; and each sign of peasant discontent gave them a new sense of confidence that the future was theirs.

* *

Throughout these years of sporadic unrest, the FNSEA pursued a tortuous course of encouraging peasant protest while collaborating closely with the government. Properly channeled, rural activism had its advantages for the syndical leaders; they could use it to warn the politicians that concessions must be made. But what concessions? To be effective, their program needed to combine immediate results with at least the appearance of long-term plans; and it needed to offer something to the small polycultural peasants as well as to the large one-crop producers. The syndicate's solution was a set of demands based on government price supports. Only by state action to raise farm prices, the FNSEA declared, could the farmers be expected to go on tooling up for higher productivity; and only by state action to restore the proper balance between agricultural and industrial prices could the peasantry be assured of social justice. "The guaranteed price," asserted one FNSEA spokesman, "is simply our equivalent of labor's minimum-wage principle." The goal of steadily rising productivity, officially adopted by the state and accepted by the farming profession, must be accompanied by the equally important goal of parity between rural and urban classes. Otherwise the peasantry would return spontaneously to its traditional Malthusian practices, limiting production in order to protect itself against disaster.

Higher prices would clearly benefit the growers of large cash crops. Just as clearly, price increases would be of only marginal help to the three-quarters of all French peasants who produced relatively little for the market. The problems of the subsistence-level peasant were too complex to be solved by price adjustments. Genuine structural reforms were needed, and drastic changes in the marketing system—notably for meat and milk products, fruits, and vegetables, the chief "money crops" of the small peasantry.

Nevertheless, the FNSEA's "prices first" policy was shrewdly conceived, and was generally accepted by French farmers both large and small. A policy of raising prices was easy to grasp; its effects promised to be immediate; and its probable inflationary consequences could be ignored or argued away. No one seemed to care that most of the gains from higher prices would go to a small group of modernized farmers. For a peasant living near the subsistence level, a few hundred or a few thousand additional francs (even of the badly inflated kind) could loom as large as millions for the big one-crop producer.

Furthermore, the FNSEA's program of "prices first" did not mean "prices only." The syndicate also pressed steadily for a variety of special concessions: rebates on the purchase of farm machinery, a reduced price for gasoline used in farm work, increased government credits for rural services and "collective equipment" (water supply lines, electrification, and so on), improved social security for farmers, and state assistance in finding new export markets. None of these proposals was particularly helpful to the small peasant. True, they did not exclude him in any way: theoretically, he was given an opportunity to mechanize, to consolidate scattered strips, to export with government assistance. But in practice, these opportunities were quite beyond his imaginative and financial grasp. The success of the FNSEA's program depended, in effect, on a continuing flow of the peas-

ant population away from the land, and the concentration of
agricultural production in fewer and larger farms. Yet not once
during the Fourth Republic did any prominent FNSEA leader
admit as much. On the contrary, advocates of a continuing rural
exodus were denounced as defeatist, un-French, anti-peasant;
and it is quite possible that the FNSEA leaders who made these
charges really believed what they said.[38]

One part of the FNSEA's program did affect the small
peasants directly: namely, its plan for better-organized marketing procedures for meat, milk products, fruits, and vegetables.
These products were still marketed in an archaic fashion; prices
fluctuated drastically, and growers were often victimized by powerful and unscrupulous middlemen. Some of the worst abuses
occurred in the marketing of livestock; the cattle-buyers (popu-
larly known as *chevillards*) worked together to share and mo-
nopolize regional markets, at the expense of the unorganized
sellers. Most of the FNSEA leaders had no intention of challenging these vested interests; their social conservatism was too
deep-rooted to permit an attack on the rights of private commerce, or on the peasant's theoretical right to sell where and
when he wished. They were long since reconciled to the
Wheat Office (now renamed the Cereals Office, and somewhat
broadened in scope), but they were opposed to extending the
system of state regulation to other products. They aimed instead at a kind of limited *dirigisme* (or, in their own phrase,
"intelligent interventionism") that would enable the state and
the profession to join forces in policing the market.[39] They favored a system resembling the wine-marketing mechanism set
up in the 1930's: agencies subsidized by the government, and
run conjointly by government, farm organizations, and inter-
mediaries, would be empowered to buy, store, and dispose of
portions of a harvest that might otherwise swamp the free market and depress prices.

Thanks to its intimate relationship with both parliament and the Ministry of Agriculture, the FNSEA managed to get much of its program adopted during the life of the second National Assembly (1951–56). Increased credits were appropriated for "collective equipment" and for agricultural expansion, and rebates were granted on the purchase of farm machinery and gasoline, thus speeding the process of mechanization. But the bulk of the government's financial aid to agriculture continued to be spent in the form of price supports, in accordance with the FNSEA's desires.[40]

The government also accepted the FNSEA's market-organization plan. By a decree of September 30, 1953 (drafted with the help of FNSEA representatives), the cabinet authorized the creation of an advisory committee and an executive agency (*organisme d'intervention*) for each of several major farm products in the free sector. The advisory committees were to guide the government in long-range planning; the executive agencies to arrange for the storage, processing, and disposal of excess production. Implementation of the decree was slowed by the opposition of commercial pressure groups, who saw it as threatening their freedom to manipulate the market. Advisory committees were set up for most major products, but only three executive agencies were created: for wine (IVCC), for meat (SIBEV), and for milk products (Interlait). These agencies were severely hampered by inadequate financing: the storage and processing facilities at their disposal, for example, were wholly insufficient to meet serious emergencies. They provided little more than a palliative to prevent disastrous price fluctuations, rather than a first step toward a system of organized marketing under state control.[41]

By the end of the legislative term in 1956, syndicalist leaders had settled comfortably into the habit of working closely with the politicians (and, to a lesser degree, with the civil serv-

ants in the Ministry of Agriculture). Few other interest groups
in the state had won so many concessions; no other group had
participated so directly in the shaping of government policy.
True, the ratio between agricultural and industrial prices still
remained unfavorable to agriculture; and evidence of small-
peasant dissatisfaction persisted. Still, the modernized sector
of agriculture was prosperous; productivity was rising steadily;
and the only serious threat to syndical unity had been put down
without much trouble. The past four years had done much to
soften the FNSEA leaders' sense of grievance toward the state;
they could look back on their lobbying record with a good deal
of complacency.[42]

Meanwhile, however, a potential rival for agrarian leadership had been emerging—a more serious rival, some thought,
than the CGA had ever been. The departmental Chambers of
Agriculture, suppressed by Vichy in 1940, had been resuscitated
in 1949, despite the vigorous protests of FNSEA and CGA
leaders combined. By a ruling of the Conseil d'Etat, Vichy's
action was declared illegal, and the prewar personnel of the
Chambers were judged to be still in office. The FNSEA decided to make the best of it by negotiating a kind of treaty with
the central headquarters of the Chambers (the APPCA), de-
limiting the respective functions of the two agencies. The Chambers agreed to refrain from competitive syndical action, and to
confine themselves to furthering professional education and technical progress.[43]

For a time it seemed that peaceful coexistence was assured.
The APPCA moved back into its old building behind the Opéra,
where it henceforth shared quarters with the FNSEA; and after
the Chamber elections of 1952, a number of men held office in
both organizations. Indeed, Blondelle himself was elected president of the APPCA in 1952, and held both that post and the
presidency of the FNSEA until 1954, when he relinquished the

syndical presidency for the somewhat less wearing APPCA task. Nevertheless, as the years went by, the two organizations gradually became rivals. One difficulty was the FNSEA's chronic shortage of funds. Syndical membership was voluntary, whereas the Chambers of Agriculture, as official state agencies, enjoyed a regular income from taxes levied by the state. The financial advantage of the Chambers was still further increased in 1954 by a governmental decree altering their tax base.

An even more important factor in the rivalry was the tireless activity of the APPCA's top permanent official, Director-General Luc Prault. Few men in recent years have played so important a role in French agricultural organizations. Prault, after advanced training as an agronomist, had begun his career as an organizer of farm cooperatives, but had then moved into the central offices of the prewar Chambers of Agriculture, where he had quickly made himself the indispensable man. Dismissed by Vichy in 1940 on charges of Masonic connections, Prault had nonetheless worked his way into the Vichy Ministry of Agriculture, and by 1944 he had risen to the highest administrative post in that organization. Dismissed again in 1944 as a Vichyite, Prault found a temporary haven in the new organization of absentee landlords (FNPA), but dedicated most of his remarkable energies to reviving "his" organization, the APPCA.

By the mid-1950's Prault's influence was greater than ever, though as always it was exercised behind the scenes. Some insiders believed that he was driven by bitter recollections of disgrace in 1940 and 1944; others, that he was simply a strong-willed administrative genius. At any rate, some FNSEA leaders began to regard Prault as a shrewd and ruthless rival bent on displacing them as spokesmen for the peasantry, and indeed by 1960 the APPCA was claiming exclusive authority to negotiate with the government on behalf of agriculture, on the ground that parliament had intended to give the Chambers such a monopoly when it set them up many years before.[44] This rivalry, however, implied no real difference of outlook between the APPCA and the FNSEA leaders (a number of whom continued to hold posts in both organizations at once). Both factions sought almost exactly the same concessions for agriculture, and shared the liberal-conservative point of view. For the moment at least, the power struggle was a matter of personal rivalries rather than doctrinal conflicts.

* *

With parliamentary elections due early in 1956, it seemed natural for the FNSEA to return to the strategy of "civic action" that had succeeded so well in 1951. Yet the syndical leaders hesitated. "Civic action" had aroused considerable antagonism within the FNSEA—especially in regions of leftist tradition, but also in Christian Democratic areas—and controversies about it might weaken or even split the organization. Besides, the originator and chief driving force of "civic action," René Blondelle, was no longer president of the FNSEA, and the organization had lost some of its toughness and unity of purpose under his successor, Jacques Lepicard. In 1956, therefore, "civic action" got little more than lip service, and the syndicate's campaign was generally restrained—especially by contrast with the flamboyant appeals of the Poujadists and the Dorgerists, which were just then building up to their peak.[45]

The outcome of the elections startled and dismayed the syndical leaders. The Independent-Peasant bloc (which numbered most of the FNSEA's political allies or agents) suffered a sharp setback, dropping from about 130 to 100 seats. The blow was doubly painful because it was so unexpected; the bloc had expected to gain strength by inheriting the votes that had gone to the Gaullist Rassemblement Populaire Français five years earlier.* It was the extreme parties of right and left, rather, that could claim victory. Communist strength increased from about 100 to 150 seats, while the Poujadists polled a wholly unexpected popular vote of two million, and claimed about 50 seats. Even the Dorgerists got themselves a toehold in parliament for the first time; both Dorgères himself and his faithful lieutenant Jean Bohuon were elected in Brittany. Although few Communist and Poujadist victories could be traced to peasant voters, the extremist groups did win surprising rural support.[46] When the Assembly convened, the Independent-Peasant bloc found itself excluded from the governing coalition for the first time in five years. Worse still, the new Socialist premier, Guy Mollet, shocked agrarian leaders by abolishing the post of Minister of Agriculture, and assigning its functions to a mere *secrétaire d'état* of subcabinet status, subordinated to the Minister of Finance.

There were sharp repercussions within the FNSEA's ruling group. Lepicard soon gave way to a more forceful figure, Joseph Courau, a polycultural farmer from the Bordeaux region with a long record of militant syndical action both in the prewar UNSA and in the Vichy Corporation. The syndicate's weekly organ, *L'Information agricole*, took on a new aggressive tone; in parliament, the APA deputies were encouraged to harass the government more vigorously. In addition, the FNSEA set out to seize the initiative in the realm of rural activism. It sponsored nationwide rural demonstrations on May 19, 1956, and boasted that more than a million peasants had responded to the call on that "historic day."[47] Throughout that year and the next it continued to stimulate or support sporadic agitation, mainly in the small-farming regions of the west, center, and southwest. By 1957 Secretary-General Albert Génin could boast with some justice

---

* The RPF had won 120 seats in 1951, but had soon disintegrated; many of its deputies had joined the Independent-Peasant bloc in the National Assembly.

that "no other organization in France, whether political, professional, or syndical, can command so large an audience."[48]

Several factors caused the FNSEA to persist in its new intransigent line. One of these was the continued exclusion of the Independent-Peasant bloc from the governing coalition under Mollet and his successor. Another was the cumulative impact of renewed inflation, brought on by the financial burdens of the Algerian war and the state's inability to take unpopular corrective measures. As prices rose, agrarian leaders concluded that the Socialists and Radicals were manipulating the upward spiral to please their urban supporters. Finally there was the bogey of agrarian demagoguery, revived in what seemed to be a more dangerous form when Dorgères, Poujade, and the unpredictable Paul Antier suddenly joined forces in May 1957 to form a new coalition, the Rassemblement Paysan. Antier's outraged colleagues in the Peasant Party promptly excluded him once and for all; but he carried almost half of the party's deputies with him into the new demagogues' axis, and retained control of the party's weekly organ (whose title, *L'Unité paysanne*, now seemed more ironic than ever).*

For fear of being outflanked, FNSEA leaders called for a new wave of peasant demonstrations, and stepped up their drumfire of complaints and criticisms of the government. To their denunciations of the cabinet's "anti-peasant" price policies, they joined a running attack on its alleged intention to regiment or even collectivize the peasantry. Mollet's agricultural advisers, headed by the Socialist Kléber Loustau, undersecretary for agriculture, had spent several months in 1956 drafting a basic law

---

* The new Rassemblement suffered from the same internal stresses that always destroyed such coalitions of demagogues. Dorgères seceded even before the Rassemblement got round to holding its first congress in 1958, and Antier and Poujade soon quarreled over the issue of supporting de Gaulle's new regime.

designed to serve as a kind of charter for the peasantry. It out-
lined an elaborate long-range program of governmental action
covering most aspects of agriculture: the planning of production,
the organization of marketing, price-fixing, education and extension services, rural equipment and housing. The proposed law
declared family farming to be the backbone of French agriculture, and promised a series of special advantages to small farmers.
No significant structural reforms or experiments in "group agriculture" were included; indeed, the bill stopped well short of
some of Tanguy-Prigent's proposed reforms of the liberation era.
FNSEA officials nonetheless pronounced it a threat. The government, they asserted, was asking parliament for virtually unlim-
ited powers to control or reform French agriculture; Loustau's
bill was "the ideal instrument of a policy that rests on the omni-
presence and the omnipotence of the state." Some rightists went
even further; a high Peasant Party official called the bill "the
most insidious attempt at collectivization that has confronted us
since the liberation."[49]

The fall of the Mollet cabinet before its agriculture bill
reached the floor of parliament freed the FNSEA of an immediate threat;* but the new Bourgès-Maunoury cabinet promised
little better from the syndicalists' point of view. Although the
premier was a Radical rather than a Socialist, his cabinet had no
Minister of Agriculture, and his young Minister of Finance,
Félix Gaillard, seemed to epitomize everything the agrarians
feared and distrusted. Not only was he a Parisian born and bred,
but he belonged to that elite corps of treasury officials called the
Inspection des Finances, most of whose members were intimately

---

* The Loustau bill, together with seven rival drafts introduced by individual deputies or groups, eventually came before the Assembly's committee
on agriculture, which worked out and adopted a compromise draft in March
1958 (Assemblée nationale, session ordinaire de 1957–58, doc. no. 6954).
But this proposal had not yet reached the floor of parliament when the Fourth
Republic fell.

connected with banking and industry. Yet by a strange paradox, it was Gaillard who was to accord the FNSEA its most important victory of the decade—the adoption of the sliding-scale principle (*indexation*) of fixing farm prices.

As always, price supports remained at the heart of the FNSEA's program; but renewed inflation since the mid-1950's had made the issue more complicated and sensitive than ever. In periods of inflation, agricultural prices are likely to lag behind unless they can somehow be hitched to changes in the general price level. Urban labor had already been accorded the sliding-scale principle; sine 1952, minimum wage levels were automatically increased with each new inflationary cycle. The FNSEA saw no reason why agriculture should not receive the same treatment, and rejected the economists' protest that a general extension of the sliding-scale system would simply build inflation into the French economy, freezing all existing relationships in the process.

Just before the Mollet cabinet fell in May 1957, the FNSEA accomplished an initial breakthrough by persuading parliament, despite the cabinet's lack of enthusiasm, to adopt the so-called Laborbe law directing the government to apply the sliding-scale principle in setting milk prices. The new cabinet, however, showed no interest in carrying out parliament's directive, and resisted agrarian pressure to do so. That resistance, combined with several other "anti-peasant" decisions on farm prices, subventions, and credits, brought on a crucial test of strength in the late summer of 1957. The FNSEA, speaking almost like a sovereign state, declared that it was "breaking off relations" with the government, and issued a call for peasant demonstrations. Both the rejuvenated Guéret Committee and the CNMCCA (the combined "technical" federations of the Boulevard St. Germain) leaped into the fray, evidently in an attempt to seize the initiative from the FNSEA. The ensuing wave of demonstrations was the most widespread and violent that the Fourth Republic experienced. Having thus made its point, the FNSEA forced the convocation of a special session of parliament in mid-September to deal with the farm crisis.[50]

The Bourgès-Maunoury cabinet—a shaky combination at best—found the heat too great to resist. On the eve of parliament's return, it promised to put the Laborbe law into operation at once; and three days later (September 18) Finance Minister Gaillard issued a much more sweeping decree that extended the sliding-scale principle to seven major farm products.[51] Strangely enough, there were no cries of triumph from agrarian leaders; they greeted the decree rather sourly as "at least a beginning."* Only in retrospect, when the Gaillard decree was rescinded, did they come to regard it as one of agriculture's greatest victories—indeed, as a pillar of the state's agrarian policy and an essential factor in the nation's rural stability.

Gaillard's concession did not suffice to save the cabinet for long; it fell two weeks later on the issue of Algerian policy. This time the crisis brought the agrarian leaders some apparent compensations. The new premier was Gaillard himself, now regarded

---

* *L'information agricole*, no. 166, Oct. 12, 1957; *L'année politique 1957*, p. 89. The APA sat "almost permanently" during the September crisis, and introduced several motions of censure. These it refused to withdraw even after Gaillard's capitulation, in order to keep up its pressure on the government. The conduct of the farm lobbyists during this episode was angrily denounced by the left-wing Catholic organ *Témoignage chrétien* (no. 690, Sept. 27, 1957). Never before, it declared, had lobbyists shown such impudence. At the outset of the debate, Courau and the directors of the large specialized associations had taken up permanent quarters in a room at the Palais Bourbon and had begun to hand down directives, "dictating terms to the adherents of the famous Amicale Parlementaire Agricole. . . . It was M. Courau and his partisans who managed the affair; the deputies merely carried out orders. It was they who warned that they would not be satisfied with empty talk. It was they who introduced motions of censure, even disposing of the signatures of certain deputies without bothering to seek them out and get their authorization." *Témoignage chrétien*, it may be noted, had close ties with certain young Catholic farm syndicalists.

as susceptible to agrarian pressures; and after two years, the Independent-Peasant bloc was invited to rejoin the governing coalition. Better still, the cabinet contained a Minister of Agriculture once more; and the post went to an Independent who belonged to the APA. It appeared that the FNSEA leaders could now safely revert to the old policy of close collaboration with government and parliament.[52]

But the political situation had already deteriorated too much to permit such a return to the past. The Fourth Republic stood on the edge of an abyss, into which it would be swept in May 1958. FNSEA leaders had often criticized "the system," yet on the whole they had found it receptive to their arguments and open to their influence. It was by no means certain that the tougher, more authoritarian Fifth Republic would be as receptive to the claims of agrarian syndicalism—and of the peasantry in general.

8
Rural Revolution: The Rise of
a New Generation

NOT LONG after the end of the Second World War, the French sociologist-journalist Raymond Aron spoke of a "silent revolution" that was under way in the countryside, a revolution that might ultimately transform France. At the time, not many of Aron's compatriots took the observation seriously. Indeed, most signs pointed the other way. Words like "stagnation" and "petrifaction" were used frequently by both French and foreign observers; and even those hardy optimists who occasionally struck a hopeful note did not often seek their examples among the peasantry.

Yet only a decade later, there were clear signs that Aron had been right. Silent revolutions are likely to reveal themselves only in retrospect, for their early stages are psychological, and their chief carriers are likely to be found in the generation that is still on the rise. This particular revolution began to attract public notice shortly after the Fourth Republic gave way to the Fifth, but its roots were at least a decade older, and its fruition was not dependent on de Gaulle's coming to power. The political crisis of 1958 helped only to the extent that the new climate favored new ideas, new attitudes, new men. Rather to the surprise of most Frenchmen, it soon became clear that the peasant world had quietly been producing a crop of such attitudes and such men.

The revolution that had been germinating throughout the 1950's was not primarily the work of either the agrarian syndicalist leaders or the politicians. Indeed, some critics have argued that while the syndicalists concentrated on protecting vested interests, and the politicians on improvising temporary solutions to successive crises, the tasks of self-examination and constructive experimentation fell altogether into other hands.

The charge is surely overdrawn. Both syndicalists and politicians made a decided contribution to the change in attitudes and the broadening of perspectives that underlay the silent revolution. Their common acceptance of economic planning at the very outset of the Fourth Republic was of fundamental importance; it gradually forced agrarian spokesmen to look beyond the current crop or crisis and view agriculture in relation to the national economy as a whole. The fact that France's experiment in planning was democratic rather than authoritarian had particular importance; democratic planning requires widespread prior discussion, and this was sure to influence the attitudes of parliamentarians and professionals alike. Representatives of agriculture participated in the Planning Commission's work at every stage. They helped to formulate intermediate and long-range goals for the nation's economy, and in the process learned to relate agriculture's needs to those of industry, commerce, and labor. They came to see the virtues of higher productivity and continued expansion, and the fearsome limits of the narrowly defensive Malthusian outlook that had dominated French agriculture in the past.* This broadened viewpoint enabled French farm spokesmen to confront the era of the European Common Market without se-

---

* The last serious attempt to reassert the Malthusian thesis as French agriculture's official doctrine was made in 1950 at the FNSEA congress. Jean Deleau, spokesman for the Wheatgrowers' Association, threatened that if the government failed to provide farm relief, the peasantry would cut back production in order to bolster prices. Deleau's position was sharply challenged by farm spokesmen committed to the Planning Commission's policy of steadily advancing productivity. Beginning about the middle of the first planning period (1948), the Commission's proposals called for the rapid development of agriculture; subsequent plans put increased emphasis on its export potential.

rious misgivings, and to persuade the peasantry generally that the experiment promised more benefits than risks.

Syndicalists and politicians also shared responsibility for the rapid mechanization of agriculture during the 1950's. The government's stress on expansion and productivity did much to stimulate the tractor craze, while the FNSEA furthered the process by its steady pressure on the state to subsidize the purchase of machinery and to furnish gasoline to farmers at cut rates. Mechanization would probably have been rapid even without these official pressures, for the younger peasant generation increasingly regarded tractors, at least, as a necessity. Not a few older peasants were forced to buy tractors in order to keep their sons on the farm. By the end of the decade, the number of farm tractors in France had risen to 625,000 (as compared with 37,000 in 1945, and 35,000 in 1938); and the number of harvesters had reached 42,000 (as compared with 250 in 1946, and 200 in 1938).[1] The tractor craze had its less attractive consequences: one was a heavy load of peasant indebtedness, and another was the mechanization of farms too small to benefit from it. This kind of uneconomic mechanization, however, was offset to some degree by state-subsidized machinery cooperatives, administered by the CNMCCA.

Several other experiments were also initiated jointly by the FNSEA and the government. In 1948, for example, an agency was established to encourage rural migration from overcrowded parts of the country to thinly populated regions. The plan was conceived by Eugène Forget, then president of the FNSEA; and the new agency was headed by him for more than a decade. With the aid of a small state subsidy, the association arranged for the transfer of some 7,000 families during the 1950's, most of them from Brittany to central or southwestern France, where large tracts of land had gone out of cultivation over the past half-century.[2] Although the numbers involved were too small to relieve population pressure in Brittany, the impact of these rural migrations in the areas of settlement was surprisingly great. Most of the migrants were young peasants with large families—men of more than ordinary vigor and imagination, open to new ideas, willing to experiment. In regions long dominated by a spirit of routine, the immediate example of a neighbor ready to try out new methods, to seek and follow informed technical advice, made the local peasants take notice, and eventually led them to more or less grudging imitation. As one grumbling old-timer remarked, "On va être obligé de faire les mêmes bêtises que lui."[3]

Another jointly sponsored enterprise was the establishment of *zones-témoins* or "demonstration areas." Inaugurated in 1952 by the Ministry of Agriculture, the demonstration areas continued and broadened an experiment in demonstration villages begun three years earlier by the Wheatgrowers' Association. By the end of the decade, 110 of these demonstration areas were in operation, mainly in poor and underdeveloped parts of the country. Supported by state subsidies and staffed by government agronomists, the experiments sought to show what could be achieved by using up-to-date techniques adapted to the region. Unfortunately, although many demonstration areas were successful enough, others were resounding failures. Some of the most dedicated rural reformers (notably among the young Catholics) believed that the demonstration-areas scheme tackled the problem wrong end to, and that the essential first step must be a psychological transformation designed to make the peasants receptive to new ideas.[4]

The syndicalists and politicians also tried to improve the nation's facilities for the education of young farmers and the advanced training of agronomists and technicians. The Third Republic had failed miserably in this realm. Farm leaders and rural politicians after the war tirelessly cited figures to show that France was far behind every other nation of western and central Europe in providing specialized training for young peasants; of all these nations, only France had not yet established an adequate network of agronomists or "county agents" to serve as farm advisers and stimulators of progress. As late as 1938, no more than 3 or 4 per cent of all peasants' sons had received even the most rudimentary instruction in agriculture. As for advanced training in agronomy, someone calculated that the number of agricultural *schools* in pre-war Germany equaled the number of agricultural *students* in France.

That the Fourth Republic ought to correct this disgraceful condition was generally agreed; yet neither the left-wing re-formers of the liberation era, nor the liberal-conservative leaders of the 1950's, managed to get very much done. One difficulty was competing demands for public funds; but the main problem was the conflict between public and "free" schools, which snarled every educational proposal of the decade. Dozens of bills were introduced into parliament; not a single one emerged from com-mittee to become law. The right and the MRP insisted on state aid for private schools engaged in specialized agricultural train-ing; the left reverted to its ancient heritage, and dedicated itself to a crusade against creeping clericalism. The effect was to block any serious improvement of public educational facilities for farm-ers' sons, and to confine expansion to private (i.e., Catholic) in-stitutions, which continued to develop in somewhat haphazard fashion.[5]

All things considered, however, neither the syndicalists nor the politicians of the Fourth Republic had reason to be ashamed of their record of achievement. Measured by the standard of past regimes, it was a good record. Only when measured by the real needs of the rural world does it seem seriously deficient. Few syndical leaders or politicians thought in terms of fundamental changes in the structure of French agriculture; their reforms, whether fiscal, educational, or technological, basically presup-posed an indefinite perpetuation of the status quo. Two agricul-tures clearly coexisted in France, but they refused to confront this fact honestly and devise separate policies to fit the situation. A single policy, designed by the modernized farmers and their political allies, could at best only speed the departure of small peasants from the land. In the end, such a policy might culminate in a single agriculture of large and prosperous farms. But no syndical leader or politician spoke in these terms. Peasantist doctrine remained too strongly entrenched in French emotions; the existence of a large mass of smallholders was still held up as a *sine qua non* of national stability and strength. Thus the accomplishments of syndical and political leaders were marred by a fundamental contradiction: they rested on the premise that France needed a mass of contented peasants on the soil, but they failed to grapple with the real causes of rural discontent.

* *

Fortunately, there were other men and groups at work in France, and in the long run their activities were to overshadow the achievements of the established syndical and political elites. Of grass-roots origin, these movements had a spontaneity that was often lacking in programs conceived and administered in Paris; their impact on rural life, and especially on rural attitudes, could therefore be far more direct and enduring.

In the realm of individual initiative, the most remarkable novelty was the so-called CETA movement. The first of these Centres d'Etudes Techniques Agricoles was set up in 1945 by Bernard Poullin, a well-to-do farmer of the Paris region. Poullin brought together a dozen of his neighbors to discuss common problems and to experiment with new techniques; they soon hired an agronomist as a counselor. After two or three years, the experiment began to attract attention, specially from the Catholic youth organization, the JAC. An editor of the JAC's farm journal conceived the idea that Poullin's scheme might be adapted to regions of small underdeveloped agriculture, and paid him a visit. Soon afterward (in 1949), the first CETA of this new type was tried in the Loire department; then others began to spring up, usually on the initiative of members or alumni of the JAC. A national CETA headquarters was established in Paris, headed by a vigorous evangelist of rural reform named Louis Estrangin, an ex-professor of literature. By 1962, more than a thousand CETAs were in operation, most of them in the underdeveloped regions. Each one was formed on local initiative, with encouragement from the Paris office; each one consisted of from ten to twenty farmers. Some were mere study circles; others employed a hired technician; still others were beginning to move into the *terra incognita* of agricultural cost accounting.[6] Although technical advancement remained their central purpose, CETA groups often found themselves drawn into the discussion of broader social and economic issues as well.

Private initiative also triumphed in the field of youth organization. The government's only enterprise in this field had been Tanguy-Prigent's unsuccessful experiment with *foyers ruraux*. The FNSEA possessed a youth branch called the Jeunes de la CGA (founded in 1945), but its activities were confined to such innocuous pastimes as sponsoring prizes at cattle fairs. Here again, it was the JAC that took the lead. This organization had undergone a profound transformation after the Second World War. In its early phase, it had been dominated by conservative social-Catholic elements. It rallied enthusiastically to Pétain in 1940, and became a kind of quasi-official agency of the Vichy regime. Yet in some regions—particularly those of Christian Democratic tradition—the Jacistes turned against Vichy and established ties with the resistance. These rebels were encouraged by a number of young priests, so that both the JAC and the Church were able to emerge from the Vichy era with a claim to a voice in constructing the new and purer postwar republic.

More important, however, was the emergence of a new kind of JAC leadership during the Vichy years. In 1942 a young peasant named René Colson from the small-farming region of the

Haute-Marne took over the post of secretary-general. An energetic and intelligent man, Colson had no interest in directing an
organization that confined itself to devotional meetings and ama-
teur theatricals. He was determined, rather, to grapple with the
tough practical problems of the small peasantry from which he
sprang. His first task was to convert the *aumônier*, or chaplain,
of the movement, Father Foreau, to his conception of the nature
and purpose of the JAC. The priests who supervised the organization, he insisted, must learn to think like peasants instead of
trying to make young peasants think like priests. Once the JAC
leaders understood the real concerns of the peasantry, they would
be in a position to recruit and train a true rural elite, and could
set it free for constructive action.

After lengthy discussions, Father Foreau let himself be convinced. Henceforth admission to the movement no longer required a fervent religious commitment, and the initiative in discussion and action was turned over to the young peasants themselves. Meanwhile Colson was recruiting a new crop of young men
and women for posts in the national or departmental JAC offices,
and was inspiring them with his own passion for practical study
and action. Rarely has a single man's dedication produced such
quick and widely diffused results; one is reminded of the enduring impact of Fernand Pelloutier on the French labor movement.
Like Pelloutier, Colson was physically frail, and burned himself
out early; but when he died in 1951 at the age of thirty-eight, he
left the JAC in the hands of a generation of leaders who bore
his stamp.[7] That generation was to complete the task of convert-
ing the organization from a kind of Boy Scout movement into the
most dynamic force for change in rural France.

This development within the Catholic laity went hand in hand
with dramatic changes in the priesthood itself. Ever since the
beginning of the century (and even before), there had been isolated signs of a new outlook, of a deep concern for the Church's

seeming failure to confront the problems of the modern age. Priests like the Abbés Trochu and Mancel in Brittany had revealed this temper, but their efforts had been premature. It was the depression decade that introduced a strong new current— particularly in the Dominican and Jesuit orders, which provided their members with a kind of training and experience far broader than that received by secular priests in the seminaries of their native departments. It was no mere accident that most *aumôniers* of the JAC and the other Catholic youth movements were drawn from the Jesuit and Dominican orders.*

Accompanying these changes were signs of an intellectual rejuvenation within the Church. During the 1930's and after, such thinkers as Jacques Maritain, Emmanuel Mounier, and Pierre Teilhard de Chardin sharply challenged the doctrines of the traditionalists and of authoritarians like Charles Maurras. This new current inspired, during the Vichy years, the creation of several "missionary" orders designed to reassert the Church's presence in the "dechristianized" areas of France, both urban and rural—notably the Mission de France, the Mission de Paris, and

---

* Jaciste leaders of the postwar era believe that the Jesuits' training school at Lyon was the most important source of renewal within Catholicism, and that its graduates powerfully influenced the new generation. One prominent ex-Jaciste puts it thus: "Nous retrouvions dans les idées philosophiques des jésuites que nous avons connus alors dans les mouvements d'action catholique la même vision optimiste de l'homme créé par Dieu à son image et appelé à créer. Cette perception du phénomène humain explique notre confiance en l'homme, et nous rejoignons la philosophie du père Teilhard de Chardin lorsqu'il écrit: 'Pourquoi n'y aurait-il pas aussi des hommes voués à la tâche de donner, par leur vie, l'exemple de la sanctification générale de l'effort humain? —des hommes dont l'idéal religieux commun serait de donner leur explicitation consciente complète aux possibilités ou exigences divines que recèle n'importe quelle occupation terrestre? —des hommes, en un mot, qui, dans les domaines de la pensée, de l'art, de l'industrie, du commerce, de la politique, etc. . . . s'attacheraient à faire, avec l'esprit sublime qu'elles requièrent, les oeuvres fondamentales qui sont l'ossature même de la société humaine?' " (Michel Debatisse, letter to the author, April 22, 1963.)

the Frères Missionnaires des Campagnes. The Mission de France, founded by Cardinal Suhard in 1941, directed its efforts at both rural and urban dechristianized areas; it sent out teams of priests to regions that could no longer recruit or support priests of their own. In 1952 it had 287 priests in the field; about half of these were assigned to rural areas. The Frères Missionnaires des Campagnes, organized by a Dominican friar in 1943, concentrated all their efforts on the rural areas. In 1956, they had about 120 priests active or in training.*

Colson's work produced no obvious effects for about a decade. Those ex-Jacistes who embarked on political or syndical action during the liberation era belonged to the prewar generation; their interest in social issues was usually counterbalanced by an ingrained conservatism of outlook, and they functioned primarily as a moderating force between the old liberal-conservatives and the anticlerical left. Meanwhile the new generation that now controlled the JAC attracted no more interest than any other band of well-meaning but somewhat impractical juveniles, except from a few conservatives who complained that "red priests" were corrupting these young innocents.

The transition from preparation to action set in midway through the 1950's. Colson's band of enthusiastic and hard-driving leaders was arriving at the age (twenty-five to twenty-eight)

---

* Adrien Dansette, *Destin du catholicisme français 1926–1956* (Paris, 1957), pp. 253, 343. The spread of rural unbelief had led one priest in 1935 to warn his fellow Catholics that the peasantry might eventually prove the most stubborn barrier to the rechristianization of France. Father M. de Ganay, *Problèmes paysans et apostolat spécialisé* (Paris, 1935), p. 47. According to the sociologist Abbé F. Boulard, *Problèmes missionnaires de la France rurale* (Paris, 1945), I, 136, only about 38 per cent of the rural population were still practicing Catholics in the sense of participating regularly in Mass and confession. More than half (57 per cent) were rated "occasional conformists," while eighty rural cantons in central France were so thoroughly dechristianized as to be labeled "missionary areas." Abbé Boulard's statistics were based not on the peasantry alone but on the entire rural population.

when Jacistes normally dropped out of the movement and took on the full-time responsibilities of establishing a family and operating a farm. They had spent ten years educating themselves in the problems confronting the peasantry; and they were persuaded that these problems were too grave to be left to the older generation of agrarian leaders and a new crop of teen-agers. How to make their influence felt was the question. There was no reason to think that the established FNSEA leaders would willingly share power with a group of youngsters whom they scarcely knew and whose aspirations they did not share. More and more, the solution seemed to be to engage in some kind of direct syndical action. For a time, the Jacistes thought of establishing a new syndicate of family farmers as a rival to the FNSEA. But they soon discarded this idea in favor of an attempt to take over the moribund syndical youth movement, the Jeunes de la CGA, which up to now most Jacistes had boycotted or ignored.

At the time, few of them foresaw the full consequences of this decision. Their chief concern was to get a hearing for their opinions, rather than to challenge their elders for control of the syndical movement itself. Between the young Jacistes and the dominant FNSEA faction, there was an age gap of some thirty years. Where normally there would have been an intermediate generation of leaders, the war had created a vacuum. The Jacistes were drawn into the vacuum almost despite themselves.*

That first step was a proposal (advanced in 1956) that the FNSEA convert the insignificant Jeunes de la CGA into a new Cercle National des Jeunes Agriculteurs (CNJA), with a more rigorous structure and more precise and important powers. Above

---

* The vacuum was not total; a few FNSEA officials like Albert Génin and Lucien Biset did come from the intermediate generation, as well as from small-farming backgrounds. Since they understood the aspirations of the rising new generation, their presence in high syndical posts probably eased the transition between the older and younger groups, and helped to avert an open clash.

all, the CNJA would be granted genuine antonomy within the syndical movement—the right to select its own officers, without interference from the senior syndicate, and to send its own delegates to sit in the highest councils of the FNSEA. In addition, the minimum age limit would be revised upward from sixteen to twenty-one, thus transforming the CNJA from a youth training group into a genuine organization of young professionals. If these terms were accepted, the Jacistes promised to throw their energies into the syndical movement, and thus to give it new life.[8]

The FNSEA leaders could see nothing but gain in the proposal. They had never quite understood their inability to draw young peasants into the syndicate; now at last it seemed that the youngsters were coming round. The details of the agreement were quickly approved, and it went into effect in March 1957. Like a disciplined army, the Jacistes moved into the new CNJA and took over virtually all its key posts.[9] For a year or two, harmony seemed complete; syndical membership rose, and the young people behaved with proper circumspection. But tensions quickly began to develop within the CNJA. A moderate element, rooted mainly in certain conservative small-farming districts but led by sons of large modernized farmers from the northeast, wanted to persist in this respectful attitude toward their seniors in syndicalism, and to express only mild aspirations toward agrarian reform. A tougher and more assertive element, drawn primarily from the underdeveloped center and south, wanted the CNJA to take a harder line, and to open the question of drastic structural reform in agriculture. The struggle culminated in 1959 in a victory for the *durs*, who secured a precarious one-vote majority in the CNJA's Conseil d'Administration and put their spokesmen—Hubert Buchou and Michel Debatisse—into the key posts of president and secretary-general.[10]

At once the CNJA's monthly organ, *Jeunes agriculteurs,* took on a more aggressive tone, and the CNJA's representatives in high FNSEA councils began to speak up more brashly. The tone of the youth group's annual congress in 1959 shook the older generation, too. A banner at the rostrum bore the slogan "Individualisme, voilà l'ennemi!"; and a series of speakers challenged many of the most cherished dogmas of the agricultural fundamentalists. Some of the elder statesmen expressed angry irritation at what they considered the excesses of these young hotheads, but no one dreamed that the newcomers might soon become serious rivals for the control of agrarian syndicalism.

* *

Meanwhile, the attention of agrarian leaders had been diverted by the fall of the Fourth Republic. In the crisis, only the youth group spoke out in defense of the threatened regime. Their seniors, despite their close association with the governments of the 1950's, had been habitual critics of "the system" (their contemptuous term for the Fourth Republic): Blondelle had even wanted to commit the syndical movement to a program of drastic constitutional revision. Most FNSEA leaders responded instinctively to the idea of strong leadership as a remedy for whatever ailed the nation. Their spokesmen publicly approved de Gaulle's assumption of power, and President Courau even proposed that the FNSEA's Conseil National adopt a formal resolution endorsing the de Gaulle regime. The proposal was blocked, however, by a few articulate leftists led by old Renaud Jean, the veteran Communist spokesman from the southwest.[11] To avoid internal conflict, the FNSEA remained officially neutral during the constitutional referendum of September 1958; but most of the syndical leaders plainly favored ratification of the de Gaulle constitution.[12]

Already, however, they had begun to experience qualms. Public statements both by the new Minister of Finance and by de Gaulle himself suggested that the new regime might jettison the system of sliding-scale prices for farm products, and in August

1958, despite FNSEA protests, the government proceeded to set the price of wheat without reference to the sliding-scale principle. The customary rural demonstrations followed, but the government stood firm. It began to dawn on agrarian spokesmen that in the absence of a parliament, much of their effectiveness as a pressure group had suddenly evaporated. For years they had been accustomed to work on and through the politicians in the Assembly; now, with the old Assembly defunct and the nature of its successor still unclear, they did not know where to turn. The Fourth Republic, it began to seem, had possessed some unsuspected virtues.

With the election of a new National Assembly impending in November 1958, the FNSEA returned almost instinctively to the strategy of "civic action." This time it joined forces with the other major agricultural organizations (notably the APPCA and the CNMCCA) to draft an "agricultural charter," whose terms would have to be accepted by any candidate desiring agricultural support. The charter included, among other things, the defense of the sliding-scale principle and the adoption of policies that would stop the rural exodus.[13] But "civic action," given the special circumstances of the time, proved to be far less effective than in the past. De Gaulle's personality overshadowed the FNSEA's recommendations, which in any event caused no great stir among rural voters. Not even de Gaulle's decision to reform the electoral system helped the FNSEA's cause very much. For years, agrarian leaders had been advocating a return to the prewar system of small single-member electoral districts, on the ground that this was the best method of protecting rural interests. But de Gaulle's adoption of this system was combined with a reduction in the size of the new National Assembly, and many depopulated rural districts were deprived of their former representation. The electoral returns disappointed syndical leaders, even though the number of agriculturists in the Assembly declined only a little (from 59 to 53); at that, the champions of agriculture in the outgoing parliament had survived better than most deputies; 52 per cent of the old APA members won re-election, as compared with only 30 per cent of the other incumbents.[14] The agrarian demagogues had suffered a total disaster: Poujadists, Dorgerists, and Antierists had been sunk without trace.[15]

A much worse blow soon followed. Late in December 1958, the new cabinet headed by Michel Debré issued a drastic set of economy decrees designed to resolve the nation's financial crisis. The decrees stripped away much of the tangle of controls and subsidies that had grown up in recent years, and opened the way for an experiment in quasi-liberalism. The principal victims, it seemed, would be the farmers and the urban workers. A number of special farm subsidies and tax privileges were abolished; and, most painful of all, the cherished sliding-scale principle for farm prices was abandoned. All the farm organizations reacted angrily; even the young syndicalists accused the new regime of annulling "innumerable years of syndical effort aimed at persuading the government to define a long-term agricultural policy."[16] Yet the FNSEA and APPCA leaders found themselves embarrassed by their eager acceptance of de Gaulle's leadership only a few months earlier, and by their approval of the Fifth Republic's new political institutions. At the FNSEA's congress in February 1959, they combined praise and denunciation in uneasy fashion, and for several months they refrained from stirring up peasant demonstrations.[17] The honeymoon with Gaullism was not quite over; but it was on the wane.

* *

In the new period of growing tension between peasantry and government, the younger peasant generation played a complex and somewhat ambiguous role. The CNJA leaders shared their seniors' irritation at the policies adopted by the Fifth Republic. The experiment in *laissez faire*, as they saw it, was consciously designed to force the modernization of agriculture by the most painful method possible—lowering prices and driving all inefficient peasants off the land. Most of the CNJA's new leaders came from the underdeveloped regions, whose peasants stood to suffer most directly from the new policies. The sliding-scale principle had provided them with at least some protection as they sought to drag the rural districts up into the modern era; therefore they shared their elders' anger at its abolition, and willingly joined the FNSEA in criticizing the government. Indeed, in the years that followed they were to demonstrate a particular talent in the sphere of rural activism; never before had peasant demonstrations been so widespread or so chronic, and never before had they been spearheaded by men in their twenties.

Yet if the young peasants and the older syndicalists joined forces in harassing the government, they differed on more fundamental matters. Indeed, in certain respects the CNJA leaders found themselves closer to some of the "technicians" around de Gaulle than to their syndical elders. Like the technicians, they were inclined to look for practical, workable solutions rather than to cling to doctrinaire conceptions. Peasant unity, they contended, was a myth that had long veiled the realities of rural existence; the contrast between rural and urban life ought to be reduced rather than preserved; and the flow of young peasants to the cities, far from being a national disaster, was an essential concomitant to the modernization of the countryside. They asked only that the rural exodus be "humanized"; that those who wished to leave be given proper training for new careers. They rejected, too, the policy of "prices first," and gave structural reforms in agriculture clear primacy over prices. Most startling of all, they questioned the hitherto sacred principles of property ownership and rugged individualism. The soil, they contended, was nothing more than a tool; what counted was the right to use it, and not its ownership. As the JAC's weekly organ put it, "The sea doesn't belong to the sailors, yet the sea is where they work."[18] They insisted that if rural life was really to be transformed, individualism would have to give way to group enterprise.

This clash of ideas foreshadowed an open conflict between generations. Neither generation constituted a monolithic bloc. Some older leaders like Eugène Forget, honorary president of the FNSEA, and Robert Mangeart, a perpetual member of its ruling councils, showed strong sympathies with the younger group; while on the other hand one wing of the CNJA (headed by delegates from the large-farming region) was bitterly hostile to the CNJA leadership and shared the outlook of the Blondelle-Courau group.[19] Neither group wanted a fight. Yet the tensions were real enough, and could be tempered only if both sides would show restraint and the senior syndicalists would grant the younger group at least some access to positions of power.

The strength of the challenge first came to public notice in the spring of 1959, when nation-wide municipal elections were held. In a great many rural communes—particularly in those small-farming regions where the Socialists or Communists were not solidly dug in—men who had long run local affairs without challenge were swept aside or partially replaced by slates of younger men. The bulk of the newcomers were ex-militants of the JAC; a large number of them (possibly as many as 4,000) promptly became mayors of their communes, by action of the new town councils.* Suddenly it seemed that the new peasant generation was coming of age, discovering itself as an organized force, putting forward its own group of spokesmen, proposing to take over public responsibilities from its elders. Looking back on the

---

* Durupt, "Action catholique et milieu rural." The full extent of this revolution was concealed by the fact that a number of older politicians chose to co-opt young men for their own lists rather than face a rival list of young activists. This may be why the press completely missed the significance of the municipal elections at the time, and discovered it only in retrospect.

situation, French political observers were to see the municipal elections of 1959 as the first great public manifestation of France's peasant revolution.[20]

The impact was soon felt within the FNSEA as well. In several departments where the CNJA was strong and the tensions with the older leaders severe, the youth group abandoned gradualism and brusquely displaced its elders. In the Breton department of Loire-Atlantique, for example, the average age of the syndicate's governing council suddenly dropped from sixty-three to just over thirty. Similar changes followed at intervals in other departments of the west, center, and south: Ille-et-Vilaine, Orne, Manche, Aveyron.[21] In most cases, the syndicate's local activity was stepped up: a stodgy and almost moribund organization was suddenly rejuvenated.

The senior syndical leaders struck back in 1960 by blocking the election of several of the young rebels to the FNSEA's central councils.[22] But their triumph was brief. Only a year later, the key post of FNSEA secretary-general fell vacant owing to Albert Génin's retirement, and the CNJA leadership entered a candidate for the succession—Marcel Bruel, of the Aveyron department. Most observers expected a deadlock between Bruel and a rival Blondelle-Courau nominee, so that victory would ultimately go to a compromise candidate. Instead, Bruel won a clear majority, giving the CNJA its first important foothold in the senior syndicate.* When the FNSEA next met in con-

---

* Bruel, an ex-Jaciste, had been departmental president of the FNSEA unit in the Aveyron, one of France's poorest departments, on the southern fringe of the Massif Central. He had won some notoriety for his plan to reorganize livestock marketing on a cooperative basis, and for his advocacy of a small farmers' coalition against the Paris basin group. Politically, he was reported to be a sympathizer of the Parti Socialiste Unifié, a small coalition of the "new left" confined chiefly to Paris intellectuals (Serge Mallet in *France-Observateur*, April 6, 1962). At one time he had been attracted by Poujade's demagoguery, and had introduced Poujade to a peasant audience in the Aveyron as "the only man capable of achieving something in France" (*Fraternité française*, no. 53, May 26, 1956).

gress in 1962, the syndicate's general report (i.e., its principal policy statement) was presented not by a member of the old guard but by one of the most dynamic and outspoken members of the new generation, Michel Debatisse, the secretary-general of the CNJA. Only three years earlier, Debatisse had infuriated many of the senior syndicalists by his general report at a CNJA congress; now they heard him reassert many of those same ideas as an official spokesman for the FNSEA.[23]

The young syndicalists' victory, however, was only partial; they had merely won the right to share in the shaping of syndical policy. The older generation still held the presidency, together with a safe majority in all the controlling organs of the FNSEA. Continuing intrasyndical tensions led to another test of strength in early 1963, when President Courau announced his intention to step down. Courau demanded that he be allowed to designate his own successor; and though the young syndicalists managed to block this move, they could not muster enough strength to impose their own presidential nominee. Courau eventually hit on a shrewd device: he chose to split the young syndicalists by proposing one of their own generation. His nominee, Gérard de Caffarelli, had been the spokesman for the conservative minority in the CNJA, and the bitter enemy of the Debatisse faction.* The scheme succeeded; in March 1963 Caffarelli narrowly won election to the FNSEA presidency. A countermove to put Debatisse into the even more important post of secretary-general, in place of the somewhat less forceful Marcel Bruel, was beaten off by the Courau-Caffarelli coalition. Until

* Caffarelli, a thirty-seven-year-old stockbreeder from Blondelle's home department of the Aisne, was a graduate of the Catholic agricultural school at Angers. Although his 75-acre farm was relatively small by the standards of his region, he shared the general outlook of the large modernized farmers of the northeast. After some years of militant action in the CNJA, he had become president of the FNSEA's departmental unit in the Aisne. In 1961 he had unsuccessfully stood for the post of FNSEA secretary-general; in 1962 he had been one of the *rapporteurs* at the FNSEA congress, and had stressed the primacy of higher farm prices over structural reforms.

now, the factional rivalries within agrarian syndicalism had taken the form of a dialogue rather than an open conflict; henceforth there was danger of a serious rift. But even though the older generation had once more managed to keep its dominance within the FNSEA, it seemed only a matter of time until full control of agrarian syndicalism would pass into the hands of the militant new generation.

* *

Meanwhile, in the new Gaullist republic, parliament's authority had been sharply reduced; the locus of decision-making had shifted to the offices of the President and the Premier, where small staffs of technicians and professional civil servants were given unprecedented freedom to push ahead with plans for reform in every sphere. The older syndical leaders were slow to react to this change. By force of habit, they continued to address their pleas and their pressures to the National Assembly and the Senate, chiefly through the rejuvenated APA, which was now larger than ever.[24] It gradually became clear that this sort of lobbying could produce little more than noisy reverberations, but the FNSEA officials could see no alternative to the old techniques: stirring up rural demonstrations, and assailing the "irresponsible bureaucrats" and (increasingly) the new "technocrats."

The young syndicalists, by contrast, quickly realized that "it was now better to know two well-placed civil servants than twenty deputies."[25] If decision-making had really passed to the "technocrats," then it seemed sensible to seek connections and to exert pressure in their ranks. Furthermore, the younger syndicalists knew that some professional bureaucrats with high posts in the de Gaulle regime shared their own general outlook. Many of these officials—especially in the Planning Commission, but also in other state agencies, notably the offices of the President and the Premier—were men of the postwar generation; young, aggressive, practical.[26] In the early months of the Fifth Republic, these officials made contact with the CNJA leaders, and consultations between the two groups became increasingly frequent. Angry conservatives charged that the "technocrats" were taking advantage of the young peasants' personal ambition or naïveté to give a false appearance of rural support for their "antipeasant" schemes. In fact, however, a genuine community of interest was partially bridging the gap between government planners and the new peasant elite.

True, the gap took some bridging. Peasant unrest continued, and the CNJA provided much of its motive force and local leadership. The typical flare-up occurred for the classical reasons: low farm income and a pervasive sense of injustice, brought to a climax by some kind of immediate grievance created by marketing difficulties, a crop failure, or a governmental decision. Increasingly, however, an important new factor became apparent: an urge for fundamental change, advance, structural reform.

For more than a year, the Fifth Republic clung to its quasi-liberal policy, with its distressing effects on the peasantry. By the end of 1959, peasant discontent was intense, and some feared that it might converge with extreme right-wing discontent over Algerian policy to produce a real threat to the regime.[27] Even the modernized large-farming region of the northeast was affected this time (doubtless because price supports were at the heart of the conflict); a mass meeting of 30,000 peasants in Amiens (February 1960) erupted into violence, and more than a hundred demonstrators and policemen were injured. The riot encouraged de Gaulle's right-wing enemies to seek peasant support for their Algérie Française campaign; they hastily created a peasant newspaper of ultra-demagogic tone, and Pierre Poujade leaped forward with a proposal for a new peasant front to which even the FNSEA was invited to adhere.[28] In an effort to head off this threat, the government decided to offer a concession; early in March, Premier Debré authorized a partial return to the sliding-scale principle for farm products. But the new price-fixing system was hedged about with so many reservations that agrarian leaders greeted it sourly. "Zero, less than zero," was FNSEA President Courau's public comment.[29]

A second concession of a broader character, however, was already in the discussion stage. Toward the end of 1959, Debré had abandoned his stance of apparent indifference to the complaints of the farmers and had spoken of the need to provide agriculture with some kind of basic charter. In December, a committee of high civil servants, economists, and representatives of the major farm organizations (including the (CNJA) was appointed to draft such a charter.[30] But the committee quickly bogged down in academic discussions and in fruitless attempts to reconcile contradictory viewpoints, and ultimately accomplished nothing. Debré soon assigned the drafting task to a small group of "technocrats," while the FNSEA and APPCA set to work independently on their own draft.

The syndicalists found their model in West Germany's "green law" of 1955, a measure designed to meet the special conditions of West German agriculture: farms uniformly small, total production far below the nation's needs, and costs of production among the highest in western Europe. If the German peasantry were to be kept on the land, social considerations would have to outweigh strictly economic ones, and the community as a whole would have to subsidize the farmer. The "green law" rested on this premise, and declared that the government's goal was parity of living standards between peasants and urban groups. The law was described by its French admirers as a kind of long-term contractual agreement between the government and the organized farmers.[31]

Such a system would obviously appeal to the older leaders of French agrarian syndicalism; just as obviously, no committee of technocrats would find it acceptable. France, unlike Germany, possessed a modernized farm sector, with high and steadily rising productivity; the prospect of large export surpluses was imminent. A "green law" for France, like any other scheme based on high prices, would be of limited benefit to the marginal smallholders of the south and west, while assuring modernized farmers a high profit margin at the consumer's expense. Furthermore, it would be likely to price French farm exports out of world markets.

The differences between the government and the profession came into the open in April 1960, when the Debré cabinet announced its draft plan. Although designed, like the "green law," to ensure parity between the farmers and other sectors of society, it subordinated price guarantees and market support to long-range development, expansion, and structural reform. The heart of the program was contained in a projected "agricultural orientation law," in which were lumped together a number of rather disparate provisions. The most novel item called for the establishment of a series of regional agencies called Sociétés d'Aménagement Foncier et d'Etablissement Rural (SAFER), which would be authorized to buy land as it came on the market, to carry out necessary improvements (including the consolidation of microfundia into viable farms), and to sell or lease this land to qualified family farmers. The bill also proposed to upgrade backward regions by authorizing the creation of "special zones of rural action," in which the government would undertake crash programs of public investment. It attempted to provide more effective market support by fusing several small funds into a single Fonds de Régularisation et d'Orientation des Marchés Agricoles (FORMA), with increased resources and broadened authority. Finally, it touched lightly on the sensitive issue of price guarantees by promising new *prix d'objectifs* for 1965 and offering to consider the farmers' costs of production in fixing annual price levels. Accompanying the orientation law were four other bills calling for increased agricultural investment by the state, the reorganization and expansion of agricultural education, and the extension of health insurance to peasant families.[32]

In the chorus of denunciation that greeted the government's plan, there was only one dissonant voice: that of the CNJA. Its members recognized at least some of their ideas in the bill; unlike their elders, they welcomed the program as a first step in the right direction, and held that its chief shortcoming was its timidity. They urged amendments to reinforce and broaden the law—to speed structural reform, for example, by granting the new SAFER a priority right of purchase for all land coming on the market, and to democratize the health insurance scheme by extending its coverage and reducing its cost to small peasants.[33] The older syndicalists, on the other hand, were inclined to reject the proposed legislation root and branch on the ground that it evaded the crucial issue—namely, parity, based on guaranteed prices and the sliding-scale principle. Rather than challenge both the government and the young syndicalists, however, they set out to amend the bill during its passage through parliament. The sections on structural reform and health insurance might, they hoped, be watered down; the single article on prices might be built up into the central item in the "orientation law."

During the long parliamentary negotiations that ensued (April–August 1960), the government made a number of concessions to its FNSEA-APPCA critics, yet the gap between them was never quite closed. The structural reform and health insurance provisions were restricted somewhat, as the older syndicalists desired; the article on price supports was strengthened somewhat, though not enough to satisfy either the FNSEA or the APPCA. The showdown came in the Senate, where Blondelle led the fight against the measure. Three times the Senate rejected the orientation law; on the fourth round of voting, the lower house finally overrode the Senate's suspensive veto.[34]

At last the peasantry had its long-awaited agricultural charter. For the older syndicalists, however, it was quite the wrong kind of charter. President Courau of the FNSEA sourly described it as "a regular grab-bag."[35] Only the young syndicalists expressed restrained satisfaction, though the law fell considerably short of their hopes. Still, it represented a significant breach in an ancient juridical edifice—a breach that might be widened in the future. For the first time, a government had faced up to the problem of structural reform; for the first time, the word *structures* itself appeared in French farm legislation. Until now, the sacred principle of property rights had always blocked any serious analysis of long-range agrarian issues; henceforth, the SAFER might open the way to a new relationship between the peasant and the soil.

* *

The orientation law itself was merely a framework or a declaration of intentions; it could have no effect until the government issued implementing decrees. In spite of repeated assurances from official spokesmen, weeks and then months went by without the promulgation of a single decree. The young syndicalists, aware that some high-ranking officials in the Ministry of Agriculture were hostile to the new law, suspected the old game of bureaucratic sabotage.[36] Their rising irritation contributed heavily to the outbreak, in May 1961, of the most extensive and violent jacquerie that modern France has known.

The trouble began in southern Brittany, touched off by a disastrous drop in potato prices. Truckloads of potatoes were dumped in town squares, and bands of peasants in a few communes disrupted local elections by seizing and burning ballot boxes. A few days later, the spark of rebellion leaped to northern Brittany—the scene of a widely reported "artichoke war" a year earlier.* Some four thousand tractor-borne peasants invaded the city of Morlaix and occupied the subprefecture for a few hours—as a symbolic gesture, and without violence. That night the two chief organizers were arrested, and government officials announced their intention of making examples of the culprits. Unfortunately for the government, these organizers were among the most prominent young syndicalist leaders of the region. One of them, Alexis Gourvennec, was an ex-Jaciste who at twenty-four was already a vice-president of his departmental FNSEA unit. Nowhere else in France were the young syndicalists so numerous and well-organized; many had fought in Algeria recently, and were familiar with guerrilla and counter-guerrilla techniques.

Word of the two arrests at Morlaix caused rural insurrection to spread like a prairie fire through the west: during the next ten days railways and roads were blocked, towns invaded by tractor-borne demonstrators, telephone lines sabotaged, the Premier repeatedly hanged in effigy. When the agitation finally quieted in Brittany, it hedge-hopped to other parts of the country: the Massif Central, the Midi, the Rhône valley. For almost six weeks, some part of the countryside was in violent upheaval; only the large-farming area of the northeast was spared.[37]

There was serious danger for a time that the FNSEA leaders (and perhaps those of the CNJA as well) might lose control of their troops; for most of the demonstrations were of spontaneous local character, without central direction from Paris.

---

* The so-called "artichoke war" of June 1960 developed out of a conflict between the relatively prosperous truck-gardeners of northern Brittany and the middlemen of the Breton coast. For about a week the growers trucked their artichokes directly to Paris and sold them at street corners, aided by a few dozen urban sympathizers (mainly from the intellectual left). The chief significance of the affair was psychological: it made many young peasants more keenly aware of the advantages of organized action and of the need for understanding the marketing system. A detailed account of the episode may be found in Mallet, *Les Paysans contre le passé*, ch. 8.

There was even some talk of an open schism within the FNSEA, or of the creation of regional federations in the west or the southwest to balance the power of the Paris basin.[38] Political extremists of both left and right also tried to take advantage of the disorders, but without success.[39] In the end, a series of piecemeal governmental concessions enabled the FNSEA and CNJA leaders to get their followers in hand, and to arrange an uneasy truce.

According to one well-informed French journalist, the 1961 agitation was the first peasant revolt since the sixteenth century that forced the government to retreat on a fundamental issue.[40] Yet the crucial fact and the most striking novelty of the 1961 upheaval was not so much its effect as its character, above all the role played in it by the angry young men of the new peasant generation. Almost everywhere they took the initiative as organizers and spokesmen for the countryside; almost everywhere their aim was to reshape rural France, to destroy the barriers that had prevented the peasantry from moving up into the modern age.

The government's concessions, worked out in a series of round-table meetings with agrarian leaders, included not only emergency measures to help such hard-pressed groups as the potato growers, but also the immediate promulgation of a long series of decrees implementing the orientation law, together with a promise to prepare several supplementary bills for early submission to parliament. Shortly after the end of the disorders, de Gaulle and Debré reshuffled the cabinet in order to get more vigorous leadership into the Ministry of Agriculture. The outgoing Minister, Henri Rochereau, was a liberal-conservative businessman of the Blondelle-Courau persuasion; his successor, Edgard Pisani, was an ex-prefect skilled in the art of human relations and shrewd enough to recognize the trends of the time. Pisani and his aides, working closely with representatives

of the CNJA, set to work at once to draft the supplementary reforms that had been promised. The product of their labors, presented to parliament early in 1962, was a *loi complémentaire* designed to reinforce the basic law of 1960 and to go well beyond
it. In its final form, this so-called Pisani Charter borrowed virtually all its provisions from the CNJA program—though often
in modified form.[41]

The bill strengthened the SAFER by according them a priority for the purchase of land placed on the market; as things
stood, much valuable land was being bought up by well-to-do
farmers or speculators before the SAFER could bid for it. The
bill also imposed restrictions on the activities of the so-called
cumulards—nonagriculturists who had been buying up whole
chains of farms in order to operate them directly with hired labor.
Many young peasants, especially in the overpopulated west,
found themselves excluded from access to the profession by the
spread of *cumuls*; and in some cases long-established tenant
farmers were evicted by the new owners.*

The bill proposed to establish a new Fonds d'Action Sociale,
designed both to alleviate the condition of certain underprivileged
groups and to speed the process of structural reform. This fund
would provide supplementary pensions to aged peasants who
had hitherto been unable to retire from active farming because
old-age benefits were inadequate. Since more than 40 per cent
of all farm operators were beyond the age of fifty-five, and 400,-

---

* During parliament's discussion of the Pisani Charter in the summer
of 1962, the CNJA sought to influence the outcome by a series of demonstrations aimed at *cumulards*. The most spectacular of these incidents occurred in Normandy, where the film star Jean Gabin was routed out of
bed at sunrise by several hundred polite but firm young peasants. Gabin
had bought and merged seven contiguous farms in France's finest dairy
region; then he had begun to buy up other farms in the area, installing hired
managers and workers to replace the evicted tenants. The CNJA demonstrators insisted that their objection was not to Gabin's purchase of farm
land, but only to his refusal to continue leasing it to peasant *exploitants*.

000 were already beyond sixty-five, such subsidies would be likely to free considerable tracts of land for eventual regrouping into larger and more workable farms. Grants from the fund would also be available to peasants migrating from overcrowded to underpopulated regions, and to those seeking re-education in order to leave farming for other employment.

Finally, in order to encourage cooperative marketing procedures, the bill authorized the formation of producers' groups with power to negotiate collective marketing agreements. By vote of two-thirds of the regional producers of a given product, these marketing agreements would become compulsory for all producers in that region. A companion bill was designed to provide a more solid legal base for the practice of "group agriculture" (i.e., joint exploitation of several adjoining family farms), and sought to encourage the further growth of group agriculture by granting certain privileges to such enterprises.

The Pisani Charter was immediately denounced both by the right and by the extreme left. The conservatives saw it as creeping socialism, the Communists as a devious capitalist scheme to transfer land from small peasants to aspiring kulaks and urban speculators.* Both groups of critics bitterly accused the young peasant leaders of collusion with the government.

These convergent attacks led the cabinet to modify certain provisions in the bill before it reached parliament; and further restrictions were inserted by the two assemblies before the *loi complémentaire* was finally approved in August 1962. The principal object of attack was the land-purchase priority accorded to the SAFER; in the end, that priority was so much hedged about by safeguards and exceptions that some of the more impatient

---

* The Communists had been harping on this point ever since 1960, when Robert Mangeart told the FNSEA congress that 790,000 farms in France (or one out of three) were too small to be really viable (*La Terre*, No. 810, April 28, 1960).

young reformers wrote off the law as "emptied of all positive content." The more responsible CNJA leaders, however, welcomed the measure as the longest single step yet taken toward genuine structural reform in rural France.[42] When the cabinet began to issue its implementing decrees only two months later, their content made it clear that there would be no governmental attempt to sabotage or further restrict the legislation.[43]

* *

All these hopeful developments posed a serious threat to the extremists. On the far right, both Dorgères and Antier had already disappeared into limbo.* The Poujadists retained a few centers of rural strength—notably in the departments of Cher and Hérault. In the Cher, they even won control of the Chamber of Agriculture in the 1959 elections. But agrarian Poujadism showed no signs of growth; indeed, its shrillness seemed to reflect a kind of desperation.[44] The Poujadists' efforts to elbow their way into control of the great peasant demonstrations of 1961–62 were failures; their attempt at a political comeback in the elections of 1962 was no more successful. Poujadism undoubtedly appealed to a deep-rooted set of prejudices and suspicions in the countryside. But this instinctive or endemic Poujadism was unlikely to flourish in an era of political stability, economic growth, and psychological transformation.

On the far left, the Communists faced a difficult decision. A decade earlier, they had wagered on the failure of constructive agrarian reform, and had let the role of leadership toward

---

* Dorgères's weekly, which had long been in serious financial difficulties, gave up the ghost in June 1959. The Amiens riot of February 1960 encouraged him to publish one last issue; since then he has not been heard from. A few diehard Dorgerists still survive in the west, and turn up occasionally to heckle the speakers at young syndicalist rallies. Antier's *Unité paysanne* managed to survive for a time by becoming a monthly, but his organization disintegrated.

reform fall into the hands of the young Catholics. By 1960, it was clear that they had miscalculated, and that France was already well into a period of unprecedented rural change. An aging and rigid Communist hierarchy had thus to decide whether to go on denying the fact of change, or to overhaul party strategy in an effort to regain the initiative.

Ultimately, no clear choice was made. The party clung to its basic policy line, but at the same time sought to strengthen its organizational activity in the countryside. The rural advances of the 1950's were grudgingly recognized, but they were written off as the work of the large-farming capitalists who were out to serve their own interests. The state's agrarian reforms of 1960–62 were intended merely to speed the rape of the small peasantry; besides, they were "strongly tinctured with corporatism." The CNJA, with its goal of a society based on democratic planning and cooperative enterprise, represented "the futile reformism of the petty bourgeoisie."[45]

The party's high command also turned its attention to the shortcomings of rural party organization proper. At the sixteenth party congress in 1961, Waldeck Rochet (now risen to the eminence of assistant secretary-general, and heir presumptive to Maurice Thorez as party leader) scolded the delegates for their indifference to peasant organization, and announced that full-time party officials would be assigned to many rural departments in an effort to strengthen rural sections and cells.[46] A year later, he was able to report that the new system seemed to be producing some results: for the first time since 1947, the number of rural cells had increased slightly.[47] But there were some humiliating setbacks. In one department of the southwest, the party announced a great mass meeting for the discussion of peasant grievances. The local unit of the CNJA promptly scheduled a rival meeting at the same hour, and imported Secretary-General Marcel Bruel of the FNSEA as their principal speaker. The

CNJA session drew an audience of fifteen hundred; the Communists attracted thirty.[48]

The party's prospect of renewed gains among the peasantry seems unpromising. Its appeal continues to be directed to the marginal and submarginal farmers, whose misery is genuine and whose future is dubious. But a disproportionate share of that group has already passed the age of fifty, and its sons have departed for the cities in overwhelming numbers.* It is hard to conceive of any other class of potential rural recruits to Communism, barring a major political or economic crisis.

* *

The new peasant generation was bound to influence political as well as syndical life in France. A decade earlier, "civic action" had led agrarian syndicalism into an informal alliance with the parties of the liberal-conservative right. Most of the younger syndicalists, and almost all of the CNJA leaders, found that path completely unacceptable. Their own leanings were toward the left; but just what form their political action would take remained uncertain.

For perhaps three-quarters of the rank-and-file Jacistes and ex-Jacistes, the Christian Democratic MRP provided the natural vehicle for political action. Founded in 1944 by exponents of moderate social and political reform, the MRP had had an unexciting history; but after the mid-1950's, the influx of young rural Catholics seemed likely to revitalize it in both spirit and structure. The MRP's *équipes rurales*, for example, were completely reorganized by the newcomers, and were turned into

---

* The 1954 census revealed that 42.7 per cent of all *chefs d'exploitation* in France had passed the age of fifty-five, and that the bulk of these older peasants operated farms of less than 25 acres. The median age of peasants tilling farms of less than 12 acres was almost sixty (L. Douroux, "Exploitation agricole et problèmes fonciers," *Paysans*, no. 24, June–July 1960, pp. 38–39).

effective agencies for local political education and action. In 1958, eight of the nine ex-Jacistes elected to the National Assembly were affiliated with the MRP.[49] In the 1959 municipal elections, the bulk of the young ex-Jaciste candidates ran on MRP tickets, and strongly reinforced the party's influence in municipal affairs.

Some of the most vigorous JAC and CNJA leaders, however, found the MRP lacking in energy, fervor, and breadth of vision. Much of its original idealism, they felt, had given way to an unedifying political opportunism. Besides, some of them were against confining Catholics to a "political ghetto," and thus frightening off potential allies of anticlerical or freethinking temper. But the existing alternatives seemed even worse. The Socialists were hopelessly sunk in Marxian dogmatism; they stood for the stubborn and narrow conservatism of the petty bourgeois, haunted by fear of change. The Communists were still more dogmatic, and had chosen to defend all that was most backward and hopeless in rural life. Midway between the two Marxian parties, several tiny schismatic groups joined to form a "new left," which in 1960 took the name of Parti Socialiste Unifié; only a few of the young peasant leaders found its principles congenial, or its prospects promising.[50]

The only hope was a new kind of political organization. Soon after de Gaulle took power in 1958, some of the CNJA leaders initiated exploratory talks with representatives of the CFTC (the Catholic trade-union federation) and of certain political parties, notably the MRP. Their goal was to strengthen the existing centrist parties by persuading them to collaborate intimately with the farmers' and workers' syndicates; they proposed that each party choose half of its parliamentary candidates from the ranks of the syndicates. But an even broader purpose seems to have been implicit in this plan. The sponsors talked of creating a Rassemblement des Forces Démocratiques (RFD) that might serve as a rallying point for all democrats convinced of the need for drastic socio-economic reform. Although the RFD would presumably have begun as a coalition of autonomous parties, its success might have led to a gradual merger of those parties into a single political organization.

In fact, the RFD never went much beyond the talking stage. Only the MRP leaders showed any serious interest in the plan; and even they were reluctant to let their well-established party be integrated into a broader *rassemblement* whose prospects were uncertain. This reluctance was powerfully reinforced by the MRP's unanticipated victories in the 1959 municipal elections— victories achieved, rather ironically, by the young peasants.[51]

Disappointed in their hopes, a number of the RFD's chief sponsors fell back (for the time being, at least) on the MRP as the least of existing evils. They admitted privately that the MRP was much more permeable to new ideas than any of the other old parties; but they were dubious about the chances of revitalizing it. The MRP's old guard, they argued, was too firmly dug in, and the party's clerical taint would be too hard to eradicate. Postponing their hopes for the moment, they turned to local experiments in farmer-labor cooperation, mainly in the west and the Massif Central.[52] This emerging sense of solidarity with urban labor, though limited and sporadic, stood in sharp contrast to the outlook of the older agrarian leaders, most of whom had preferred to seek tactical alliances with the well-to-do urban bourgeoisie or with the small businessmen's and artisans' organizations.

During the summer of 1962 there was another meeting to discuss the prospects of a broad political realignment. This time the session was confined to representatives of various farmers', workers', and students' syndicates (CNJA, CFTC, FO, UNEF); no politicians were invited. This time, too, the goal was more clearly conceived: the participants hoped to create a broad new party of the non-Communist left—a party in which syndical officials might participate actively, with the formal support of their organizations. Once again, the time did not seem ripe. Although the processes of economic, social, and psychological change were clearly preparing the way for a new politics, they had not yet gone far enough to wipe out old barriers and old suspicions. For a while yet, concluded the sponsors of the meeting, de Gaulle's leadership would be indispensable to prevent a return to political instability.[53]

A few weeks later came the unexpected political crisis of September 1962, set off by de Gaulle's sudden decision to amend the constitution and his brusque appeal to the people over the head of parliament. Most of the young syndicalist leaders were distressed by de Gaulle's autocratic tactics, but were convinced that de Gaulle's leadership would be essential for several more years. In the end, the CNJA leaders parted company with the bulk of the French left, which vigorously opposed de Gaulle in the subsequent constitutional referendum and general elections. Instead, the CNJA adopted an official position of strict neutrality.[54] Rejecting both docile Gaullism and doctrinaire anti-Gaullism, the young agrarians clung to a kind of pragmatic Gaullism —but only for the years of transition. If any label can catch the spirit of their political outlook, perhaps that label would be "post-Gaullist."

* *

Thirty years after the Great Depression first shook the foundations of France's agrarian structure, the nation's rural revolution is still far from complete. Indeed, a casual visitor to the countryside might find the changes there much less dramatic than the word "revolution" suggests. Although the proportion of peasants in the total active population has declined from about 35 per cent in 1930 to approximately 20 per cent today, this figure remains one of the highest in western Europe. There is a healthy trend toward concentration of the soil in larger units, but 80 per cent of all French farms are still below 50 acres in size, and more than half are below 25 acres.[55] Much remains to be done in the way of mechanization, experimentation, education. The old complaints about prices and marketing difficulties are still heard.

Yet a revolution there has been, one without precedent in the history of the French countryside. Most peasants of 1930 probably had more in common with their predecessors of Balzac's time than with their successors of 1963—both in techniques and in general outlook.[56] Indeed, the essence of the change to date is psychological rather than material. In one sense, the whole process amounts to nothing more than a much delayed adaptation of the rural world to the modern era—an adaptation that might have begun seventy-five years ago if it had not been artificially repressed by the dominant elites of the Third Republic with their peasantist dogma.

Perhaps the outcome will be—as it might have been seventy-five years ago—the replacement of the great mass of precapitalist peasants by a smaller, more coherent, more prosperous stratum of independent farmers, rather like those of Britain or the American Middle West. Such a prospect is suggested by Henri Mendras, one of France's ablest rural sociologists, when he describes the Catholic youth movement, somewhat ironically, as the vehicle of an emerging kulak class.* If he is right, then French

---

* Interview with Professor Henri Mendras, July 1960. M. Mendras also suggests that the complex social hierarchy of rural France is rapidly giving way to a simpler but equally rigid stratification that sharply distinguishes the *exploitants* (both landowners and tenants) from the wage-earning farm workers. The new class of *exploitants* is brought together by its members' mutual concerns, and the process is speeded up by such new organizations as the CETAs. But one consequence, he contends, is to destroy the old ladder of rural social mobility; the cost of modernized farming is now so great that a landless worker can no longer hope to become a smallholder or even a tenant farmer. Class division therefore increases in the village, and the farm workers grow steadily closer to urban labor in their general outlook. Henri Mendras, *Sociologie de la campagne française* (Paris, 1959), pp. 77–83.

society may be simply following in the steps of other Western industrialized systems, while divesting itself of its outmoded peasant myth.

For some of France's young farmers, such a goal would be both sensible and sufficient. But many others conceive of a far broader and higher goal: they look to the transformation of the countryside as a way station to the transformation of the nation. The CNJA, in particular, has long since moved beyond the narrow sphere of village life and farm prices. In their chosen realm of rural socio-economic reform, the young peasants' plans have been growing steadily more elaborate and sophisticated; and these plans bear little resemblance to the highly individualistic aspirations of a potential kulak class.

"Group agriculture" and "the organization of production" are the current keynote phrases. "Group agriculture," as originally conceived a decade ago, scarcely went beyond the idea of cooperative cultivation and ownership of machinery by a handful of peasant neighbors. Now it has expanded into a far more complex conception that embraces a whole hierarchy of cooperative groups engaged in the production, processing, and marketing of farm products. As for "the organization of production," it is conceived on a Western European rather than a national scale, with regional specialization and development, regional plans and advisory councils, and regional rather than national price-fixing and marketing support.[57] Syndical organizations representing all sectors of the economy would participate actively in this planning process, and would play a direct role in supranational political life as well.

The sole alternative, as the CNJA leaders see it, would be an accelerated growth of what they call "capitalist integration" in the French countryside. They mean by this the development of a system of contractual agreements between middlemen or large processing corporations on the one hand and individual peasants on the other. The contracting firm engages to provide the peasant with his essential supplies, and to buy his product at an agreed price; the peasant is assured of an outlet, but assumes most of the profit-and-loss risks. This arrangement (which has already made some headway in France) bears some resemblance to the "putting-out" system of the early industrial era, except that the product is no longer thread or cloth but eggs or vegetables. CNJA leaders readily admit the need for "integration" in agriculture—i.e., the linking of production, processing, and marketing. But they contend that it ought to be carried out by the peasants themselves, joined together in a voluntary cooperative fashion. "Oui au progrès, non à la prolétarisation" was their slogan at the 1962 CNJA congress. If such a system of "cooperative integration" should prove workable, it would give French agriculture a socio-economic framework without exact parallel in any other country, though with considerable resemblance to some of the Scandinavian experiments. Furthermore, its success might encourage the gradual transformation of nonagricultural segments of the economy; and it would presumably strengthen the taproot of political democracy in France.

Such ambitions may be beyond attainment. To accomplish them, even in part, would require the combined energies of elite groups from every segment of society: peasants, workers, upper and lower bourgeoisie, managerial cadres, bureaucrats, intellectuals. Some tentative steps have already been taken toward bridging the gaps that have always separated these groups— toward a *regroupement inter-syndical* and an eventual regrouping of political forces. The widest gap of all has been the one dividing the peasantry from the rest of the nation; and it is this gap above all that the young peasant leaders are bent on closing. Fortunately, they have been met halfway by men of similar temper in the labor movement, the business world, the bureaucracy, and intellectual circles.

It is true that in certain respects the young peasant leaders expect to be met more than halfway. Like the older generation of agrarian leaders, they advocate what they call a "transfer of revenues" from other branches of the economy into agriculture, in the form of transitional price supports, subsidies to agricultural social security, and government investment in rural equipment. They believe, too, that it is time for the nation to provide real equality of treatment for its peasantry, notably in medical care (where the statistics on disease and infant mortality are startling)* and in education. Most peasant children even today can expect no more than a few years of primary education in an ill-equipped village school, plus (at best) a few weeks of sketchy and inadequate post-elementary agricultural instruction.[58] Recently the CNJA has begun to agitate for a system of *ramassage scolaire* that will permit farm children to be transported by school bus to elementary and secondary schools in the larger towns. Obviously the material revolution has a long way to go.

As for the psychological revolution that has undoubtedly occurred, some observers are still skeptical. They point out that the new rural elite constitutes no more than a tiny minority of the whole peasant population, and that the forces arrayed against change are far too great to be overcome. They sometimes add that the rural reformers themselves do not form a single cohesive bloc, and that personal or doctrinal rivalries will be likely to hamper their effectiveness. Certain critics even claim to find in the new peasant generation a powerful and disturbing corporatist tendency, or a persistent survival of peasantist dogma — either of which might corrupt the urge toward modernization and toward bridging the urban-rural gap.

Each of these charges has at least some plausibility, and no one can yet be sure that the critics are wrong. Still, the hopeful

---

* Official surveys show that urban children and army draftees are taller than those from rural areas, and that infant mortality is higher in the country than in the cities. Privately conducted studies of mental disturbances and of alcoholism show a higher incidence in the countryside (Latil, *Evolution du revenu agricole*, pp. 291–92). Alfred Sauvy has pointed out that better milk is available in the workers' quarters of Paris than in most rural districts.

signs are sufficient to counterbalance the doubts and fears, and to leave the future open. Small the rural elite may be, yet it is far larger and more influential that anyone dared to hope only a decade ago, and its effect as leaven in the peasant mass has already produced surprising results. Divided it may be, too; yet differences of opinion do not destroy all chance of fruitful accomplishment. As for the allegations of corporatist and peasantist tendencies among the young peasants, there would seem to be only slight reason for concern. If faint echoes of a corporatist attitude do persist, there is little sign of a narrow and jealous exclusivism, or of a desire to reconstruct society on corporative lines. And so far as the peasantism of the young peasants is concerned, it contrasts sharply with the traditional doctrine; for it challenges the dogma of a separate and morally superior peasant world, and demands for its members the right to be citizens "à part entière."

"The French peasantry," Serge Mallet tells us, "is an unknown world. The object of everybody's concern, the leitmotif of every electoral speech, the peasants still live in isolation. . . . Nevertheless, in these last few years, the French countryside has been profoundly shaken. A technical revolution of unequaled scope, comparable in its economic and political consequences to the nineteenth-century industrial revolution, is in progress in the countryside. . . . But the political ripening of the peasant follows the laws of nature. The germination process occurs underground. To follow the development of the seed, one must look beneath the soil."[59] Mallet's phrases are those of the journalist rather than of the cautious and plodding scholar. Yet at this point in the historical process, midway through an absorbing rural revolution, his judgment provides a tentative conclusion as apt as any that might be offered by an historian. One can at least be sure that the French peasantry has outgrown its passive and negative role; that its voice will be heard henceforth in the shaping of its own future, and that of France.

APPENDIX

APPENDIX

On the Trail of Arthur Young:
Six Village Sketches

ALMOST two centuries have elapsed since the eminent agronomist Arthur Young set forth on those travels in France that were to make him immortal. Probably immortality—at least in the literary and scholarly world—is in part a matter of luck. At any rate, it was Young's good fortune to arrive in France at a moment of impending revolution, and to record an aspect of French life that other observers, fascinated by the dramatic developments in Versailles and Paris, were inclined to overlook.

France in our day, whatever the uncertainties of its future, is surely not confronted by another 1789. But in our day as in Young's, drastic changes are taking place in France's economic, social, and psychological structure, and the backwash of change has reached into the most remote corners of provincial France. With some justice, then, the rural traveler of our day, seeking insights into a neglected but important side of France's modern history, may invoke the shade of Arthur Young as a kind of spiritual predecessor.

My first extensive foray into the countryside took place in 1950–51, when the barest beginnings of fundamental change could be detected. Indeed, "detected" is probably too positive a word; the signs of change could best be guessed at, intuited, rather than seen or proved. My second visit, in 1960, took me to many of the same villages I had seen a decade earlier, and to a few new ones as well. Some of them were chosen as examples of peasant Communism—a paradoxical phenomenon that has a special fascination for the naïve American observer. Others were selected because they seemed likely to throw light on a quite different phenomenon—the emergence of a new elite in the countryside. Perhaps some aspects of France's rural revolution, of the complex forces at work in our era, can best be conveyed by a series of brief glimpses into six of these tiny, remote communities.

* *

Midway between Paris and the Belgian frontier, nestled in a small valley in the heart of the Soissons plateau, lies the hamlet of Epagny. The region has long been one of the principal breadbaskets of France; the plateau's rich soil produces grain crops that would be the envy of the American west. Many of its farms (gigantic by French standards) are highly mechanized, thoroughly modern, and remarkably prosperous. Epagny's 320 inhabitants are isolated from railways and main roads; those who want to visit the metropolis of Soissons must walk a mile to catch the once-a-day bus. Yet they live in relative comfort, thanks to the fact that Epagny was blown to bits during the First World War. No house is more than forty years old, and most houses are miraculously equipped with electricity and running water. Such *confort moderne* is rare indeed in rural France.

Nevertheless, the commune has steadily lost population during the past few decades. Mechanization is partly responsible; it has reduced the demand for labor. But far more important, the young people of Epagny rebel against life in the village. Leisure-time diversion is almost nonexistent; so is opportunity for the future. Three-quarters of the children migrate to the towns or cities as soon as their schooling is over. As a community in the organic sense, Epagny is dying.

Epagny's social structure could scarcely be reduced to simpler terms. In 1950, the business community consisted of a harness maker, a blacksmith, a grocer, and a tavernkeeper. There were five retired persons who had come home to spend their declining years. A priest from a neighboring village passed weekly to say Mass. Beyond this, there were landowners and farm laborers: nobody else.

A closer look at this solidly agricultural community shows at once that it violates all the usual generalizations about France, the nation of smallholders. There are only four farms in the entire commune. Three of them are giants, ranging from 600 to 800 acres each; the fourth is a pygmy of 35 acres. The de Fay family, whose aristocratic forebears have long inhabited the region, controls two of the large farms. The rest of the adult population is made up of farm laborers—mostly native Frenchmen, with a considerable minority of Poles. Here, then, is an example of large-scale capitalistic agriculture tinged with feudal survivals.

Immediately after the Second World War, when Charles de Gaulle's provisional government restored free elections, Epagny shifted to the extreme left in brutal fashion. In 1945, 45 per cent of the voters who went to the polls chose the Communist ticket; in 1946 (when two elections occurred), it was 59 and 60 per cent; in 1951, 61 per cent; in 1956, 55 per cent. The parties of the moderate left and center were virtually wiped out; only the rightist Independent-Peasant bloc survived as a feeble counterpoise to Communism.

Communism's postwar success in Epagny was all the more striking because the movement was so new there. During the Third Republic, Communist candidates had rarely received a single vote; it was the Socialists, rather, who had swept the polls.

Back as far as 1914, a Socialist spellbinder had launched the trend when he told these landless workers: "It's easy to know the right way to vote; just see what the boss does, then vote the opposite way." For the next twenty-five years, Socialism had seemed sufficiently opposite to express the workers' discontent. After 1945, it dwindled to near-extinction; the Socialist ticket got only four votes in 1951. Here, it would seem, was a simple case of a proletarianized farm population that gradually became ripe for revolutionary action, and that finally took the natural step from herbivorous to carnivorous Marxism.

Yet the story is not all told. What of the social relationships in the village as the Red tide rose? Prior to 1940, the big landlords had always controlled the local political machinery of the commune. Jean de Fay was mayor in that era; his son Pierre sat on the town council; the third of the big owners, M. Ancellin, was assistant mayor. Municipal elections in 1945 gave the workers their chance to take over the town hall. But the balloting produced astounding results. The voters chose a town council consisting of seven conservatives and three Socialists, without a Communist in the lot; and the council promptly chose Pierre de Fay as mayor, with Ancellin back in his old post as assistant. During the years that followed, the conservatives' grip on the municipality was never challenged. In 1947, Pierre de Fay led the field with 126 of 130 votes cast; his brother Jean followed with 118; Ancellin got 92. When the Fourth Republic gave way to the Fifth in 1958, de Fay and Ancellin stayed on in their perpetual posts in the town hall.

Here is clear enough evidence that the farm workers of Epagny, however discontented they may be, fall somewhat short of fire-eating class-consciousness. How can it be that these proletarians, who persistently support the Communist ticket in national elections, remain loyal to a landowning aristocrat like de Fay? Most of them will answer that question candidly. "He's not like most of the big shots; he's a *chic type*. And besides, who else around here could be mayor?" Who else, indeed? Most of the able young men go off to the cities, leaving the "rejects" to work on the farms. And when a spark of leadership does appear in some farm laborer, it has precious little chance to develop. Workers who develop political ambitions in villages like Epagny have rarely been able to win the votes of their jealous neighbors. "Why should I vote for Jacques? I'm as good a man as he is."

The fact that peasant Communism exists in a village like Epagny needs little explaining. What is curious here is its flabbiness, its lack of intensity; for these proletarians seem made to order for the Leninist formulas. Someday, perhaps, Epagny may furnish troops for a Communist revolution. It is unlikely ever to furnish leaders.

* *

In the valley of the Lot, some three or four hundred miles south and west of Epagny, lies the village of St. Pierre-Toirac. The rich, flat floor of the river valley, 250 acres of which are within the boundaries of the commune, strikes one as a kind of oasis. To the north and south stretch miles of *causses,* those eroded dry hills that remind one of parts of the American southwest. Farming in many parts of the region is a harsh and grim struggle; but on the bottom land of St. Pierre, even the routine methods of the local farmers produce rich cash crops. Tobacco, sold to the state monopoly at a fixed price, is the chief moneymaker. Not only is St. Pierre prosperous, but it is open to currents from the outside world. An important railway line runs through the valley, so that St. Pierrians can easily visit Figeac, Cahors, or even distant Toulouse.

St. Pierre is a village of equals. The land is owned by forty peasants, none of whom holds more than thirty acres, and few of whom hold less than five. Both cash tenantry and share tenantry are unknown. The only non-peasants are the local doctor, a few station employees, and a dozen retired railway workers or civil servants. Even the shops and *bistros* (such as they are) are kept by the wives of peasant owners.

Like so much of southwestern France, St. Pierre is leftist by long tradition. That tradition is vigorously anticlerical and individualistic; during the Third Republic, it was accurately translated into politics by the doctrines and leadership of the Radical Party. Prior to 1940, Anatole de Monzie, the district's favorite adopted son, always got his largest majorities at St. Pierre. The fact that he called himself an Independent Socialist probably gave him added glamor, especially since St. Pierrians knew as well as anybody else that de Monzie's socialism went no deeper than the label. When Marxist candidates appeared in the region, they were almost totally ignored by St. Pierre's voters. De Monzie's highly individualistic pseudosocialism was good enough for them. Then came war, occupation, and liberation. St. Pierre went to the polls in 1945 to choose among five tickets, all adroitly equipped with leftist labels and programs. The village, which had never before cast a single vote for an avowedly Communist candidate, went overboard for Communism. Sixty per cent of the voters chose that party's list, and they continued to do so in four successive elections from 1945 to 1951.

St. Pierre's brusque turn to Communism is far less understandable than that of Epagny. What produced this sudden transmutation of inveterate Radical smallholders into Communists? One factor, no doubt, was Radicalism's collapse in 1940, which left a kind of vacuum just to the left of center; another was de Monzie's tortuous attitude toward Vichy. But a more logical choice for St. Pierrians would have been the mild Socialism of Blum rather than the rigid Communism of Thorez. The explanation does not lie in the impact of some outstanding personality —a native son who suddenly espoused the cause, or led a resistance group in heroic fashion, or proved to be an organizer of genius. Instances of this sort did occur here and there in France; but in the valley of the Lot, the caliber of Communist leadership remained as low as it had always been. The only new source of Marxian ideas was the handful of retired railway workers who settled down here during and after the war; and none of them was a leader.

Was there, then, a real change of heart among these violently individualistic peasants? Were they somehow converted into tough-minded sectarians, or utopian visionaries? A brief visit sufficed to destroy any such hypotheses. During my stay in St. Pierre in 1951, a government land survey was in progress, for the first time in a century. Hanging about the surveyors from dawn to dusk were four peasants, who turned out to be the leading Communists of the village. The surveyors were approaching their plots, and each peasant meant to make sure that no neighbor would gain a six-inch strip of soil at his expense. In a different way, the fellow-traveling mayor also showed a lack of the sectarian rigor that marks the true rural Communist; he went so far as to welcome an American visitor to his *bistro,* and to set up drinks on the house. True, his tolerance and credulity had their limits—as when somebody attributed expansionist tendencies to the Soviet Union, and referred darkly to the fate of the kulaks in Bulgaria. "Ça," he announced with finality, "c'est pour les poires." Only a sucker will swallow that stuff. Nobody, it appeared, was going to make *poires* of these hardheaded peasants of St. Pierre-Toirac.

If it was true that St. Pierre's Communism reflected nothing more than an old tradition of self-assertive individualism, when and how would that fact be demonstrated at the polls? The first indication came in 1956, when the impassioned demagoguery of Pierre Poujade (a native of the region) offered the St. Pierrians an alternative avenue of protest against all forms of external authority. The Communist share of the vote dropped from 60 to 39 per cent; and about half of the party's deserters clearly went over to the Poujadist list. Two years later came an even more telling sign. In the 1958 elections that followed de Gaulle's return to power, the first day's voting ended in a stalemate between the Communist and the Socialist candidates. A week later, in the runoff ballot, St. Pierrians showed their true colors; they opted for the Socialist, 67 to 44. After more than a decade of pleasant and riskless flirtation with the idea of social revolution, the village found itself safe at home again.

* *

When one arrives in the village of Samazan (population 765), nothing seems to distinguish it from a hundred other sleepy towns of old Gascony, just north of the Pyrenees in southwestern France. True, it appears more prosperous than most; yet what brought me there was not its economic achievements but its political behavior. Forty years ago, Samazan and the surrounding district sent the first peasant Communist to parliament; and since that time, without interruption, Samazan's voters have never failed to back the Communist ticket. In 1935 they gave the party control of the city hall as well, and they have kept it there to the present day. Here is a clear example of rural Communism solidly implanted, and adopted by the free choice of its citizens.

Neither crushing misery nor class exploitation can explain the party's hold on Samazan. Two-thirds of the peasants are smallholders; the rest practice that ancient form of share tenantry called *métayage*, which survives mainly in the southwest. Although *métayage* is widely regarded as a kind of feudal survival, the *métayers* of Samazan make out about as well as the smallholders, and in most cases they cultivate a larger acreage. These Gascon peasants, fiercely individualistic by nature, suspicious of aristocrats, Church, government, and even of their own neighbors, ought properly to be Radical Socialists of the purest tradition. And that is exactly what they were until they shifted brusquely to Communism, just after the First World War.

Why it happened, and what the results have been, were the things that first attracted me to Samazan. In a pleasant farm-house on a ten-acre tract of his own I found the mayor, Renaud Jean, a tough and grizzled old figure with a twinkle in his eye and with the Gascon's ready tongue. I went in the hope he might suggest some reasons for Samazan's attachment to Communism; I came away convinced that I had found the reason in Monsieur Jean himself. The mayor was the son of Jean Jean, a local *métayer* who had managed, by a lifetime of hard work, to scrape together a nest egg big enough to buy his own farm. The son saw active service in the First World War, and returned from the trenches gravely wounded in body and intensely pacifist in spirit. During convalescence, he began the process of self-educa-tion that was to divert him from dirt-farming to Marxian politics. In 1920, he astounded the experts by getting himself elected Socialist deputy for his home district; and shortly afterward, when the French Marxians split, he became a charter member of the French Communist Party. The next two decades saw his steady rise in the Communist hierarchy. He crusaded persistently for a program of mass action among the small and middle peas-ants, who, he claimed, were ready to accept the gospel if it were properly presented to them. Although he met both active oppo-sition and deep inertia in the party's ruling circles, he eventually began to get a hearing in the depression era. The party's rural successes in the 1936 elections seemed to prove his foresight. By 1939 he was solidly established as Communism's expert and spokesman on peasant questions; and in the Chamber of Deputies he had risen to the chairmanship of the powerful committee on agriculture.

But throughout these years Jean was shrewd enough (and

sincere enough) to keep his roots in Samazan. When, in 1935, he added the post of mayor to that of deputy, he was always on hand for village council meetings, whatever the press of business in parliament. No citizen's complaint was too petty to go unnoticed. While we sat talking in his parlor in 1951, an old peasant arrived, bowing and scraping, cap in hand: the postal authorities had chopped down one of his trees to put up a new telephone line. When he had departed, with assurances that his rights would be protected, I asked about the visitor. "Oh, he's not from Samazan," replied the mayor with just a touch of embarrassment. "He's from the village over that way. Somehow, when they don't know where to turn, they always seem to wind up here."

Jean's career as a top-rank Communist and as a deputy ended abruptly in 1939. The Stalin-Hitler pact outraged him, and he said so frankly. Besides, he played no part in the wartime resistance movement, but preferred to remain in quiet obscurity as a farm laborer in southwestern France, working under an assumed name. The party bosses did not forget; after the war they blackballed him as a candidate for his old parliamentary seat, and "parachuted" an outside candidate into his district. If Jean's pride was hurt, his loyalty to the Communist cause was unshaken; he backed the party's slate, and reconciled himself to a career of purely local scope. There in Samazan he was unchallengeable: at each municipal election his ticket of councilors far outdistanced all rivals, until at last no challengers even dared to enter the lists. And within the new farmers' syndicate, the FNSEA, Jean built himself a second career; he quickly emerged as secretary-general of the syndicate's departmental unit in the Lot-et-Garonne, and remained its dominant figure long after every other Communist had been dislodged from a position of leadership in the department.

When I returned to Samazan in 1960 after a decade's absence, it was clear that the years had been good to the villagers. There were ample signs of prosperity and progress: tractors droning in the fields; an occasional threshing machine maneuvering awkwardly past strips of vineyard, like a fat man trying to get into a Fiat; a modernized schoolhouse that might have done credit to an American town; a fine new tomato-packing plant; a surprising number of children, for a region that had almost invented planned parenthood. It appeared that village Communism had been a smashing success.

But an afternoon of renewing acquaintance with Mayor Jean left me far less sure of it. "You've certainly gone in for mechanization here," I remarked. "How many tractors are there now?" "You're right," Jean replied. "Fifty tractors for a hundred farms —and not a dozen farms big enough to support one." "But don't you have tractor cooperatives?" I asked. "After all, one finds them everywhere in France now." "Oh, they tried one," he said with a shrug, "but it didn't last long; the peasants around here are too individualistic for that." "And the tomato-packing plant? Surely that's a municipal cooperative?" "No indeed; it's built and owned by Monsieur X." "What about organizations? Is there a unit of the young farmers' syndicate in Samazan?" "Not here; the young people are too busy having a good time." "You seem to have had your own population explosion since my last visit. Isn't that something new for this region—a sign, perhaps, of rising optimism and confidence?" "Frankly," said the mayor, "that's one of my biggest worries. School enrollment is up 60 per cent over the last ten years. What are we going to do with all these youngsters when they finish their studies?"

Has the village, then, gained nothing from a generation of Communist control? To say so would, I think, be quite unfair. Renaud Jean could properly claim that he had given Samazan two things: a school and a priest. Of that model school plant he could speak with touching pride; his stubborn and persuasive action got it out of the villagers and the Parisian bureaucrats, and it may well stand as his monument. His more ironic achievement is the presence of the *curé*. Some years ago the long-time *curé* (who rejoiced in the name of Patrick Kelly) was transferred, and the living fell vacant. Like so many other rural parishes, Samazan was served sporadically by a priest from a neighboring commune. Although Samazan is anticlerical to the core, some parishioners complained: Didn't they have as much right to a priest as the next village? Mayor Jean's convictions did not stand in the way of his duty; he went to see the bishop. "Monsignor," he said politely, "my constituents want a priest. For several years the rectory in Samazan has been standing empty. If you don't send us a priest shortly, I intend to convert the building into a shelter for indigent families." Within a month, Jean recollected triumphantly, there was a new *curé* in Samazan.

Just before leaving, I raised the delicate question of the future. "Is there a vigorous new generation," I asked M. Jean, "raised in the Marxian faith and ready to carry on your work?" "Of course, of course!" came the impatient answer. "They'll carry on, they see how history is moving." Yet somehow there seemed to be more ritualism than conviction in his voice. The next day, in the regional metropolis of Agen, I expressed my doubts to a well-informed government official in the bureau of agricultural services. "You're quite right to be skeptical," he said. "Renaud Jean has run his commune for forty years, and he has recruited and trained a remarkable number of young men who have gone high in national party councils. But in Samazan there's absolutely no one to take his place."

I thought of this comment recently when news came of Renaud Jean's death, at the age of seventy-four. The obituaries in some of the non-Communist farm journals were even warmer than those in the party organs—and perhaps rightly so. After forty years as a Communist fief, Samazan is scarcely more Communist in spirit than it was at the outset. It continues to vote Communist, almost by reflex; but whatever the election results, the village is likely to remain what it has been for a century: the epitome of Radical Socialism.

* *

High on the western slope of the rugged Massif Central lies the bleak plateau of Millevaches. Few parts of France are more isolated or more forbidding of aspect during the long winter months. When friends in the south learned of my intention to go there, they threw up their hands in horror: "Mais vous allez voir le moyen âge!" "The only natural resource is rainfall," a government official in the prefecture at Tulle told me. "Rain alone saves the area from being a desert." It is the kind of country that inspired one well-known French agronomist, René Dumont, to propose a drastic solution for France's farm problem: outlaw agriculture in the hill regions, deport all the peasants to the lusher river valleys, and convert the uplands into the world's largest national park. To anyone who has visited the plateau of Millevaches, the idea is not completely absurd.

Poverty is both the tradition and the rule on the plateau. More than a century ago, population pressure started a stream of emigration that has drained the Massif of much of its best blood. Its sons became celebrated throughout France as masons and lumberjacks; they flooded into Paris to serve as horsecab drivers and taxi drivers. Often they returned for part of each year; some retired to end their lives in their native villages. In either case, the ideas they brought back from the distant cities were revolutionary and potentially explosive.

There is a marked uniformity about the villages of Mille-vaches. Their social structure, their conditions of life, and their political tradition and behavior are pretty much cut from a single pattern. Take, then, an example chosen more or less at random:

the hamlet of Viam. Not quite 300 people inhabit this lonely spot and scratch out a living on its meager soil. There were almost three times as many a century ago: Viam's population in 1876 was 872. How so many mouths could have been fed on such scanty resources remains a mystery. Doubtless the crushing poverty of that era will go far to explain the fact that the plateau long ago began to slide toward the left.

Viam in 1876, like most of the mountainous areas in France, was an intensely religious community. Four of every five adults were regular churchgoers, and passively accepted clerical guidance. Viam was also an intensely ignorant community; only 8 per cent of the adults in 1876 could read and write. Today, three generations later, the village is literate, and almost totally without religion. A tiny remnant of Catholics take Easter Communion. Two-thirds of the children are not baptized; most of the dead are buried after a semi-political harangue by the Communist mayor.

The decline of Catholicism and the rise of Communism in Viam are closely intertwined. Well before 1900, some of the early migrants to the cities brought back an intense hatred of a religion which to them represented blind routine and obscurantism. In that epoch, their indictment of the Church had some validity—as many of the younger priests of our day are quick to admit. Poverty and resentment opened the way to a fanatical anticlericalism, which expressed itself politically in a steady trend to the left, via Radicalism to Socialism and then to Communism.

The final step in that leftward process was accomplished in the 1920's. Communism's Millevaches apostle, a man of more persistence than genius, was bush-bearded Marius Vazeilles. This native son settled down as a horticulturist on the edge of the plateau some forty years ago, and devoted himself to the propagation of trees and Communism. He crusaded unceasingly for the reforestation of the plateau, and for the expansion of his regional peasant syndicate, Les Travailleurs de la Terre. By 1925 almost every village on the plateau had its local unit of the syndicate. When Vazeilles stood for election to the Chamber in 1928 against the Radical incumbent Henri Queuille, the peasants of Viam gave him 54 per cent of their votes. In 1936 the figure rose to 64 per cent, and similar successes throughout the plateau swept him triumphantly into office. But if Vazeilles was the symbol of Communism in Viam, he was not its creator or its real source of strength. When he abjured the party in 1940 for somewhat obscure reasons, Viam's Communist supporters were unruffled. In every election from 1945 to 1958, the Communists' proportion of the vote ranged between 65 and 71 per cent.

Viam in our day is Communist almost in the sense that Mississippi is Democratic, or Vermont Republican. Communism is the party of "the best people," the village leaders. Most of the largest landowners (ca. 80–100 acres) are either in the party or for it. In the years just after the war, six local farmers managed to buy tractors (which, on the plateau, lends them a kind of Cadillac-level prestige); most of them stolidly continue to vote Communist. True, they understand Marxian doctrine no better than their forebears a century ago understood Aquinas. Almost no resident of the plateau even pretends to an acquaintance with Marxian theory. Theirs is an orthodoxy that contains more dogmatic conformism than reasoned comprehension. Their first postwar deputy, Clément Chausson, faithfully reflected their spirit. One of his proudest boasts was that by coasting down the hills of the region during an election campaign, he used two liters a day less gasoline than his rival candidates. Viam admired Chausson: he was a sharp operator, who knew the value of a sou.

Here again, as in Samazan, a generation of Communist control has failed to produce impressive results. A single village street, bearing ample evidence that animals outnumber men in the region; a tiny general store, out of whose entryway a scrawny chicken strolls; a weed-choked village square, with the inevitable *monument aux morts* bearing its appalling record of fifty-two victims of the First World War; a moldering, lichen-covered, decrepit town church, verging on total collapse. All this leaves the visitor with a sense of stagnancy, sterility, decay; a sense that nothing has happened here in the memory of living man save such catastrophes from outer space as the Great War of fifty years ago.

Yet the outer world has begun, in the last decade, to impinge on the life of Viam in at least a marginal way. Two farms in the commune have been bought by outsiders—immigrants from more crowded parts of France, where land is hard to find. These two newcomers have joined with a dozen other farmers from neighboring villages to found the first CETA in the region. The striking thing about this cooperative is that of its fifteen participants, only two are natives of the plateau; the rest are French or Dutch immigrants with wider horizons and more open minds. The old families of Viam look on these experimenters with the jaundiced eye of a Southerner threatened by Yankee freedom riders.

A second influence also comes from the outside world. Some years ago the Church classed the plateau of Millevaches as a missionary area, and began to send teams of young priests into the district. From their headquarters in the regional metropolis of Bugeat (population 1,063), these "missionaries" fan out in all directions; one of them comes to Viam once or twice a month to say Mass in the half-ruined church. They are energetic and intelligent young men—quite different in spirit and training from the old school of priests who were recruited from the immediate region. They are remarkably well-informed about questions of local sociology and economics, and fully aware of the difficulties of their task.

Yet the impact of their work, after a full decade or more, is not easy to detect. Mass at Viam still draws only a dozen worshipers, most of them older women. The church building molders away, almost beyond the point of usability, while priests and town council remain locked in a permanent cold war over who shall bear the cost of its repair. The missionaries show no great enthusiasm for implanting a village chapter of the JAC—perhaps because they feel it would be hopeless to try, or possibly because they share the suspicion and hostility of many French priests toward these young lay-action groups that often rebel at clerical control. On such crucial issues, the clergy remains divided against itself. Viam proves—if proof were needed—that French Catholicism is far from being a monolithic unit. It also proves that poverty and frustration can produce their own form of messianic faith: the ritualized conviction that a kind of primitive magic labeled Communism may some day bring salvation.

* *

From Viam to Palladuc is not very far, at least as the crow flies: about eighty miles due east, across some of France's most rugged terrain. This, too, is hill country—the region called Auvergne, whose tough and self-reliant sons have long made their way in Paris as chestnut merchants, coal heavers, *bistro* owners, or (if they happen to be named Pierre Laval) politicians. Just over the ridge from Palladuc lies Laval's home town of Châteldon, with a bust of this most eminent Auvergnat still standing in its village square.

Palladuc's favorite son is a quite different type. It would not have occurred to me to visit him (or Palladuc either) in 1950; the place was remote, the man as yet unknown. Michel Debatisse was then a teen-age peasant boy, just past his meager schooling and about to take over his father's small farm. For a teen-ager, the village offered literally nothing in the way of recreation or inspiration. A new priest sought to fill the void by organizing a local branch of the JAC. Debatisse and his friends joined, and promptly infused their own dynamism into the group; from recreation they turned to study and to action. All these young men were dirt-poor, without resources to mechanize or modernize; progress had to come out of their minds, not their pockets. Their efforts were turned toward cooperative enterprise in cultivation, the joint purchase of machinery on long-time credit, and such experiments as hauling their animals to the higher mountains to graze in summer.

It was a slow and painful process. Even the agricultural technicians of the region scoffed at the enterprise as misguided; after all, had not government agronomists a few years earlier crossed the Palladuc hill country off their agricultural map of France? Besides, Debatisse was finding his time increasingly taken up with the Young Catholic movement. Soon he was regional president of the JAC; then came a call to Paris to edit the group's national journal. He left reluctantly, for there was still so much to do in Palladuc. But as his outlook steadily broadened, from village to region to nation and beyond, the problems of peasant life took on greater scope and challenge, and the fate of Palladuc began to seem dependent on decisions made elsewhere. Somehow, he felt, a total transformation had to be attempted: a transformation that would alter social and economic structures, and, even more profoundly, mental attitudes.

Almost no one, it seemed, had thought seriously about these problems. Most of the politicians had been content with piecemeal reforms and barren oratory. The agrarian syndical movement reflected the interests of the large mechanized farmers of the north. Nobody, Debatisse felt, was trying to help the mass of small peasants.

He and his friends accordingly set out to infiltrate the farmers' syndicate. As we have seen, they persuaded its leaders to let them form an autonomous young farmers' branch of the FN-

SEA; Debatisse accepted the key post of secretary-general. From this rostrum the young men began to astound their elders with some of the most unorthodox ideas the syndical leaders had ever heard. They complained that wheat prices, instead of being set too low, were probably too high for the long-run good of the peasantry; that the steady drain of population from farm to city ought to be applauded, not deplored; that the peasants' passion for land ownership had long been their undoing; that the government, instead of being viewed as a kind of vulture with teats, should be encouraged to tear down the existing agrarian structure and build a better one in its place. By 1960 the Jacistes had begun to take over a few regional branches of the FNSEA itself; and some experts were predicting that within a decade—perhaps even sooner—they would control the national syndicate as well. Debatisse found himself consulted regularly by the government's agricultural planners, and he became one of the youngest members of the Fifth Republic's Economic Council.

"If you want to visit Michel Debatisse in Palladuc," one of his friends warned me, "it had better be on Sunday." That, he pointed out, was Debatisse's only day of so-called rest at home, at the end of a harassing week of travel to every corner of France, interspersed with eighteen-hour working days in Paris. He receives an alien visitor graciously in the kitchen of his half-modernized farmhouse, which is set on a hill in the middle of his half-modernized farm. There is running water in the kitchen (a luxury not shared by three-quarters of France's peasant homes); there is a modern stove and a well-scrubbed concrete floor. The view outside is magnificent, but the soil seems thin and the pasture sparse. One gets a sense of man locked in unending struggle with nature, with the odds heavily in nature's favor.

Perhaps Debatisse ought to have stayed in Palladuc to finish the job he had begun, instead of decamping for Paris to take on the nation's problems; so say some of his elders in the farmers' syndicate, even those few who really sympathize with the younger group's goals. Yet as I sat in the Debatisse kitchen and listened to this tough young Auvergnat talk of the issues facing the peasantry and the nation, of problems of social structure and economic change and political action (and as his young wife, another ex-Jaciste from French Flanders, interjected some vigorous opinions of her own), I got the sense that here was a rare kind and degree of talent, of dynamism and conviction, that ought not to be confined to a single village; that these are the qualities that might, at the proper moment, help to transform an entire society, and to carry dozens of Palladucs out of one epoch of history into another.

* *

The village of Teillé lies on the southern edge of Brittany, in the pleasant grazing country not far from Nantes. The village postmaster, with a touch of pride, points the way to the farm of Bernard Lambert, second-youngest deputy in the French parliament.

This is a region where feudalism, if it died a legal death in 1789, has survived in spirit and mores right down into our own day. Much of the land was sharecropped until 1945; landowners might drop in unannounced to look over the harvest, to see what was cooking in the kitchen, to take home a chicken from the poultry yard. Some of the older peasants still bow and scrape at such a visit, and greet the landlord as "Monsieur not' maître." Bernard Lambert recalls that in 1938 his father, a *métayer,* won a radio in a raffle—the first set in Teillé, the wonder and delight of the whole village. Two days later the landlord appeared: "Lambert, you owe me money. No luxuries for you while you're in debt. I'll take the radio and credit it to your account." "A good way to make Communists," remarks the younger Lambert dryly.

In politics, the old aristocrats have kept a powerful grip on the region; boxcar names are common in the departmental council, and they often go to parliament as well. After the turn of the century the old elite was challenged by the bourgeois Radical Socialists, who found enough support in the cities and towns to elect a few deputies. Neither Christian Democracy nor Marxism ever made much headway in the area. Here was a classic example of the old rural pattern: on the one side, aristocrats, church, and peasantry; on the other, the anticlerical bourgeoisie.

Lambert was an early rebel against this pattern; he rejected it at the age of twelve. Until then, he had taken for granted his role as a share tenant's son and an obedient Catholic; the priest, he recalls, turned him into a good royalist and even, for a time, into "un petit Pétainiste." Then something opened his eyes (as he now puts it); in 1942 he abruptly stopped going to Mass—abruptly, and permanently. Yet the breach was never complete on either side; after the war, when a new priest founded a local chapter of the JAC, Lambert was welcomed as a member even though he refused to return to the fold. Here Lambert got his first chance to discuss questions of agronomy, economics, politics, in an atmosphere of remarkable freedom. He read voraciously, discovered that he possessed a natural articulateness of speech, was drawn (like Michel Debatisse) into regional and then national positions of leadership in the JAC. Meanwhile he and a few young neighbors took to working their small rented farms conjointly, and founded a small cooperative slaughterhouse to buck the powerful cattle-dealers' monopoly. They next moved in on their elders who had run the regional farmers' syndicate, and took over complete control. Within a year, the average age of the syndicate's regional governing body dropped from sixty-three to thirty. Their butchering cooperative, harassed by the angry cattle-dealers who controlled all marketing outlets, managed to survive by creating its own markets in cities like Nantes, where it arranged for direct sales to organized consumer groups and trade unions.

After the fall of the Fourth Republic in 1958, de Gaulle convoked the electorate to choose a new National Assembly. Four candidates turned up in the district: an aristocrat, a Radical Socialist, a Poujadist (something new in these parts), and the customary Communist railway employee, who ran for the record. The Radical candidate, André Morice, appeared unbeatable; he had sat in parliament for more than a decade, had recently served as Minister of War, and was generally regarded as a front-runner for the premiership. A wealthy Nantes contractor, he was assured of the bourgeois vote by his social role and his Radical label. But he had kept his fences mended on the right, too, and had recently proved his broadmindedness by supporting the clericals on a school bill. No one in France seemed a surer bet for re-election.

Morice made only one mistake: he challenged the local young farmers' group. A few days before the campaign began, he publicly denounced the organizers of the cooperative slaughterhouse, accusing them not only of pinko leanings but of financial dishonesty as well. The young fire-eaters who were now in control of the regional farmers' syndicate were outraged. Morice, they agreed, must be taught a lesson. But how? At the end of an all-night meeting, they decided to enter a peasant candidate, and to draft Bernard Lambert as their champion.

Lambert himself took no part in the discussion; he was just back from two years as a sergeant in Algeria, fighting a war in which he did not believe and winning a decoration for valor in the process. When a delegation waited on him the next day, he was astounded, and tried to beg off: "I'm just back from the war, I'm in debt, I'm too young, and what do I know about politics anyway?" They persuaded him to think it over for a week, got up a petition signed by a thousand young peasants of the region, and, in the end, won his consent.

The story of that campaign is like something out of Horatio Alger. Everybody who counted lined up behind either Morice or the aristocratic candidate: the well-born, the business group,

the prefect and subprefect (whose careers Morice could presumably further), the cattle-dealers to a man, all the important
members of the clergy. Back of Lambert there was nobody except
a horde of young peasants and a considerable number of young
priests, who virtually deserted their farms and flocks for a month
to cultivate the district politically. At the end of the first day of
balloting, Lambert and Morice were neck and neck; the others
lagged far behind. The aristocrat promptly withdrew and threw
his support to Morice; for the first time in local memory, the
Blue and the Black joined in a solid bloc. The young peasant
phalanx, undiscouraged, flung itself into a week of day-and-night
action—and the miracle was accomplished. When the runoff
ballots were totaled, the count stood 19,636 for Lambert, and
19,229 for Morice.

The manner of Lambert's election was no more unorthodox
than his subsequent political behavior in the National Assembly.
During his first years as a deputy, he violated virtually every
taboo of French politics. He outraged the nationalists by calling
for a negotiated peace in Algeria. He voted to end the peasants'
ancient privilege of home distillation of alcohol—an act of courage rarely performed by any rural deputy in history. He asserted
quite openly that his own party, the Catholic MRP, ought to be
liquidated as soon as possible, since Catholics ought not to isolate
themselves in a confessional party. He proposed the creation of
a state agency that would regularly buy up all farm land that
came on the market, with a view to leasing it to small peasants
for cooperative cultivation. "The myth of peasant land ownership," he contends, "has bankrupted the peasants; since 1789 they
have bought all the land in France three times over." Lambert
and his friends have pioneered in an unprecedented kind of
farmer-labor action in their region of southern Brittany: the
farmers' syndicate and the trade unions there frequently join
forces to push their common aims, and to engage in joint demonstrations. Even the Communist-controlled labor movement, the

CGT, participates in this common action. "Why not?" asks Lambert. "After all, there are only two things wrong with the Communists—they're too sectarian and too conservative."

Only a miracle, perhaps, could have permitted such a maverick to survive long in politics. When de Gaulle and the National Assembly locked horns in 1962 over the issue of constitutional revision, Lambert joined those who voted for a motion of censure against de Gaulle's Premier. Along with many other young farm syndicalist leaders, Lambert shared de Gaulle's desire for a reinforced presidency, but objected to de Gaulle's indifference to constitutional procedures in achieving that end. The Gaullists did not forgive such *lèse-majesté*. In the elections that followed, all factions except the Communists joined forces behind a single anti-Lambert candidate of the moderate right. Before this solid coalition of conservatives, Radicals, and Gaullists, Lambert went down to defeat by a vote of 18,512 to 15,306 (with another 2,310 votes wasted on the Communist candidate). Lambert's friends consoled themselves by reflecting that his total vote at the first ballot exceeded that of 1958, and that his old rival André Morice, putting discretion ahead of valor, had chosen not to risk a second defeat.

Perhaps Lambert's brief political career was no more than a spectacular accident. Yet possibly it was more than that: a harbinger of new forces at work in French society, of new ideas and mores, of a kind of grass-roots political action that France has never known before. Perhaps even the radicalism of tomorrow will find its home in the countryside rather than in the cities. As the journalist Jacques Fauvet puts it, "While the world of labor grows less and less revolutionary, the peasant world grows less and less conservative." The locus classicus is as always Tocqueville, who remarked a century ago, "The peasants are the last of all to rise, but they are also the last to sit down."

NOTES

Notes

1. Alfred Cobban, "France—A Peasants' Republic," *The Listener*, XLI (1949), 429.

2. Quoted in *Le Temps*, Jan. 31, 1938.

3. Pierre Frédérix, *Etat des forces en France* (Paris, 1935), pp. 41–42; Charles Bettelheim, *L'Economie allemande sous le nazisme* (Paris, 1946), p. 36; E. Labat, *L'Ame paysanne* (Paris, 1919), p. 26; J. Teilhac (quoting Guesde), "Les Paysans ont-ils leur place dans la société moderne?," *La Revolution prolétarienne*, June 25, 1935, pp. 210–11.

4. Louis Chevalier, *Les Paysans* (Paris, 1947), pp. 9, 71.

5. Marc Bloch, *Les Caractères originaux de l'histoire rurale française* (Oslo, 1931; new ed. Paris, 1955); Georges Lefebvre, *Les Paysans du nord et la révolution française* (Paris, 1924; new ed. Bari, 1959), and *Etudes sur la révolution française* (Paris, 1954). My account in the next few pages depends heavily on the work of Bloch and Lefebvre.

6. The first serious attempt at an agricultural survey was conducted in 1862; since then, surveys have been made at irregular intervals (1882, 1892, 1929, 1946, 1955). Time and experience have not corrected all the faults of the early surveys; almost everyone who has written on French agriculture has paid his ironic respects to the variations and inconsistencies of the statistics. Part of the trouble is that categories change from one survey to the next (often without adequate explanation). But equally important are the volatile impulses of those who fill out questionnaires. Minister of Agriculture Georges Monnet told the Senate in 1936 that in his home canton the statistics submitted by the mayors changed from year to year, even with respect to the total acreage of the commune (*Journal officiel, débats du Sénat*, July 24, 1936, p. 838).

7. This figure excludes all farms of less than 2½ acres. Agronomists in recent years have tended to make this correction in all the survey figures, on the ground that many or most of the tiny farms were either part-time

operations or mere Sunday gardens. Their exclusion distorts the picture somewhat, but their inclusion would probably distort it more.

Michel Augé-Laribé points out that the 1882 survey showed a total of 5,672,007 *exploitations* but only 4,835,246 *exploitants* (including those with less than 2½ acres); he confesses his bafflement at the contradiction (*L'Evolution de la France agricole*, Paris, 1912, p. 102). For what they are worth, the 1882 figures break down thus:

Farms of less than 2½ acres 2,167,667
Farms of 2½ to 25 acres 2,635,030
Farms of 25 to 100 acres 727,222
Farms of over 100 acres 142,088

Approximately 80 per cent of the *exploitants* owned their land, while 20 per cent were cash tenants or share tenants. The tenants, however, worked 40 per cent of the total area (cash tenants 27 per cent, share tenants 13 per cent). A considerable number of peasants were simultaneously landowners and tenants, but the survey ignored this embarrassing complication.

8. Albert Soboul, "La Question paysanne en 1848," *La Pensée* (1948), new series No. 18, pp. 55–66, No. 19, pp. 25–37, No. 20, pp. 48–56; Rémi Gossez, "La Résistance à l'impôt: Les Quarante-cinq Centimes," *Etudes*, XV (1953), 88–132; Claude Lévy, "Notes sur les fondements sociaux de l'insurrection de décembre 1851 en province," *L'Information historique*, XVI (1954), 1942–45.

9. Marx's judgment, which appeared in his pamphlet *The Eighteenth Brumaire of Louis Napoleon*, may be found in the collected works of Marx and Engels published by the Institut für Marxismus-Leninismus in Berlin: *Karl Marx Friedrich Engels Werke*, VIII (Berlin, 1960), 201. Engels's travel notes also appear in the *Werke*, V (Berlin, 1959), 475. Renan's comment is quoted in Roland Maspétiol's *L'Ordre éternel des champs* (Paris, 1946), p. 393.

10. Michel Augé-Laribé, *La Politique agricole de la France de 1880 à 1940* (Paris, 1950), p. 124.

11. *Karl Marx Friedrich Engels Werke*, VIII, 198.

12. Albert Demangeon, *France économique et humaine* (Paris, 1946–48), I, 4–7, 95.

13. Jean Chombart de Lauwe, *Bretagne et pays de la Garonne* (Paris, 1946), p. 115.

CHAPTER TWO

1. France's census classification of "rural population" is often mistakenly confused with "agricultural population"—even by Ministers of Agriculture

(e.g., Georges Monnet, in a speech in London in 1937). The census classifies the entire population of a commune as rural if its chief town has fewer than 2,000 inhabitants. By this definition, all the inhabitants of about 36,000 of France's 38,000 communes are rural; but many of these residents are obviously not engaged in agriculture. Unfortunately, estimates of the active agricultural population are neither consistent nor very reliable. Sometimes they include only the number of adult males engaged in farming; sometimes they include women and teen-agers as well, sometimes all members of the family who are dependent on agriculture.

2. During the Third Republic, more than 30,000 of France's communes had populations of less than 1,500. Each of these communes had one senatorial elector, while Paris (with a population of almost 3 million by 1914), had only 30 electors.

3. Marcel Faure in *Paysans*, No. 1, Aug.-Sept. 1956, p. 57.

4. Figures on the numbers and kinds of agrarians in parliament may be found in Jacques Fauvet and Henri Mendras, eds., *Les Paysans et la politique* (Paris, 1957), p. 215.

5. Chevalier, *Les Paysans*, pp. 31–33.

6. One of the most consistent anti-Mélinists within agrarian ranks was the noted agricultural historian Michel Augé-Laribé. A recent statement of the pro-Méline case may be found in Roland Maspétiol's *L'ordre éternel des champs* (Paris, 1946), pp. 216–17. According to J. F. Gravier (*Mise en valeur de la France*, Paris, 1949, p. 31), Méline's aim was not to shield French agriculture against change, but to provide it with the temporary protection that any expanding industry needs during its growth to maturity. Méline's praiseworthy purpose was frustrated, according to Gravier, by the slackening of France's population growth, which narrowed the domestic market for farm products and led to technical stagnation.

7. A handful of syndicates had been created extralegally before 1884. It is part of France's agrarian folklore (based on fact, in this case) that agricultural syndicates were authorized as a kind of afterthought, by a last-minute amendment offered from the floor during the parliamentary debate in 1884.

8. The FNMCA grew out of an earlier organization, the Société Nationale d'Encouragement à l'Agriculture, founded by Léon Gambetta and other republicans in 1880. It was customarily headed by a Radical Socialist politician, and had close ties with the Ministry of Agriculture.

Syndical and cooperative membership figures are harder to find for the pre-1914 period than for more recent periods. One estimate credits the right-wing syndicates and their affiliated mutual-insurance groups with a membership of a million families in 1914, and the left-wing movement with 600,000 (Neil Hunter, *Peasantry and Crisis in France*, London, 1938, p. 220). But Augé-Laribé, who knew the situation much more intimately, suggests that there were probably no more than a half-million *syndiqués* of all sorts in France before 1914 (*La Politique agricole*, p. 136).

9. This so-called Ruau proposal was also a response to pressures from private commerce, which resented "unfair" competition from the cooperatives and syndicates. After years of deadlock, a compromise statute on the scope and powers of farm cooperatives was finally adopted in 1920.

10. Augé-Laribé, *L'Evolution*, p. 80.

11. For an excellent account of Jaurès's position on the peasantry, see Harvey Goldberg, *The Life of Jean Jaurès* (Madison, Wis., 1961), pp. 179–94. Also Carl Landauer, "The Guesdists and the Small Farmer: Early Erosion of French Marxism," *International Review of Social History*, VI (1961), 212–25.

12. Stanley Hoffmann *et al.*, *In Search of France* (Cambridge, Mass., 1963), p. 409.

13. Trochu's enemies finally evicted him (in 1930) from the staff of *L'Ouest-Eclair*, and he died a frustrated and embittered man. An account of his long conflict with his ecclesiastical superiors and with the conservative Catholics who dominated Breton politics may be found in his book (written under the pseudonym Paul Delourme) *Trente-cinq Années de politique religieuse* (Paris, 1936).

14. These figures omit all farms under 2½ acres (see n. 5, ch. 1). For what they are worth, here are the official statistics of 1892 and 1929:

	1892	1929
Farms of less than 2½ acres	2,235,405	1,014,731
Farms of 2½ to 25 acres	2,617,558	1,863,867
Farms of 25 to 100 acres (25 to 125 in 1929)...	711,118	973,520
Farms of over 100 acres (over 125 in 1929).....	138,671	114,312

The number of cash tenants declined from 1,061,401 in 1892 to 728,131 in 1929; the number of share tenants, from 344,168 to 198,783. Once again, however, the survey made no provision for listing peasants who straddled these categories.

15. One factor in disorderly marketing was the practice of "sugaring" substandard wine, to which some unscrupulous growers resorted. For a detailed account of the winegrowers' problems, see Charles K. Warner, *The Winegrowers of France and the Government Since 1875* (New York, 1960).

16. *Journal officiel, débats de la Chambre des députés*, Dec. 9, 1938, p. 1712.

17. Michel Augé-Laribé, *Le Paysan français après la guerre* (Paris, 1923), pp. 43–46. Three and a half million peasants were mobilized; 673,700 were killed or listed as missing, and about 500,000 suffered grave

permanent injuries. After 1918, many conservatives argued that Méline, by keeping a numerous peasantry on the soil, had won the war for France. Jacques Bainville, *La Fortune de la France* (Paris, 1937), p. 358.

18. Augé-Laribé, *Le Paysan français*, p. 241.

19. Michel Augé-Laribé, *La Révolution agricole* (Paris, 1955), p. 308.

20. Daniel Halévy, *Visites aux paysans du centre* (Paris, 1935), pp. 267–68.

21. The laws of 1918–19 on the regrouping of land parcels were effective only in the war-devastated areas, where the old pattern of land division had been blasted out of existence. Elsewhere, regrouping depended on the consent of a majority of the landowners involved—and that was hard to obtain. The law of 1918 on agricultural education, from the elementary to the advanced level, was well-conceived; but adequate credits were never appropriated to carry out the plan.

Government credits for the re-equipment of war-devastated farms enabled the farmers of the fertile northeast to restore full productive capacity by the mid-1920's. Some farmers, however, did not return to the land, so that the war speeded up the process by which land was concentrated in fewer and bigger farms. An undetermined proportion of these credits was diverted away from agriculture by a *sub rosa* traffic in war claims; some farmers sold their claims to urban speculators, who used the money for new construction in the towns.

22. Pierre Caziot, *La Terre à la famille paysanne* (Paris, 1919).

23. See below, pp. 165–66.

24. Chéron is supposed to have turned up at least one family with a claim to a thousand years of unbroken occupancy. Most Frenchmen viewed such claims with even more than their usual skepticism.

25. Augé-Laribé, *La Paysan français*, pp. 115–16. Augé-Laribé was one of the CNAA's top officials.

26. Much has been written in recent years on the power of the alcohol lobby and the economic and social consequences of its activities. The beet-growers, numbering only about 150,000 and concentrated mainly in the large-farming area of the northeast, have been the chief beneficiaries; they appear to have used the mass of 1,600,000 winegrowers as their shock troops for political action. For a recent analysis in English, see Bernard E. Brown, "Alcohol and Politics in France," *American Political Science Review*, LI (1957), 976–94.

27. This sentiment was expressed in 1926. *L'Europe nouvelle*, XI (July 14, 1928), 969.

28. "Delourme" [Trochu], *Trente-cinq Années*, p. 306. Further details on Breton syndicalism in the 1920's may be found in Henri Pitaud's *La Terre au paysan* (Paris, 1936) and in an exchange of correspondence

(including letters from Trochu and Mancel) in *L'Europe nouvelle,* XI (June 2, June 16, and July 14, 1928), 757, 834–36, and 967–69. Henri Pitaud, a young Vendean peasant of strongly left-wing Catholic sympathies, was an active crusader for "peasant emancipation" in the west. For a time he joined Mancel's youth movement and attempted to implant it in the Vendée. After several other abortive ventures in grass-roots organization during the 1930's, Pitaud gave up the fight and emigrated to Paraguay. He seems to have been one of those lonely pioneers who are born a quarter-century too soon.

29. Louis L'Hévéder, quoted in *L'Europe nouvelle,* XI (July 14, 1928), 969. "Sillonist," of course, refers to Marc Sangnier's Christian Democratic movement, the Sillon.

CHAPTER THREE

1. Marcel Faure in *Paysans,* No. 22, Feb.-March 1960, pp. 7–8.

2. J.-M. Jeanneney's calculations, which compare agricultural prices to the general price level (1913 = 100), show that in 1930 farm prices moved above the general price level for the first time in almost a decade, and that they fluctuated between 101 and 119 during the depression years (Jeanneney, *Tableaux statistiques relatifs à l'économie française et l'économie mondiale,* Paris, 1957, p. 67). Some economists, however, contend that wholesale food prices remained steadily below those of industrial products from 1930 through 1936; see, for example, R. Forestier in Société Française d'Economie Rurale, *L'Economie agricole française 1938–1958* (Paris, 1959), p. 222.

3. There are no dependable figures on the rural exodus for this or any other period. One economist makes the following estimate of the average annual shift from agriculture to other employment:

	Men	Women
1918–1930	50,000	40,000
1931–1935	25,000	15,000
1936–1939	60,000	30,000
1940–1944	25,000	35,000
1945–1949	55,000	50,000
1950–1951	70,000	60,000

Marc Latil, *L'Evolution du revenu agricole* (Paris, 1956), p. 82.

4. Jean Dessirier in *La Conjoncture économique et financière,* XI (Nov.-Dec. 1939). Dessirier calculated that the decline in total peasant buying power was partly offset by a decline of 15 per cent in the farm population.

5. *Le Temps,* Sept. 21, 1936.

6. The Paris demonstration of November 28, 1934 (like that of Chartres in 1933), was sponsored by the Parti Agraire; it also had the sanction of the new Front Paysan. Some ten thousand peasants crowded into the Salle Wagram to applaud a series of orators who denounced falling farm prices as a boon to the Marxists "and their protectors, the international bankers." Despite the efforts of a large riot squad, some of the peasants broke through to the Etoile and succeeded in marching down the Champs Elysées. *Le Temps,* Nov. 29 and 30, 1934; Pierre Dominique, "Les Paysans à Paris," *L'Europe nouvelle,* XVII (Dec. 8, 1934), 1205.

7. Halévy, *Vistes aux paysans,* p. 268.

8. Michel Augé-Laribé, "De la France d'avant-guerre à la France d'aujourd'hui: Structure agricole," *Revue d'économie politique,* LIII (1939), 149–51.

9. Association Générale des Producteurs de Blé, *Bulletin de documentation,* No. 8, April 16, 1935.

10. On the wine problem in the depression years, see Warner, *The Winegrowers,* chs. 7–8.

11. Farm income in 1938 was derived from the following sources: meat, 22.5%; wheat, 17.0%; milk, 13.5%; wine, 11.5%; fowls and eggs, 11.5%; vegetables, 9.5%; other crops, 14.5%. J. Klatzmann in Société Française d'Economie Rurale, *L'Economie agricole française 1938–1958,* p. 152.

12. J. Teilhac, *La Révolution prolétarienne,* June 25, 1935, p. 210. The most vigorous and persistent spokesman for the neo-physiocratic doctrine was René Dumont, a brilliant young faculty member at the Institut National Agronomique; see, for example, his lively pamphlet *Misère ou prosperité paysanne?* (Paris, 1936). Since the Second World War, Dumont's influence in French agricultural planning has been very great.

13. Wilhelm Roepke, *International Economic Disintegration* (London, 1942), pp. 158–59. Although the phrase comes from a German author, it beautifully sums up the French peasantist view. The phrase from Ramuz was frequently cited by French peasantists: e.g., Louis Salleron, *La Corporation paysanne* (Paris, 1943), p. 25.

14. In 1930 the Socialists, for the first time since 1911, gave agricultural problems a central place on the agenda of their party congress. "The red harvest is there, ready to be reaped!" cried Compère-Morel, to salvos of applause. The party's reformulated policy called for the defense of both small- and middle-sized rural property, even after a Socialist victory. It also urged the creation of state marketing agencies (*offices*) and the encouragement of producers' cooperatives for the joint use of machinery. Parti Socialiste S.F.I.O., *XXVIIᵉ congrès national, compte rendu sténographique*

(Paris, n.d.), pp. 325–68; Parti Socialiste S.F.I.O., *Programme agricole* (Paris, 1931).

15. Union Nationale des Syndicats Agricoles, *Vers la corporation agricole* (Paris, 1934), pp. 32–37. This volume contains the proceedings of the UNSA's first congress.

16. Louis Salleron in UNSA, *Vers la corporation agricole*, pp. 143–44; Jacques Le Roy Ladurie in R. Grand *et al.*, *Questions agricoles* (Paris, 1936), pp. 212–14. Le Roy Ladurie described Italian corporatism as not much different from Stalinism, and suggested that it might be wise to invent a new word for nontotalitarian corporatism.

17. *Syndicats paysans*, No. 1 (July 1, 1937). This was the new weekly organ founded by the activists of the UNSA, and jointly edited by Louis Salleron and Jacques Le Roy Ladurie. Salleron, an intense young intellectual employed in the offices of a farm organization, was already emerging as the chief theorist of corporatism. Le Roy Ladurie, scion of an old royalist family of large landowners in Normandy, was secretary-general of the UNSA.

18. Advocates of modernization on the Danish-Dutch model rarely got their ideas into print until after the Second World War, but those ideas were already emerging in the 1930's. For a postwar exposition, see Jean Chombart de Lauwe, *Pour une agriculture organisée: Danemark et Bretagne* (Paris, 1949). Other specialists whose ideas anticipated this point of view were René Courtin, Pierre Fromont, and Louis Malassis.

19. The principal sources for the history of the Parti Agraire are Henri Noilhan's *La République des paysans* (Aurillac, 1931) and the files of the two leading weekly journals of the party, *La Voix de la terre* and *La République agraire du massif central*. Noilhan, though trained as an agronomist, was a Parisian lawyer with political aspirations; he barely missed a seat in the Chamber in a 1935 by-election.

20. Interview with Henri Dorgères, August 1951. Dorgères denied the allegation that he had once been a member of the Action Française, but admitted that he had been strongly influenced by Maurras until Maurras's anti-Christian views gradually alienated him. At the outset, Dorgères formed an alliance with the Parti Agraire, but this broke down within a year owing to electoral rivalries. Dorgères blamed the "intrigues" of the Abbé Trochu for the misunderstanding. In fact, every political alliance in Dorgères's long career was to break down in similar fashion.

21. The Dorgerist movement attracted more contemporary attention than the Agrarian Party, and has been treated more extensively by historians. See, for example, J. M. Royer's chapter "De Dorgères à Poujade" in Fauvet and Mendras, *Les Paysans et la politique*. A well-known Parisian journalist of the era, L. G. Robinet, wrote an admiring pamphlet on Dorgères and his movement, *Dorgères et le Front paysan* (Paris, 1936); Henri Pitaud's *La*

Terre au paysan is a hostile account that contains some interesting details. Dorgères himself published three books: *Haut les fourches!* (Paris, 1935), *Révolution paysanne* (Paris, 1943), and *Au XXe siècle 10 ans de jacquerie* (Paris, 1959). Other sources include Dorgères's weekly journal, *Le Cri du sol*, and his monthly "theoretical" organ, *Le Cri du paysan*.

22. Pitaud, *La Terre au paysan*, p. 173. Dorgères's enemies commonly described him as a paid puppet of Le Roy Ladurie and Lemaigre-Dubreuil. Dorgères denied that he accepted a penny from either man (except for newspaper advertising for Lemaigre's vegetable-oil firm). Ninety per cent of his funds, he insists, came from membership dues and subscriptions, and the rest from a benevolent society of nonagriculturists (interview, August 1951).

23. Interview with Henri Dorgères, August 1951. Dorgères recalled, with some pride, that his partisans had manhandled about thirty deputies; one was thrown out of a window. Dorgères's "beefsteak" speech drew a crowd of 15,000; he shared the rostrum with Le Roy Ladurie (*La République agraire du massif central*, Sept. 8, 1935).

24. Pierre Dominique, "Les Paysans à Paris," *L'Europe nouvelle*, XVII (Dec. 8, 1934), 1205. See also *La République agraire du massif central*, Aug. 11, 1934.

25. Such passions were aroused by the schism that it is difficult to reconstruct the story. My account rests primarily on the contemporary press—notably *La Voix de la terre* (representing Agricola's faction) and *La République agraire du massif central* (representing the Noilhan-Guillon faction). See also Pierre Dominique, "La Guerre des fourches," *L'Europe nouvelle*, XIX (Feb. 15, 1936), 147. An interview with Henri Noilhan in 1951 threw no additional light on the episode.

26. Interview with Renaud Jean, 1951.

27. The subsidy enabled the editors to send out large numbers of free copies, and thus to inflate the subscription figures (which reached 30,000 as compared with the previous maximum of 10,000 for *La Voix paysanne*). Some critics charged that the Party had suppressed *La Voix paysanne* because of its independent tone, but Jean insisted that his paper had merely succumbed to financial difficulties (*La Terre*, No. 15, May 8, 1937). For a fuller account of the Communists' rural activities between the wars, see my essay "Communists and Peasantry in France" in E. M. Earle, ed., *Modern France* (Princeton, 1952).

28. Pitaud, *La Terre au paysan*, p. 178. Pitaud was active in the CNP from 1933 to 1937, when he broke with Calvayrac because the latter allegedly permitted the CNP to become "merely the agrarian branch of the Socialist Party" (*L'Effort paysan*, No. 32, Sept. 25, 1937).

29. CNP brochure quoted in *La Voix de la terre*, No. 391, Aug. 27, 1936.

30. Quoted in *La Terre*, No. 16, May 15, 1937.

31. In 1937, when the Blum government organized the National Wheat Office, two seats on its council were allotted to the CNP as a representative farm organization, even though other farm groups far exceeded it in membership. Calvayrac, who took one of the council seats, promptly enraged the other agricultural representatives by voting with the government's delegates against a higher wheat price.

Several young members of the CNP were to win prominence in agricultural affairs after 1944. Pierre Tanguy-Prigent became Minister of Agriculture during the liberation era, and Henri Canonge became a high official in the postwar farm organization, the CGA.

CHAPTER FOUR

1. Joseph Cadic, deputy for Morbihan, in *Journal officiel, débats de la Chambre*, Feb. 19, 1937, p. 643.

2. Louis Bodin and Jean Touchard, *Front populaire 1936* (Paris, 1961), p. 146.

3. François Goguel, *La Politique des partis sous la IIIe république* (Paris, 1946), II, 263–64.

4. This statement is supported by Georges Dupeux. For details on peasant voting in 1936, see G. Dupeux, *Le Front Populaire et les élections de 1936* (Paris, 1959), pp. 149–71.

5. Forty-seven deputies in the 1936 Chamber listed themselves as farmers (*cultivateurs*) or landowners (*propriétaires*); in addition, there was an agricultural worker, an agricultural cooperative director, and an agricultural engineer. The Radicals and the Socialists had the largest contingents of farmers, with fifteen and thirteen, respectively; see Chambre des députés, *Notices et portraits 1936* (Paris, 1936). The 1932 Chamber had contained fifty-three farmers and landowners, and three agricultural engineers. Some of these listings were ambiguous: e.g., one deputy described himself as "cultivateur et négotiant."

6. The Communists' "programme de sauvetage de l'agriculture française" called for higher farm prices and the defense of working peasants' property. The Socialists' platform strongly resembled that of the Communists, save for putting more emphasis on the interrelationship between the farm crisis and the general crisis. The Radicals, after asserting, "Le parti agraire, c'est nous," proposed similar remedies, but added references to tariff protection and to the need for organizing the profession. The right-wing groups were more inclined to rate the farm crisis as the nation's outstanding problem, and hinted at a corporatist solution by their references to *la classe*

paysanne. From left to right, every party put higher farm prices at the top of its list of goals. Dupeux, *Le Front Populaire*, pp. 103–17.

7. *Ibid.*, p. 182.

8. *Journal officiel, débats de la Chambre*, July 3, 1937, pp. 1722–1817.

9. *Journal officiel, débats du Sénat*, July 21–24, 1936, pp. 723–888.

10. *Journal officiel, débats de la Chambre*, Aug. 13, 1936, p. 1371.

11. See above, p. 56. This incident occurred shortly after the devaluation of the franc in 1936, which led the growers to demand an emergency price adjustment.

12. Pierre de Pressac in *Revue politique et parlementaire*, CLXXX (Aug. 10, 1939), 305. On the difficulties of the Wheat Office in 1938–39, see also *Le Temps*, May 4, June 22, July 31, and August 3, 1939; and Louis Salleron *et al.*, *La Corporation paysanne* (Paris, 1943), pp. 185–90.

13. Association Générale des Producteurs de Blé, *Bulletin*, No. 23 (Dec. 9, 1937); see also *Journal officiel, débats du Sénat*, Dec. 29, 1937, p. 1368.

14. *France-Documents*, n.s., No. 65, June 1952, p. 9.

15. In an address delivered in London early in 1937. Georges Monnet, "The Place of Agriculture in the Economic Policy of the French Government," *International Affairs*, XVI (1937), 425.

16. Bills for the protection of tenants' rights had been introduced repeatedly, but unsuccessfully, ever since 1848. Monnet's proposal fixed the lease period at nine years, with a guaranteed right of renewal; assured the tenant of a pre-emptive purchase right if the farm was put up for sale; and required owners, at the termination of a lease, to pay an indemnity covering the value of improvements made by the tenant (*Journal officiel, débats de la Chambre*, March 23, April 27 and 29, May 21, 1936, pp. 1170, 1365, 1401–13, 1581–85). A similar measure was eventually to be adopted in 1945.

17. *Ibid.*, Feb. 11, 12, and 16, 1937, pp. 475, 529, 570.

18. *Ibid.*, Feb. 11–25, 1937, pp. 475–713 (esp. pp. 477, 478, 486, 528, 538). Some right-wing farm journals alleged that most of Monnet's reform bills had been drafted in a trade union office in Paris, and that they were "all more or less of Russian or sovietist inspiration" (*L'Effort paysan*, No. 4, March 13, 1937).

19. *Journal officiel, débats de la Chambre*, Feb. 11 and 16, 1937, pp. 479–83 and 570–72.

20. Pierre Dominique, "La Province devant Paris," *L'Europe nouvelle*, XIX (July 25, 1936), 754; *La Voix de la terre*, No. 387, July 22, 1936; *La République agraire du massif central*, July 20, 1936.

21. Jean Moquay, *L'Evolution sociale en agriculture: La Condition des ouvriers agricoles depuis juin 1936* (Bordeaux, 1939), pp. 139–41.

22. Dorgères, *La Révolution paysanne*, pp. 71–72; *L'Effort paysan*, Nos. 25, 27, 29, Aug. 7 and 21, Sept. 4, 1937; *Journal officiel, débats de la Chambre*, Dec. 13, 1937, pp. 2951–52.

23. Dessirier, a violent critic of the Popular Front, was virtually the only contemporary statistician who published estimates of current price levels and real buying power. See his monthly publication *La Conjoncture économique et financière* for the Popular Front period—especially the graphs in the issues dated October 1937 and November-December 1939.

24. R. Forestier in *L'Economie agricole française 1938–1958*, p. 226; Dessirier in *La Conjoncture économique*, December 1938. Dessirier observed that while total buying power had fallen by almost 20 per cent since 1913, the agricultural population had also declined by 15 per cent. According to J. M. Jeanneney (*Tableaux statistiques*, p. 67), the index of agricultural prices compared to the general price level (1913 = 100) stood at 110.5 in 1936, 103 in 1937, 103.6 in 1938, and 99.0 in 1939. During 1931–34, however, it had ranged somewhat higher—between 110 and 120.

25. J. Klatzmann, "Le Revenu de l'agriculture française avant la guerre et aujourd'hui," *Etudes et conjoncture*, I (Nov. 1946), 85, 101–5. Klatzmann's very rough estimates (to be used with caution, he warns) would suggest that annual net income per adult male in 1937–39 averaged 13,000 francs for owner-operators, 10,500 francs for cash tenants, and 6,500 francs for share-tenants. He estimates the average annual income of an adult male farm laborer at 7,000 francs.

Another study—this one by economists in the Planning Commission—estimates 1938 per capita incomes as follows: farm laborers, 7,000 fr.; *exploitants*, 7,100 fr.; nonagricultural population, 9,700 fr. (Latil, *Evolution du revenu agricole*, p. 343). These figures, unlike Klatzmann's, are based on the number of persons living off each type of activity rather than on the number actively engaged in it.

In 1939 three private groups broke precedent by embarking on efforts to survey the condition of the peasantry by means of questionnaires. The UNSA led the way with a lengthy inquiry labeled "Cahiers générales de la paysannerie" (*Syndicats paysans*, No. 42, March 16, 1939). The Communists countered with their own elaborate questionnaire, designed to emphasize class relationships and rural social conditions (*La Terre*, No. 129, July 22, 1939). Finally, the JAC began a smaller-scale but more detailed inquiry among young peasants, the results of which were eventually published in Suzanne Sailly-Laisné, *Orage sur le moisson* (Paris, 1941). The JAC inquiry examined the budgets of 104 agricultural workers' families, with incomes ranging from 4,000 to 23,000 francs per year, and of 64 small-owners, half of whom reported budgets in deficit or in "precarious balance."

26. Dorgères later claimed that his adherents reached a figure of

400,000 on the eve of the Second World War (*La Révolution paysanne,* p. 51). Some years later he remarked privately that all published figures should be cut approximately in half (interview, August 1951). Even that figure would probably be somewhat inflated.

27. *Le Temps,* May 5, 6, 7, 11, and 24, 1937. A similar stand was taken by the conservative deputy M. Coquillard, who pointed out in a speech in the Chamber that when the Roman peasantry disappeared, Rome promptly fell before the barbarians (*Journal officiel, débats de la Chambre,* June 17, 1938, p. 1452).

28. This episode produced bitter recriminations on both sides: see the exchange of insults in *L'Effort paysan,* No. 108, March 11, 1939. Dorgères remained convinced that the UNSA bought off Chantérac by offering him a vice-presidency, and that the Count callously betrayed his trust (interview, August 1951). Chantérac's retrospective explanation was much more cynical. He had used Dorgères at first, for one has to work with the tools at hand; but he had dropped him as soon as possible (interview with the Count de Chantérac, March 1951).

29. One-third of the delegates to the UNSA general assembly in 1939 came from Chantérac's region (*L'Effort paysan,* No. 124, July 1, 1939). Other large UNSA units were the Landerneau group, which claimed a membership of 50,000 families in 1938 (Office central des Syndicats, Landerneau, *Lettre mensuelle,* Dec. 1938), and the Union du Sud-Est, which was said to have 200,000 adherents (Louis Salleron, *Un Régime corporatif pour l'agriculture,* Paris, 1937, p. 96).

30. *L'Effort paysan,* No. 78, Aug. 13, 1938. A Vichy propagandist later alleged that the purpose of this "satanic project" had been to clear out the peasants in favor of "exotic illiterates" who would not resist collectivization (Henri Mounier, *Le Communisme contre le paysan français,* Paris, 1942, p. 14).

31. *Syndicats paysans,* No. 31, Sept. 28, 1938; *L'Effort paysan,* No. 86, Oct. 8, 1938. There is no way to measure the extent and intensity of peasant pacifism in 1938–39. Almost all politicians at the time were convinced that the peasants exceeded any other group in their fear of war and their antagonism to a strong foreign policy. The Munich crisis produced a sharp split among Socialist Party politicians: most of those who represented rural districts strongly supported the Munich settlement, whereas the urban deputies were more dubious. Pierre de Pressac in *Revue politique et parlementaire,* Oct. 10, 1938, pp. 106–9; P. E. Flandin, *Politique française 1919–1940* (Paris, 1947), p. 307.

32. *L'Effort paysan,* No. 130, Aug. 19, 1939.

33. *La Terre,* No. 131, Aug. 5, 1939.

CHAPTER FIVE

1. Fauvet and Mendras, *Les Paysans et la politique*, pp. 159, 288. Most peasants undoubtedly responded to Pétain's appeals, at least during the first year or two. One rural patriarch was heard to remark, "What I like about him . . . is that he's like me . . . —a good liar!" (Robert Aron, *Précis de l'unité française*, Paris, 1945, p. 79.)

2. Augé-Laribé, *La Révolution agricole*, p. 274.

3. Marc Bloch, *L'Etrange défaite* (Paris, 1957), pp. 190–92.

4. Interview with Louis Salleron, August 1951.

5. Caziot testimony in *France During the German Occupation*, p. 258.

6. *Ibid.*, pp. 258–60; Chambrun collection, Hoover Library (undated memorandum attached to the testimony of Adolphe Pointier); interview with Louis Salleron, 1951; Chevalier, *Les Paysans*, p. 82. The German and Italian corporations were vertical rather than horizontal; there was a separate federation for each product, with middlemen and industrialists participating alongside the growers. Occupied Belgium was given such a system by German decree; the French averted a similar system by proposing their own model. The Germans apparently preferred the vertical system because it was better adapted to food requisitioning. Nevertheless, the postwar republic charged that the Peasant Corporation had been "imported into the country by the tanks of the invaders" (*Journal officiel, lois et décrets*, Oct. 13, 1944.)

7. The text of the law was published in *Journal officiel, lois et décrets*, Dec. 7, 1940, pp. 6005–8.

8. Louis Salleron *et al.*, *La Corporation paysanne* (Paris, 1943), p. 38.

9. *Ibid.*, p. 52.

10. Louis Salleron, *Naissance d l'état corporatif* (Paris, 1941), p. 237.

11. *Journal officiel, lois et décrets*, Aug. 22, 1942. Nominees for the post of regional syndic seem to have been selected pretty generally by this process of election: see, for example, *L'Effort paysan*, No. 327, July 8, 1943, which reported the Count de Chantérac's election in the Tarn by 268 of 274 votes cast. In September 1943, Minister of Agriculture Bonnafous announced that nominees for the post of local syndic would be elected on October 17; but Laval (who was evidently nervous about the outcome) canceled the elections at the last minute. *L'Effort paysan*, Nos. 337 and 338, Sept. 30 and Oct. 7, 1943; *La Défense paysanne de la Corrèze*, November 1943; *La Terre* (Limoges), August 1944.

12. Caziot later declared that the final text "bore no resemblance" to the original draft—a view that seems somewhat excessive (*France During the German Occupation*, p. 258). See also Michel Cépède, *Agriculture et alimentation en France durant la IIe guerre mondiale* (Paris, 1961), pp. 74–75.

13. Cépède, *Agriculture et alimentation*, pp. 89–92.

14. Fauvet and Mendras, *Les Paysans et la politique*, p. 235. *L'Effort paysan* (No. 300, Dec. 24, 1942) later complained that the Commission had been made up of men "without a common doctrine, and often with none at all."

15. Salleron, *La Corporation paysanne*, pp. 62–64.

16. *Syndicats corporatifs paysans*, No. 6, Sept. 1, 1941.

17. Interview with Louis Salleron, 1951. Salleron persuaded his collaborators on *Syndicats paysans* to suspend publication in protest against German interference. A few Corporation officials, according to Salleron, were prepared for all-out collaboration.

18. Bonnafous told a German official in December 1942: "So far the Peasant Corporation has been merely an organization for peasant demagoguery, and has hampered the government. It has been necessary to convert it into an organization that helps the government" (Cépède, *Agriculture et alimentation*, p. 92).

19. The text of the law is published in *Journal officiel, lois et décrets*, Dec. 17, 1942, pp. 4121–24. For an extended analysis of the reform as viewed by a Corporation official, see Salleron, *La Corporation paysanne*, pp. 68–84.

20. Albert Dollinger in Salleron, *La Corporation paysanne*, p. 74.

21. Maspétiol, *L'Ordre éternel des champs*, p. 538. Indications of the continuing feud between the Corporation and the Ministry of Agriculture appeared frequently in *L'Effort paysan*, which became the principal corporatist organ after the demise of *Syndicats paysans*. Soon after Vichy collapsed, the former National Syndic asserted that "the Corporation was almost continually in opposition to the Ministers of Agriculture and Food Supply, who constantly neglected professional opinion." (Pointier memorandum, dated Sept. 21, 1944, Chambrun collection, Hoover Library.)

22. One prominent syndical leader recalls, for example, that before 1940 the 23 peasants in his home village were divided 13 to 10 between the Catholic syndicate and the Radical *comice agricole*; cooperation between them was impossible. Since the war, all 23 have remained united in a single syndicate (interview with Robert Mangeart, July 1960).

23. From Article I of the "Peasant Charter" of 1940.

24. *France During the German Occupation*, pp. 259–61. This official added, however, that the troublemakers were not the syndics but the "professional bureaucrats" who had gotten a grip on the Corporation (Cépède, *Agriculture et alimentation*, p. 93).

25. Chevalier, *Les Paysans*, p. 82. Even *L'Effort Paysan*, which had always been deeply committed to the corporatist ideal, quoted one critic's accusation that the Corporation had become merely "a device for collecting food" (No. 323, June 10, 1943).

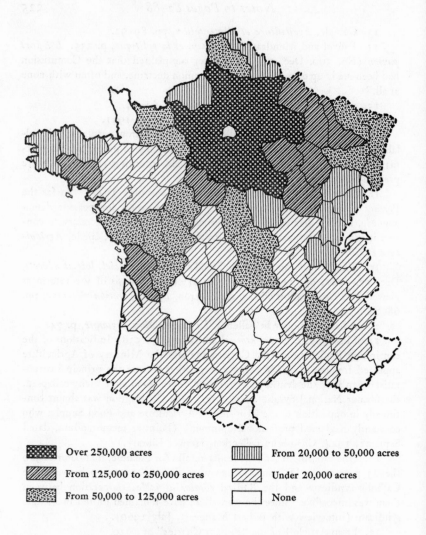

Over 250,000 acres   From 20,000 to 50,000 acres

From 125,000 to 250,000 acres   Under 20,000 acres

From 50,000 to 125,000 acres   None

PROGRESS IN REMEMBREMENT THROUGH 1961
(Calculated by department)

From *Paysans*, No. 37 (1962), p. 38.

26. Salleron, *Naissance de l'état corporatif*, p. 107; *Syndicats corporatifs paysans*, No. 3, July 1, 1941.

27. Mgr. Chaptal, *Lettres à un curé de campagne* (Paris, 1942). Although the Corporation enjoyed Church support, there was some Catholic resentment at its attempts to interfere in the realms of family organization and youth training (N. Drogat, *La Corporation paysanne*, Paris, 1942, pp. 38–39; Jean Serve, *Le Syndicalisme agricole*, Paris, 1945, p. 8).

28. Louis Salleron, "Introduction aux problèmes du plan en agriculture" (May 1944). This mimeographed document, prepared for the final session of the National Corporative Council, is in M. Salleron's possession.

29. *L'Effort paysan*, Nos. 358 and 363, March 23 and May 18, 1944.

30. Mimeographed copy of M. Pointier's circular letter, dated March 24, 1944 (Chambrun collection, Hoover Library).

31. The statute was drafted by Louis Salleron, who worked at lesser jobs in the Corporation after his dismissal as delegate-general (interview, 1951).

32. Cépède, *Agriculture et alimentation*, p. 188. Vichy's return-to-the-soil campaign produced more raillery than results. One peasant paper commented sourly that city youngsters talked of a return to the farm "between a permanent wave and a visit to a bar . . . , as one plays with a yo-yo or plays ping-pong—just to be in the vogue" (*Défense paysanne de la Corrèze*, Jan. 15, 1941).

33. Maspétiol, *L'Ordre éternel des champs*, p. 492.

34. For progress in *remembrement*, see the map opposite.

35. H. Mendras in *L'Economie agricole française 1938–1958*, p. 154.

36. When the government finally carried out a currency exchange on June 4, 1946 (confined to 5,000-franc notes, the denomination most commonly used for hoarding), farm proprietors turned in slightly more than one hundred billion francs (*Etudes et conjoncture: Union française*, Vol. I, No. 1-2, Aug.-Sept. 1946). The category of farm proprietors included absentee landowners. The total figure fell far short of the amount needed to finance the postwar modernization of agriculture.

37. The Comité d'Histoire de la Deuxième Guerre Mondiale has compiled statistics on political arrests and deportations for about a dozen departments. In some departments, peasants represented the largest single group of deportees: e.g., Creuse (47 of 158 deportees) and Yonne (187 of 1,219 political arrests). In Finistère, on the other hand, the total of 597 deportees included only 39 *cultivateurs* and 5 agricultural workers (*Bulletin du comité d'histoire de la deuxième guerre mondiale*, Nos. 66 and 69, June and October 1958, and special issue dated March 1959; see also Nos. 62, 75, 77–79, and 82 for the records of other departments). According to the Communists' underground organ *La Terre* (Oct. 1943), evasion of the German forced-labor draft was general in agricultural regions; it quoted prefectoral

estimates of 90 per cent in Finistère, 95.5 per cent in Côtes-du-Nord, and 99 per cent in Puy-de-Dôme.

CHAPTER SIX

1. Some attempt was made to inflate the CGA's resistance activity after the liberation; e.g., the first issue of *La Libération paysanne* (No. 1, Oct. 21, 1944) claimed that the CGA had been founded in 1941. According to Tanguy-Prigent, however, no steps were taken until late in 1943, when a group of about fifteen resisters brought out the first issue of *La Résistance paysanne* (interview with Pierre Tanguy-Prigent, August 1951).

2. A decree abolishing the Corporation and re-establishing the prewar organizations was issued from Algiers on July 26, 1944 (*Journal officiel de la république française*, No. 64, Aug. 5, 1944, p. 674).

3. Interview with Roger Dusseaulx, April 1946.

4. Jean Laurenti, the CDAP's leading organizer, in *La Voix paysanne de l'Hérault*, No. 6 (Nov. 1, 1944).

5. *La Terre*, No. 4, Oct. 28, 1944; Serve, *Le Syndicalisme agricole*, p. 12.

6. *Journal officiel, lois et décrets*, Oct. 13, 1944, pp. 924–26. Tanguy's description of the Corporation—contained in his first speech after the liberation and published in *La Liberation paysanne*, No. 1, Oct. 21, 1944—outraged its former leaders, who retaliated by describing the CGA as "a counterfeit copy of the Corporation" (Adolphe Pointier in *France During the German Occupation*, p. 275).

7. *Journal officiel, lois et décrets*, Oct. 21, 1944, p. 1036. Father Serve alleged at the time (in *Le Syndicalisme agricole*, p. 14) that only five of the seventeen members were peasants. In fact, twelve were listed as *cultivateurs* in the *Journal officiel*.

8. Confédération Générale d'Agriculture [CGA], *Congrès de l'unité paysanne* (Paris, 1945), p. 52.

9. This antisyndicalist position was vigorously argued by the agricultural specialist Professor Jules Milhau in an interview in February 1951; indeed, he contended that the time for the disappearance of agrarian syndicalism had already arrived. For a more general analysis of the syndicalist-vs.-services controversy after 1944, see "XXX" in *Droit Social*, XVII (1954), 257–63.

10. Information on the first stage of CGA development—especially at the local level—is spotty and scattered. According to *La Terre* (No. 23, March 10, 1945), only two-thirds of the departments had held their local congresses (in which delegates were selected) before the national congress

met. Many local farm journals contain useful details; they indicate that there was no standard pattern or sequence of events. See also a contemporary MRP pamphlet, *Jalons pour renover notre agriculture* (Paris, 1945), pp. 37–38.

11. CGA, *Congrès de l'unité paysanne*, pp. 9–21, 59–65.

12. What may have been one last attempt to keep control of the CGA in the hands of the technicians occurred shortly before the FNSEA elections. On Oct. 8, 1945, Tanguy issued an ordinance forbidding agricultural syndicates to engage henceforth in economic activities. Rightists protested that his purpose was to emasculate the syndicates in order to reinforce the hold of the "service" federations on the peasantry (E. de Felcourt, "La Législation agricole depuis la libération," *Monde français*, May 1948, p. 198). It may be, however, that Tanguy was merely trying to end the confused overlapping of syndical and cooperative functions inherited from prewar days. In any event, the ordinance was never enforced. As it happened, the subsequent growth of the cooperative movement gradually pushed the syndicates out of the "service" realm and produced an increasingly clear separation of functions.

13. Waldeck Rochet in *La Libération paysanne*, No. 47, Jan. 6, 1946. In some regions where right-wing syndicalism had deep roots (e.g., the Landerneau area), the old syndicates had simply ignored the CGA after the liberation and had continued to operate extralegally. This infringement on syndical unity was finally ended sometime in 1946, when an accommodation was worked out and the rebellious syndicates were quietly integrated into the FNSEA.

14. René Cercler in *Revue politique et parlementaire*, CLXXXVI (1946), 141; E. de Felcourt in *Monde français*, May 1948, p. 199. Two high CGA officials reported at the subsequent congress that the proportion of voters had been 70 per cent (CGA, "Congrès national du 12 au 16 mai 1946: "Rapports," mimeographed).

15. *Le Paysan du sud-ouest*, May 15, 1951.

16. FNSEA, *2ᵐᵉ congrès national: Rapport moral sur l'activité de la F.N.S.E.A. par M. Blondelle* (Paris, 1947); N. Drogat, "Y a-t-il une crise de la C.G.A.?," *Travaux de l'Action Populaire*, No. 16, Jan. 1948, pp. 34, 38–39.

17. Interview with Octave Bajeux, president of the SNPBR, August 1951; also *Le Monde paysan*, Nos. 61 and 80, April 30 and Sept. 24, 1947, and *La Terre*, Nos. 104 and 154, Sept. 26, 1946, and Sept. 25, 1947. The Tenants' Section was balanced by a Landlords' Section, established in 1947 to represent the interests of non-absentee landowners who rented out part of their land or who had retired from active farming.

18. *Le Monde*, March 10, 1950.

19. Tanguy once declared that "peasant property is the most glorious creation of our history" (P. Tanguy-Prigent, *La Terre aux paysans*, Paris, 1946, p. 12).

20. Tanguy's program was embodied in a Socialist Party pamphlet, *La Rénovation paysanne* (Paris, 1945), for which Tanguy himself wrote the introduction in September 1944.

21. The number of share tenants fell from 133,000 in 1945 to 72,000 in 1955 (*L'Information agricole*, No. 221, March 1960).

22. The number of CUMAs declined from 12,000 in 1948 to half that figure in the early 1950's. By 1956 the total had climbed again to 6,300, and by 1958 to 8,000 (*Paysans*, No. 20, Oct.-Nov. 1959, p. 34).

23. *Cahiers d'action religieuse et sociale*, No. 18, July 1, 1947, pp. 569–76; interview with A. Labardin, former national president of the JAC (1951). Soon after the liberation, the JAC secretary-general proposed joint action with the Ministry to create youth centers for groups of villages, but suspicion on both sides blocked the plan. Vichy had anticipated the *foyers ruraux* in a small way by setting up a few "maisons des jeunes," administered by the Secretariat à la jeunesse (*Chef paysan*, Nov.-Dec. 1945, p. 23).

24. For a typical attack on the "collectivizers," see Antony Rougié, *Peints par eux-mêmes: La Vague marxiste sur l'agriculture* (n.p., 1947). Almost every right-wing paper or periodical carried scare stories, and even the MRP's farm journal *Monde paysan* (No. 11, April 30, 1946) declared flatly that the Land Office would expropriate all peasants.

25. Tanguy-Prigent, *La Terre aux paysans*, pp. 7–15, 31. Probably the real trouble was, as an "insider" put it a few years later, that the sponsors of the Land Office had never really known just what they meant by it (interview, 1951, with an ex-official of the CGA who had been in close touch with Tanguy during the liberation period). If they had thought the plan through in advance, they might have made a really effective case for the Office as a valuable agency for reorganizing the nation's farm structure.

26. Mallet, *Les Paysans contre le passé*, p. 36n.

CHAPTER SEVEN

1. The FNSEA claimed 1,750,000 members in 1949; 900,000 in 1953; and 675,000 in 1958. *Annuaire de la CGA 1949–50* (Paris, n.d.), p. 18; *Le Monde*, Feb. 25, 1953; *Paysans*, No. 15, Dec. 1958–Jan. 1959, p. 75.

2. Sénat, 2e session ordinaire de 1959–60, Doc. No. 190, pp. 9, 19. The official total of 2,267,704 farms in 1955–57 included 150,260 farms

of less than 2½ acres. They are properly included here because this survey, unlike most earlier ones, excluded week-end garden plots and counted only genuine farms. The land was distributed as follows:

	% of all farmers	% of total farm acreage
Farms of less than 2½ acres	6.7	0.3
Farms of 2½ to 25 acres	49.1	16.1
Farms of 25 to 125 acres	40.0	58.1
Farms of over 125 acres	4.2	25.5

According to the best estimate of the rural exodus (Latil, *Evolution du revenu agricole*, p. 82), departures from agriculture for other employment averaged 55,000 men and 50,000 women annually from 1945 through 1949, and rose to 70,000 men and 60,000 women in 1950 and 1951. The exodus probably continued at about the same rate during the 1950's. For the proportion of total active male population engaged in agriculture, see the map overleaf.

3. *Journal officiel, avis et rapports du Conseil économique*, 1953, No. 24. J.-M. Jeanneney's figures on the relationship of agricultural prices to the general price level (*Tableaux statistiques*, p. 67) run as follows:

1945 .... 103.1		1951 .... 80.4
1946 .... 110.3		1952 .... 84.0
1947 .... 121.4		1953 .... 84.2
1948 .... 103.7		1954 .... 85.2
1949 .... 92.9		1955 .... 83.9
1950 .... 88.0		1956 .... 84.8

4. *Journal officiel, avis et rapports du Conseil économique*, 1953, No. 24; Sénat, 2ᵉ session 1959–60, Doc. No. 190, p. 25.

5. An additional source of urban-rural stress was the sharp contrast between the peasants' self-image and the image the urban groups had of the peasants. An opinion poll in 1949 divided the population into seven socioeconomic groups and asked respondents to rank these groups according to their relative economic status at the time. All nonpeasant groups rated the peasantry in rank 1, 2 or 3; peasant respondents rated the peasantry in rank 5, 6 or 7 (with the largest number choosing rank 6). *Sondages*, XI (August 1949). Ten years later, the pollsters asked a similar question: Are the farmers' current difficulties worse than those of other Frenchmen? Fifty-three per cent of the peasant respondents answered, "Much worse," whereas only 7 per cent of the urban working-class respondents gave this answer. *Sondages*, XXII (1960), 37–38.

6. Sénat, 2ᵉ session 1959–60, Doc. No. 190, p. 33; also Joseph Klatz-

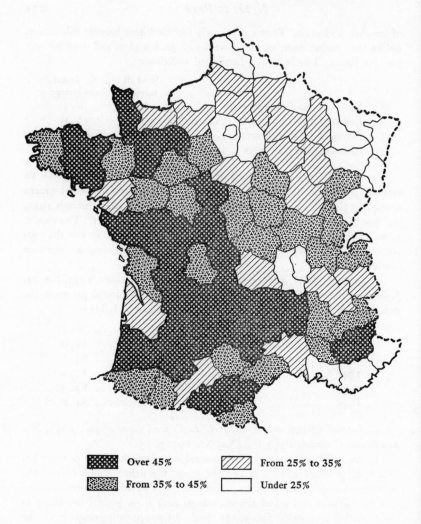

	Over 45%		From 25% to 35%
	From 35% to 45%		Under 25%

PROPORTION OF TOTAL ACTIVE MALE POPULATION
ENGAGED IN AGRICULTURE, 1954
(Calculated by department)

From *Paysans*, No. 37 (1962), p. 14.

mann and L. Malassis in *L'Economie agricole française 1938–1958*, pp. 150, 241.

7. Altogether, 22 of the FNSEA's departmental federations were deprived of a vote in the 1950 congress because they had paid no dues; 19 of them were south of the Loire. FNSEA officials at the congress reported that each of the delinquent units had lost at least 50 per cent of its members. Communist spokesmen charged that the FNSEA leaders had expelled the 22 federations for championing the family farmer rather than the large capitalist farmer. Blondelle and his friends angrily replied that many family-farming departments had remained loyal to the syndicate, and added that three-quarters of the members of the FNSEA's national council elected in 1950 were family farmers. On this controversy, see *La Libération paysanne*, Nos. 256, 259, 260, March 9 and 30, April 6, 1950; *La Terre*, No. 282, March 9, 1950; and *Cahiers d'action religieuse et sociale*, April 1, 1950, p. 218.

8. *La Gazette agricole*, Dec. 16, 1950. Blondelle, added the author enthusiastically, "has the fiber and the wisdom of a real leader." Before 1951, the CGA statutes had not permitted syndical officials to run for political office.

9. Peasant candidates had never before been so numerous; according to *Le Monde*, they totaled about 650, or one out of six. True, most of them were mere showcase candidates, listed fourth or fifth on a ticket that could not possibly win more than one or two seats; but it was significant that almost every party felt impelled to include a peasant candidate or two in each rural or semirural district. Some solidly peasant lists were also entered.

10. Of the 88 agriculturists elected, exactly half ran as Independent-Peasant bloc candidates or on tickets with vaguely corporatist labels. Among them were 27 prominent syndical officials, headed by Jean Laborbe, secretary-general of the FNSEA. There had been 70 agriculturists in the preceding Assembly; not one of them had been a syndical official. For a more detailed account, see G. Wright, "French Farmers in Politics," *South Atlantic Quarterly*, LI (1952), 356–65.

11. Quoted in *L'Information agricole*, No. 10, Dec. 20, 1952.

12. *Ibid.*, No. 4, Nov. 8, 1952.

13. According to Philip Williams, *Politics in Post-War France* (London, 1958), p. 114, in the economically advanced departments 18 Independents and 3 Peasants were elected; in the most underdeveloped departments, 2 Independents and 15 Peasants; and in the middling departments, 27 Independents and 22 Peasants.

14. The theme of the two agricultures and the widening gap between them was most consistently argued by the editors of the review *Paysans*,

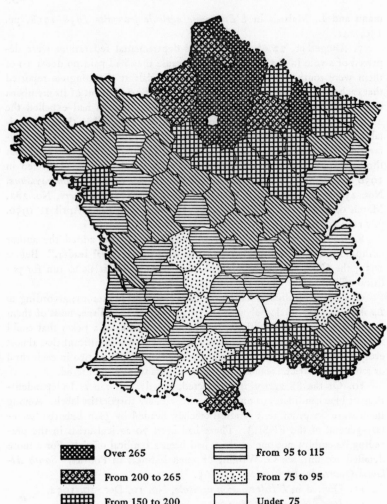

	Over 265		From 95 to 115
	From 200 to 265		From 75 to 95
	From 150 to 200		Under 75
	From 115 to 150		

RELATIVE STANDING OF DEPARTMENTS IN PER
CAPITA FARM INCOME, 1951
(Average for France: 140)

From *L'Espace économique français* (Paris, 1955), published by the Institut
National de la Statistique et des Etudes Economiques.

which began to appear in 1956. See also *Revue du ministère de l'agriculture,* No. 81, 1953, p. 328, which shows that agricultural investments under the first Monnet plan went mainly to the more highly developed agricultural departments. For the government's efforts to correct this imbalance, see G. Sévérac, "Les Disparités régionales," in *L'Economie agricole française 1938–1958,* pp. 161–67. Regional differences in per capita farm income are portrayed in the map opposite.

15. At the 1954 congress of the FNSEA, four seats on the Conseil d'Administration were assigned to those underdeveloped regions that had been virtually unrepresented because they paid insufficient dues (*Le Monde,* Feb. 26, 1954). Shortly afterward, President Lepicard invited journalists to a press dinner to hear the FNSEA's case. His long and heavily documented exposé sought to refute all charges of domination by the large-farming element. Dividing France into northern and southern halves by a line drawn from Nantes via Orléans to Geneva, he produced the following statistics:

	North	South
Average size of farm	50 acres	50 acres
% of all farmers	40	60
% of FNSEA members	47	53
% of FNSEA budget paid	67	33
Average yearly contribution per member	93 fr.	43 fr.
Example of dues paid by departments with equal syndical membership but different economic status	1,896,000 fr. (Oise)	290,000 fr. (Savoie)
Members of FNSEA Conseil d'Administration	12	16
Members of FNSEA Bureau	7	10

It was entirely inaccurate, Lepicard argued, to set up two hostile categories—the large, modernized, rightist north and the small, oppressed, leftist south. All categories overlapped and crisscrossed, and two-thirds of the departments did not fit into either category. Agriculture's only hope, he concluded, was "to remain united in diversity" (*Le Rassemblement,* No. 340, April 1–7, 1954).

FNSEA officials, in the course of interviews in 1960, continued to insist that the organization had never been controlled by the large-farming group. Indeed, they declared, the underdeveloped areas were heavily overrepresented in the FNSEA's central councils. Of the 28 members of the Conseil d'Administration in 1960, only 8 came from the large-farming departments, while the southwest alone—though the weakest of all regions in syndical strength—had 4. Representation was based on the number of *syndiqués*

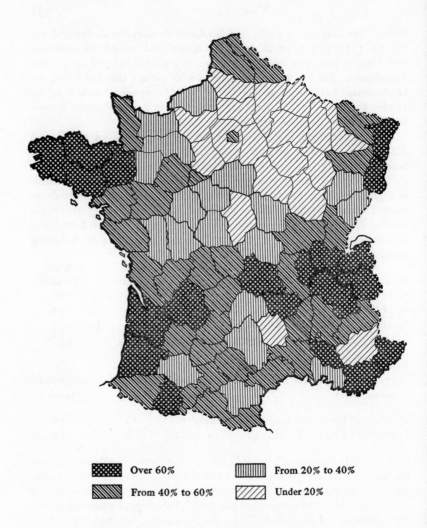

▦ Over 60%   ▥ From 20% to 40%

▨ From 40% to 60%   ▧ Under 20%

SMALL-FARMING AREAS: PROPORTION OF AGRICULTURAL
LAND IN FARMS OF LESS THAN 50 ACRES, 1955

From *Paysans*, No. 37 (1962), p. 47.

alone, even though richer departments were assessed a higher share of syndical dues (interviews with Guy Cotton and M. Delorme, July 1960). For the distribution of the small-farming areas, see the map opposite.

16. M. Galard, "Le Malaise paysan," *Paysans*, No. 23, April-May 1960, p. 13. Officials of the FNSEA, during interviews in 1960, readily confirmed the fact that the Paris basin group often holds preparatory meetings just before FNSEA sessions.

17. *Le Paysan d'Auvergne*, No. 168, Oct. 1–15, 1953.

18. Compulsory distillation was extended to many small growers as well as large ones; the use of certain grape varieties was outlawed; the right to plant new vines was strictly limited; and indemnities were promised to growers who would uproot their vines in favor of other crops. An agency called the Institut des Vins de Consommation Courante (controlled by the growers) was set up to supervise the functioning of the new system (Warner, *The Winegrowers of France*, pp. 180–89). It received indemnity requests from about 90,000 winegrowers, who uprooted almost 250,000 acres of vineyard—i.e., about 7 per cent of the total acreage (IVCC circular dated Dec. 31, 1962). The uprooting program was suspended in 1957 after two successive bad crop years; but a bumper crop in 1962—the second largest in French history—again created a large surplus, and demonstrated that a reduction in acreage was not enough to solve the chronic wine problem.

19. *L'Information agricole*, No. 204, June 13, 1959.

20. *Le Paysan d'Auvergne*, No. 169, Oct. 16–31, 1953; also Jacques Fauvet in *Le Monde*, Oct. 11–12, 1953.

21. "XXX" in *Droit social*, XVII (1954), 263. President Martin of the CGA had tried the same tactic again early in 1953—this time at the FNSEA congress—but the suggestion had been quickly buried (*Paysans*, No. 5, April-May 1957, p. 10).

22. *L'Information agricole*, No. 22, May 30, 1953; *Le Monde*, June 27, 1952, and May 27, 1953.

23. *Le Monde*, Oct. 17, 1953; *Le Paysan d'Auvergne*, No. 170, Nov. 1–15, 1953.

24. *Le Paysan d'Auvergne*, No. 173, Jan. 1954; *L'Information agricole*, No. 56, Dec. 5, 1953. One consequence of the shake-up was the transfer of the three "service" or "technical" federations—cooperatives, mutual-aid societies, and farm-credit groups—from the CGA building behind the Opéra to the old cooperative headquarters in the Boulevard Saint-Germain. The direct lineage between the prewar FNMCA and the new CNMCCA thus became even more obvious. The FNSEA stayed on in the Rue Scribe, sharing offices there with the revived APPCA.

25. *Le Paysan d'Auvergne*, No. 171, Nov. 16–30, 1953.

26. *Ibid.*, Nos. 171 and 174, Nov. 16–30, 1953, and Feb. 1954; *L'Information agricole*, No. 58, Dec. 19, 1953.

27. *Le Paysan d'Auvergne,* No. 173, Jan. 1954.

28. *Combat,* Oct. 31, 1946; *Le Monde,* Nov. 1, 1946.

29. Dorgères was clearly adrift during the early postwar years, and could find no clear-cut line to follow. His principal theme was that "in a democratic regime . . . the only useful organization is one that can frighten the government into capitulating" (*La Gazette agricole,* March 24–31, 1951).

30. Some early attempts at collaboration between Poujade and Dorgères quickly turned sour, since neither virtuoso was willing to play second fiddle. See J. M. Royer in Fauvet and Mendras, *Les Paysans et la politique,* pp. 164–67; Stanley Hoffmann, *Le Mouvement Poujade* (Paris, 1956), pp. 337–41.

31. *La Terre,* No. 575, Oct. 27, 1955.

32. Fernand Clavaud, "La Situation à la campagne et les tâches du Parti," *Cahiers du communisme,* XXXVII (1961), 1743.

33. Waldeck Rochet in *Cahiers du communisme,* XXXVII (1961), 138.

34. *La Terre,* Nos. 477, 478, 480, 483, Dec. 10, 17, and 31, 1953, and Jan. 21, 1954.

35. See Waldeck Rochet's report to the party's central committee at a special session on peasant problems, *ibid.,* No. 575, Oct. 27, 1955.

36. *Ibid.,* No. 515 (Sept. 2, 1954).

37. E.g., Waldeck Rochet in *ibid.,* No. 554, June 2, 1955; Jean Flavien, "L'Evolution de la situation à la campagne," *Cahiers du communisme,* XXXVIII (1962), 164.

38. Although specialists like René Dumont and Alfred Sauvy had long been urging the need to continue and even to speed up the rural exodus, agrarian leaders rarely had the courage to support the idea even when they agreed with it. In 1951, agrarian spokesmen from left to right savagely denounced former Secretary-General René Colson of the JAC for an article entitled "A Million Too Many Peasants" that appeared in *Témoignage chrétien* (April 15, 1951); yet many of them privately admitted the validity of his thesis (interview with M. Boursier of the Beetgrowers' Association, August 1951).

39. See the FNSEA's brochure *Le Livre vert de l'agriculture* (supplement to *L'Information agricole,* No. 35, June 12, 1953).

40. According to the OEEC, 60 per cent of the French government's credits to agriculture went for the support of prices; the proportion in other western European countries ranged from 24 to 42 per cent (L. Malassis in *L'Economie agricole française 1938–1958,* p. 246).

41. Sénat, session de 1959–60, Doc. No. 190, p. 44.

42. There had been one painful interlude of conflict between the FNSEA and the government when Pierre Mendès-France headed a cabinet in 1954–55. Although Mendès retained an Independent as his Minister of

Agriculture, his anti-alcohol campaign quickly alienated such powerful groups as the beetgrowers and the *bouilleurs de cru* (home distillers), and led them to denounce him as the "No. 1 enemy of French agriculture" (Fauvet and Mendras, *Les Paysans et la politique*, pp. 116–17). Mendès was enthusiastically supported, however, by left-wing agrarian leaders like Philippe Lamour and Roland Viel, who asserted that his government had done more for the peasantry than any government in the preceding thirty-five years. *Le Monde*, Jan. 27, 1955 (quoting Viel); also *Le Paysan d'Auvergne*, No. 163, June 1–15, 1953 (quoting Lamour).

43. *La Terre nouvelle*, Feb. 17, 1951; *L'Information agricole*, No. 19, Feb. 21, 1953.

44. APPCA, *L'Intérêt national exige une loi verte* (Paris, 1960), p. 48. In this pamphlet, the APPCA claimed that unless such a monopoly existed, the state would continue to play off one peasant organization against another. On the APPCA-FNSEA rivalry, see also *Paysans*, No. 5, April-May 1957, pp. 1–12.

45. Blondelle, acting now outside the FNSEA, did try to resurrect the old strategy in somewhat different form. Under the label *action civique républicaine*, he arranged a loose alliance of petty bourgeois interest groups, linking the FNSEA, the artisans' organization, the small businessmen's movement, and the so-called Confederation of the Middle Classes (*Le Monde*, Oct. 29 and Nov. 25, 1955). But the FNSEA gave only lip service to this alliance, on the ground that the program of constitutional reform put forward by these groups would be likely to split the syndicate (*L'Information agricole*, No. 158, May 11, 1957). Subsequent attempts by Blondelle to breathe some life into his proposed coalition were not much more successful —though *L'Information agricole* (No. 160, June 15, 1957) did publish an appeal for cooperation by Gingembre of the small businessmen's association. Cooperation was tried briefly during the crisis of 1958, when the Fourth Republic gave way to the Fifth; but the FNSEA and Gingembre's group soon went their separate ways again.

46. There are varying estimates of the number of peasant votes cast for Poujadist candidates. Poujade himself claimed 400,000 (*Les Paysans et la politique*, p. 201); Stanley Hoffmann (*Le Mouvement Poujade*, p. 335) sets the figure at 350,000. The statistician Joseph Klatzmann, using sampling techniques, estimates that 14.5 per cent of all peasant voters backed Poujadists, and that the proportion exceeded 25 per cent in twelve departments in the west, the Midi, and the Paris basin (*Les Paysans et la politique*, pp. 48, 58–60). No peasant was elected on a Poujadist ticket.

According to Klatzmann (*Paysans*, No. 19, Aug.-Sept. 1959, p. 75), the distribution of the peasant vote in 1956 was as follows: Communists, 17.5%; Socialists, 14.0%; independent leftists, 2.5%; Radical Socialists, 9.0%; RGR, 2.5%; MRP, 12.5%; Independents-Peasants,

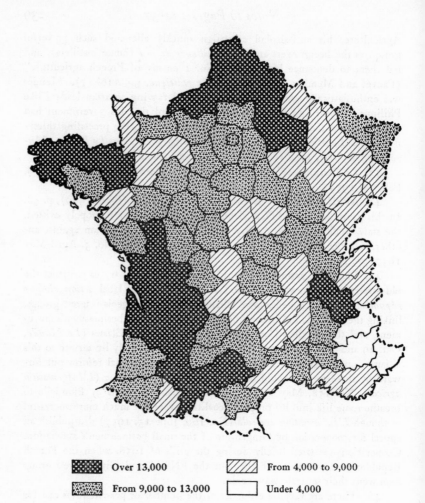

Over 13,000

From 9,000 to 13,000

From 4,000 to 9,000

Under 4,000

NUMBER OF TRACTORS PER DEPARTMENT, 1962

From *Paysans*, No. 37 (1962), p. 41.

20.5%; Gaullists, 3.5%; Poujadists (UDCA), 14.5%; extreme right, 2.0%; unclassifiable, 1.5%.

47. *L'Information agricole*, No. 137, May 26, 1956. The FNSEA's call to action was ignored, however, in some leftist departments of the Massif Central, where syndical leaders alleged that the republic was being threatened.

48. *Ibid.*, No. 160, June 15, 1957.

49. *Ibid.*, No. 156, April 15, 1957; *L'Année politique 1957* (Paris, 1958), p. 24 (quoting Eugène Berthé, secretary-general of the Laurens wing of the Peasant Party); and *Chambres d'agriculture*, the official organ of the APPCA, which was still sputtering angrily three years later (No. 194, April 15, 1960, pp. 13–15).

50. *L'Année politique 1957*, pp. 86–87; *L'Information agricole*, No. 164 (Sept. 14, 1957).

51. The price-fixing mechanism set up by the Gaillard decree was exceptionally complex, for it was geared in with the third modernization plan, and, strictly speaking, it did not "fix" prices except for cereals and beets. The government was authorized to set both a *prix d'objectif* for each product (to be attained at the end of the planning period in 1961) and an annual *prix indicatif* (designed to bring prices by stages to the 1961 level). If the market price diverged too greatly from the annual *prix indicatif*, the various marketing agencies set up in 1953 would undertake to buy, store, or seek export outlets in an effort to shore up the market. The *prix indicatif* was to be set after taking into account the general price level, the index of agricultural wages, and the cost of items essential to agriculture. This last provision of the decree was what gave it its sliding-scale or *indexation* feature.

52. *L'Information agricole*, Nos. 168 and 178, Nov. 9, 1957, and April 5, 1958. The FNSEA continued to work closely with the APA. In December 1957, for example, FNSEA officials attended an APA session and presented several long reports on the various pending versions of a basic law. The APA president invited these visitors to prepare a set of amendments, and promised that the APA would introduce and support them in the National Assembly (*ibid.*, No. 173, Jan. 31, 1958).

CHAPTER EIGHT

1. *L'Economie agricole française 1938–1958*, p. 35. See the map opposite.

2. *L'Information agricole*, No. 215, Dec. 19, 1959. The 7,000 families included 900 from Morocco and Tunisia; but a number of wealthy North African *colons* migrated without aid, and bought large tracts in the southwest. Migrants assisted by Forget's Association Nationale des Migra-

tions Rurales took up 750,000 acres of land in central and southern France, 45 per cent of which had been partially or completely out of cultivation.

3. Marie-Joseph Durupt, "Action catholique et milieu rural" (manuscript draft of thesis, Institut d'Etudes Politiques); also see below, p. 200. Mlle. Durupt's *grognard* was referring to a young Jaciste experimenter rather than a migrant, but the traditionalists' reaction was the same toward both kinds of modernizer. Experts who visited one southwestern department noted that the five best farms they saw there were run by migrants (J. C. Tirel in *Académie d'agriculture*, No. 16, Nov. 1957, pp. 861ff).

4. Durupt, "Action catholique et milieu rural." Most of the demonstration areas that failed were set up at the request of a deputy or a local politician who demanded fair shares for his department. When the subsidy ran out, such experiments often collapsed without leaving a trace.

5. According to the 1955 census, only 3.3 per cent of all *chefs d'exploitation agricoles* had received professional training of any kind. But the proportion ranged from less than 2 per cent among the higher age groups to 16.4 per cent in the lowest age group; by the end of the decade, between 10 and 20 per cent of all future farmers were receiving adequate elementary training (Y. Desjonquères, "Quelques chiffres sur la formation professionelle agricole," *Paysans*, No. 11, April-May 1958, pp. 19–28). The most successful of the Catholic *post-scolaire* institutions, the *maisons familiales*, numbered 316 in 1958–59; there had been only 150 ten years earlier, and only 2 in 1940 (Durupt, "Action catholique et milieu rural"). There was little expansion of advanced training facilities; by 1962, only 500 agricultural engineers were being turned out annually by state schools, and 200 more by private schools (*Le Monde*, Oct. 5, 1962).

6. "Agriculteurs et techniciens," *Economie et humanisme*, No. 85, May-June 1954, pp. 46–47; Durupt, "Action catholique et milieu rural" (which estimates that 50 per cent of the CETA presidents in 1960 were former Jacistes). The fact that the CETA's central offices were housed in the building of the Société des Agriculteurs de France (Rue d'Athènes) caused a good many leftists to regard the movement with suspicion in the early years. Most of them came to accept the CETAs, but a few rigidly doctrinaire leftists continued to boycott them in favor of the demonstration areas run by the Ministry of Agriculture.

7. My account of Colson's unique role in reshaping the JAC is based primarily on conversations with people who worked with him, and on Mlle. Durupt's study. In 1944 Colson founded the JAC's influential weekly magazine, *Jeunes Forces rurales*, which he developed as a vehicle for rural reform. In 1946 he established the so-called Centre National d'Etudes Rurales to encourage the collection of data on France's agrarian structure, and in 1951 he formed the Union des Ententes et Communautés Rurales

to stimulate experiments in group agriculture. Colson's brief but solidly documented monograph *Motorisation et avenir rural* (Paris, 1950) was one of the first dispassionate attempts to examine the various courses that lay open to the peasantry.

8. Durupt, "Action catholique et milieu rural"; *L'Information agricole*, No. 155, March 30, 1957; and interviews with various CNJA officials.

9. Mlle. Durupt has calculated that in 1960 Jacistes or ex-Jacistes held 45 of the 85 departmental presidencies in the CNJA, 24 of the 30 posts in the national Conseil d'Administration, and 8 of the 10 posts in the Bureau.

10. Interviews with CNJA officials.

11. *La Terre*, No. 717, July 17, 1958.

12. *L'Information agricole*, No. 187, Sept. 27, 1958. The FNSEA had authorized one of its vice-presidents, Fernand Vangraefschepe, to serve on de Gaulle's constitutional advisory committee in 1958. Only two representatives of professional groups were invited to participate.

13. *L'Information agricole*, No. 189, Oct. 25, 1958; *Le Monde*, Oct. 18, 1958.

14. *L'Information agricole*, No. 192, Dec. 6, 1958.

15. In the 1958 crisis, Antier came out at once for de Gaulle as "the only savior" and "the indispensable man." Poujade, on the other hand, took a sour attitude from the start, and in September 1958 declared, "De Gaulle is in power, but it's Rothschild who governs" (*L'Unité paysanne*, Nos. 634, 636, 645, May 17 and 31, Sept. 6, 1958). Dorgères approved the Gaullist coup of 1958 and voted for the new constitution, but he shortly began to denounce "the technocrats, the planners, the knights of the slide-rule," who surrounded de Gaulle. His most violent epithets, however, were reserved for the leaders of the CNJA, whom he described as "camouflaged Communists" (*La Gazette agricole*, Nos. 479, 485–86, March 28, May 30, and June 27, 1959).

16. *Paysans*, No. 17, April-May 1959, p. 74; also *Le Monde*, Dec. 28–29, 1958, and *L'Information agricole*, Nos. 194 and 195, Jan. 12 and 24, 1959.

17. *La Terre*, Nos. 749 and 752, Feb. 26 and March 19, 1959. The Communists accused FNSEA leaders of trying to repress spontaneous peasant demonstrations. Whatever the validity of this charge, by autumn the syndicate was once more giving its official blessing to the activists.

18. *Jeunes Forces rurales*, No. 328, March 1, 1960.

19. Interviews with various national and regional officials of the FNSEA and the CNJA, 1960.

20. E.g., Jacques Fauvet in *Le Monde*, Sept. 25, 1962.

21. Mallet, *Les Paysans contre le passé*, p. 32n; interviews with CNJA officials.

22. Interviews with CNJA officials, 1960; Serge Mallet in *France-Observateur*, March 3 and 24, 1960; *Jeunes Forces rurales*, No. 329, March 15, 1960. FNSEA leaders engaged in a variety of corridor maneuvers to influence the voting: e.g., they persuaded certain delegates from the Catholic west that such candidates as President Buchou of the CNJA were really crypto-Communists. Although several CNJA candidates were defeated, the FNSEA's 46-member Conseil d'Administration nevertheless included 9 former or current Jaciste militants, and the 21-member Bureau included 7 ex-Jacistes (Durupt, "Action catholique et milieu rural").

23. FNSEA, XVIe congrès fédéral, *Rapport général: L'Expansion et l'organisation de la production* (Paris, 1962). Debatisse's report was a remarkably tough-minded analysis of French farm problems in an era of rising productivity; such sensitive issues as overproduction, the rural exodus, the contrast between advanced and underdeveloped regions, and the need for structural reforms were discussed with refreshing candor. "It is best," concluded Debatisse, "to look important truths in the face. They don't endanger our syndical unity nearly so much as a silence filled with equivocation. The oneness [*unicité*] of agriculture is a myth, but its unity is real."

24. The APA rose from about 100 members in the Fourth Republic to 273 in the Fifth (*Le Monde*, Aug. 9, 1961). Gaullist leaders had at first thought of outlawing all such parliamentary interest groups, but finally permitted them to continue.

25. *Jeunes Forces rurales*, No. 310, May 15, 1959.

26. The contrasts in talent and outlook between these new civil servants around de Gaulle and Debré and the old-guard bureaucrats in control of the Ministry of Agriculture are briefly illuminated by Yves Tavernier in his article "Le Syndicalisme paysan et la politique agricole du gouvernement," *Revue française de science politique*, XII (1962), 626. Premier Debré's principal adviser on agricultural problems, Antoine Dupont-Fauville, is a good example of the new technocratic elite; born in 1927, he was an Inspecteur des Finances and had worked for a time in the Planning Commission.

27. De Gaulle's popularity among the farmers dropped from 74 per cent in April 1959 to 58 per cent in January 1960. No other group recorded so great a decline. *Sondages*, XXII (1960), 84.

28. *Fraternité paysanne*, No. 47, Feb. 18, 1960. The new right-wing organ, which openly advocated the OAS cause in Algeria, was called *Promotion paysanne*. It carried front-page editorials by the notorious French-Algerian activist Robert Martel, and advocated a return to the Peasant Corporation of Vichy days. Despite the denials of FNSEA officials, a number of political agitators—including Dorgères himself—participated in the Amiens demonstration, and may have been responsible for turning it toward violence

(*Moniteur agricole*, No. 151, Feb. 18, 1960; *La Gazette agricole*, No. 487, Feb. 22, 1960).

29. *L'Année politique 1960* (Paris, 1961), p. 26.

30. Y. Tavernier in *Revue française de science politique*, XII (1962), 634; *Moniteur agricole*, No. 145, Jan. 14, 1960.

31. Joseph Courau in *L'Information agricole*, No. 202, May 16, 1959; APPCA, *L'Intérêt national exige une loi verte* (Paris, 1960). The German "green law" contained no provision for guaranteed prices or a sliding-scale principle, but relied on other devices to achieve parity. French syndicalists proposed to adapt the German system to their needs by inserting price guarantees.

32. For the text of the government's proposed *loi d'orientation agricole*, see Assemblée nationale, session de 1960, Doc. No. 565. There is a good summary of the accompanying projects in *Paysans*, No. 26, Oct.-Nov. 1960, pp. 14–66.

33. *L'Année politique 1960*, p. 39; F.-H. de Virieu, "La Crise agricole et les projets gouvernementaux," *Paysans*, No. 24, June-July 1960, pp. 4–18.

34. Y. Tavernier in *Revue française de science politique*, XII (1962), 633–46; M. Faure and G. Champagne in *Paysans*, No. 26, Oct.-Nov. 1960, pp. 2–29.

35. *L'Année politique 1960*, p. 233.

36. Y. Tavernier in *Revue française de science politique*, XII (1962), 626.

37. For an excellent analysis of the 1961 peasant disturbances, see Henri Mendras and Yves Tavernier, "Les Manifestations de juin 1961," *Revue française de science politique*, XII (1962), 647–71; also *Le Monde*'s daily reports, especially those of June 18 to 26.

38. *Le Monde*, June 18–19, Aug. 15 and 22, 1961. Regional federations were eventually organized both in Brittany and in the southwest, but they have scarcely developed beyond the paper stage.

39. In the Midi, it was the Communists who sought to politicize the demonstrations; in other areas (notably Brittany), agents of the right-wing OAS hoped to recruit the peasants as shock troops for their Algérie Française campaign. The disgruntled rightists later claimed that the young peasant leaders had been bought off by the government for five million francs a month (Mendras and Tavernier, in *Revue française de science politique*, XII, 655–56).

40. Mallet, *Les Paysans contre le passé*, p. 196.

41. Marcel Faure, "La Colère paysanne," *Paysans*, No. 38, Oct.-Nov. 1962, p. 10.

42. Information provided by CNJA officials; also Marcel Faure in

Paysans, No. 38, Oct.-Nov. 1962, pp. 10–14. Serge Mallet, on the other hand, contended that the bill had been completely emasculated ("La Lutte des classes à la campagne," *France-Observateur*, Sept. 13, 1962).

43. *Paysans*, No. 39, Dec. 1962–Jan. 1963, pp. 75–77; F. de Virieu in *Le Monde*, Oct. 23–24, 1962. The decree defining the authority of the SAFER, for example, interpreted their powers about as broadly as the basic law permitted. The initial funds put at the disposal of the SAFER were another matter. *Paysans* pointed out that to restructure one-fourth of France's farm acreage in the next ten years, SAFER would need an annual sum twenty-five times the initial year's allotment.

44. Poujade's weekly organ, *Fraternité paysanne*, specialized in philippics against the evil forces that were alleged to be exploiting, misleading, and betraying the hapless peasantry. The FNSEA officials were "ensaucissonés de la système," or "sheep-dogs who bark to please their masters"; the CNJA leaders were "imbeciles" or "zazous" who had managed to "recruit a fair number of bird-brained little MRPs and genuine collectivists." Interspersed with these pleasantries were denunciations of the international bankers, the Jews, the greedy and infantile Americans, rival agitators like Dorgères and Antier, and other assorted villains. Poujade also exploited the passions and divisions created by the war in Algeria; he became a frank apologist for the fascist-tinged OAS. Occasionally the flow of vituperation was interrupted by a kind word about someone: e.g., a citizen of Plains, Montana, who spoke for what *Fraternité paysanne* called "an anti-Communist peasant organization" in that state. This gentleman had written to Poujade to propose a joint crusade in defense of the white man and his culture, which "stand on the brink of disaster" (No. 13, May 8, 1959; also other issues *passim*).

45. Jean Flavien, "La Prolétarisation de la paysannerie travailleuse," *Cahiers du communisme*, XXXVI (1960), 1125–37; F. Clavaud in *ibid.*, pp. 1717–45; Louis Perceval, "Les Paysans contre le passé ou paysans sans avenir?," *ibid.*, XXXVIII (1962), 107–29.

46. Waldeck Rochet in *Cahiers du communisme*, XXXVII (1961), 134–39. The importance of organizational activity in rural districts was pointed out by another party official, who noted the curious fact that the party's influence was greater in such moderately prosperous departments as Allier, Lot-et-Garonne, and Vaucluse than in such poor regions as Aveyron, Cantal, and Morbihan. The principal reason, he contended, was the good work done in these regions over the years by Communists and other progressives (F. Clavaud in *ibid.*, p. 1741).

47. Waldeck Rochet in *Cahiers du communisme*, XXXVIII (1962), 15–17. In 1959 the Communists also founded two new "front" organizations: the Mouvement de Coordination et de Défense des Exploitations Familiales and the Union de la Jeunesse Agricole Française. The former

was apparently designed to unify and rejuvenate the various regional *ligues* and *mouvements* that had been steadily losing their impetus as agitational weapons. The youth group, headed by a member of the party's central committee, was frankly dedicated to the task of building a backfire against further JAC progress in the countryside. All the evidence suggests that neither group has made a significant impact. The party's failure to build a young-peasant following was illustrated at the 1961 party congress, when an attempt was made to rejuvenate the party leadership by adding sixteen young members to the central committee. Not one of these neophytes came from the peasantry. *Cahiers du communisme,* XXXVII (June 1961), 298, 595; see also *La Terre,* No. 738, Dec. 11, 1958, and No. 755, April 9, 1959.

48. Interview with a CNJA official, 1962; see also *France-Observateur,* August 9 and 23, 1962. The young syndicalists in the Tarn had originally proposed to attend the Communist meeting and to challenge the speakers from the floor. They were overruled by their elders in the departmental FNSEA unit, who did not care to risk a head-on encounter with the Communists. The young leaders therefore appealed to CNJA headquarters in Paris, which urged them to act rather than sit by.

49. Durupt, "Action catholique et milieu rural."

50. My account is based on interviews with a number of CNJA leaders in 1960.

51. On the RFD episode, see *France-Observateur,* Feb. 5, 1959, and Michel Debatisse, "Syndicalisme et politique," *Paysans,* No. 14, Oct.-Nov. 1958, pp. 78–82. My account rests primarily on interviews with participants and well-informed observers in 1960.

52. The most successful of these local experiments in peasant-worker cooperation took place in the Loire-Atlantique, where the CFTC was strong, and where the lives of many of the factory workers and peasants were interwoven through family ties. The young peasants' chief theoretical organ, *Paysans,* had been preaching this kind of collaboration from its earliest issues in 1956. Recently the CNJA and the CFTC organized a joint research group for the study of common problems (*L'Information agricole,* No. 280, Dec. 1962).

53. My account is based on information provided by one of the participants.

54. *Le Monde,* Oct. 27, 1962. In some departments, however, the CNJA units recommended that their members vote No in the referendum. For different reasons, both President Blondelle of the APPCA and the leading officials of the FNSEA also favored a negative vote (*Le Monde,* Oct. 19 and 24, 1962; *L'Information agricole,* No. 276, Oct. 1962).

55. *Paysans,* No. 37, Aug.-Sept. 1962, p. 46. According to the most recent census figures (1955), the distribution of French farms is as follows:

	Number of farms	% of all farmers	% of total farm acreage
Farms of less than 2½ acres	150,300	6.6	0.3
Farms of 2½ to 25 acres	1,114,770	49.2	16.1
Farms of 25 to 125 acres	907,600	40.0	58.1
Farms of over 125 acres	95,100	4.2	25.5

The government statistical office, on the basis of sampling techniques, estimates that by 1960 the number of farms had fallen to slightly below two million, and the proportion of farmers and male farm laborers in the active male population to 16.0 per cent and 5.9 per cent, respectively (*Paysans*, No. 39, Dec. 1962–Jan. 1963, p. 83). The sample suggests that almost a million men and women left agriculture in the six years from 1954 to 1960.

56. Minister of Agriculture Henri Rochereau declared in 1960 that French agriculture had changed more in a decade than in the preceding two centuries (*Le Monde*, Nov. 20–21, 1960).

57. Serge Mallet, "Le C.N.J.A. face au néo-capitalisme," *France-Observateur*, Sept. 20, 1962.

58. According to figures for 1956–57 assembled by Common Market authorities, France was still far behind its neighbors in providing basic agricultural education after primary school. The number of students enrolled in such courses (per thousand active persons engaged in agriculture) was 14.9 in France, as compared to a range of from 31.3 to 56.8 in the other Common Market nations (*Paysans*, No. 37, Aug.-Sept. 1962, p. 91). Of all French students entering the lowest grade of secondary school in 1956, only 7 per cent came from farm families (Marcel Bruel in *La Nef*, n.s., No. 11, 1962, p. 12). Of all French students attending universities in 1959, only 5.7 per cent were children of farmers or farm workers; this proportion was scarcely higher than it had been in 1939, when the figure was estimated at 4.9 per cent (S. Hoffmann *et al.*, *In Search of France*, p. 418). Even in the advanced agricultural schools engaged in training agronomists, only a minority of the students (38 per cent) are peasants' sons (*Paysans*, No. 12, June-July 1958, p. 68).

The young peasant spokesmen are keenly aware of their own deficiencies in formal education, and are determined to give their successors a better chance. In 1959 they established a special training school for young peasant leaders (the Institut de Formation des Cadres Paysans) in a suburb of Paris. Sponsored by such men as Michel Debatisse and Marcel Faure (editor of the monthly review *Paysans*), the Institute admits some thirty regional or local officials of the CNJA for its annual three-month winter course. The subjects for study range over every aspect of French society, economics, and politics; the volunteer lecturers and discussion leaders (some of whom are eminent scholars or technicians) have been profoundly impressed, as one of them puts it, by the participants' "insatiable thirst for knowledge on every conceivable subject." Graduates of the Institute take a particularly active part in furthering the CNJA's grass-roots educational activities. Each year, CNJA headquarters selects a topic for discussion in the local CNJA units, and provides study materials for this enterprise.

59. Mallet, *Les Paysans contre le passé*, pp. 7–9.

Bibliography

The student of contemporary history commonly suffers from one of two severe disabilities: either his sources may still be inaccessible, or they may be so accessible (and so voluminous) as to seem overwhelming. The student of the present-day French peasantry plainly belongs in the second category; the sources of information are so bulky and so heterogeneous that they threaten to bury him under a sheer mass of paper. Specialized agricultural periodicals alone numbered 147 in 1936, and by the middle 1950's the figure had risen to 440. Fortunately, one of the things in which they specialize is redundancy, so that with a little care the researcher can learn to pick his way through the jungle without stopping to examine every tree.

For general guidance, and for much of my most useful information, I have relied on interviews with farm organization officials (or ex-officials), politicians, government officials, academic specialists, activists in various Catholic rural movements, and agricultural journalists. The list that follows is too long to permit proper identification, but some of the names will be familiar to anyone who has read this book:

Paul Antier, Octave Bajeux, M. Barret, Abbé J. Belliveaud, Philippe Bernard, Emile Bocquet, Jean Bohuon, Gustave Cadenne, Benjamin Caillaud, Etienne Causse, Count Alain de Chantérac, Maurice Chassant, M. Chaulet, Louis Chevalier, M. Combabessouse, Guy Cotton, Pierre Coutin, Jean Crouan, Michel Debatisse, M. Delorme, Henri Déramond, Henri Dorgères, René Dumont, Marie-Joseph Durupt, Roger Dusseaulx, Marcel Faure, M. Feunteun, Eugène Forget, M. Fournoux, François Goguel, Georges Gorse, Jean Gottmann, Alphonse Guimbrétière, M. Guitard, Pierre Hallé, Léo Hamon, F.-M. Jacq, Renaud Jean, A. Labardin, M. Labbé, Bernard

Lambert, Philippe Lamour, C. Langlade-Demoyen, Robert Lautier, M. Lemeunier, Jacques Le Roy Ladurie, Robert Mangeart, P. Marsaux, Henri Mendras, Jules Milhau, Charles Parisot, Félicien Pateau, Yves Pérotin, Camille Poli, René Rémond, Raphaël Rialland, Dr. Léopold Robert [Jean Yole], Louis Rosenstock-Franck, Abbé Jean Roux, Louis Salleron, Father Jean Serve, J.-B. Sévérac, Pierre Tanguy-Prigent, Abbé Tourelle, Marius Vazeilles, J.-P. Vizentini, M. Zermatti.

From the almost inexhaustible hoards of periodicals and newspapers, I have singled out the following journals for special attention, and have gone through extensive runs of each. The dates indicate the years I have read, rather than the beginning and terminal dates of the publication.

Bulletin communiste. 1920–24. The Communist Party's theoretical organ.

Cahiers du bolchévisme. 1924–39. Successor to the foregoing.

Cahiers du communisme. 1939–62. Successor to the foregoing.

Chambres d'agriculture. 1935–38, 1953–62. Organ of the APPCA.

La défense paysanne de la Corrèze (Tulle). 1938–44. Organ of the prewar farm syndicates and the Peasant Corporation in Corrèze.

Droit social. 1944–55.

Economie et humanisme. 1942–62. Dominican.

L'Effort paysan (Albi). 1937–44. Organ of Chantérac's syndical movement in the southwest.

Etudes et conjoncture. 1946–62. Government publication

Fraternité paysanne. 1955, 1959–62. Poujade's organ.

La Gazette agricole. 1950, 1958–60. Dorgères's organ.

L'Information agricole, 1952–62. Official organ of the FNSEA.

Jeunes Forces rurales. 1944–62. Organ of the JAC.

La Libération paysanne. 1944–52. Organ of the CGA.

Le Monde. 1944–62.

Le Monde paysan. 1946–49. The MRP's farm weekly.

Paysans. 1956–62. Published by former Jacistes.

La République agraire du massif central (Aurillac, Clermont-Ferrand). 1934–36. Regional organ of the Parti Agraire.

Revue de l'Action populaire. 1946–55. Jesuit; entitled *Travaux de l'Action populaire* prior to 1950.

Revue d'économie politique. 1930–43.

Revue du ministère de l'agriculture. 1946–58.

Revue économique. 1950–62.

Syndicats paysans. 1937–42. Organ of the UNSA.

Le Temps. 1930–40.

La Terre, 1937–62. The Communists' farm weekly.

Le Travailleur de la terre (Tulle). 1920–25. Organ of the
 Communists' earliest agrarian syndicate.

L'Union paysanne (Tulle). 1944–51. Regional organ of the
 FNSEA in Corrèze.

L'Unité paysanne. 1954–60. Organ of Antier's Parti Paysan.

La Voix de la terre (Paris). 1936–39. Organ of the Parti
 Agraire.

La Voix de la terre (Agen). 1945–51. Regional organ of the
 FNSEA in Lot-et-Garonne.

La Voix paysanne de l'Hérault (Montpellier). 1944–46. Regional organ of the FNSEA in Hérault.

I have read more selectively in a large number of other national
or regional periodicals and newspapers, and have found the following
most useful:

Cahiers d'action religieuse et sociale. Jesuit.

Cahiers du clergé rural. Sponsored by the JAC and MFR.

Chef paysan. The JAC's organ for leaders.

Le Cri du sol. Dorgères's prewar and wartime paper.

France-Observateur. Weekly of the non-Communist left.

Jeunes Agriculteurs. CNJA weekly.

Le Paysan d'Auvergne (Clermont-Ferrand). Regional organ of
 the FNSEA in Puy-de-Dôme.

Le Paysan du Midi (Montpellier). Regional organ of the FNSEA
 in Hérault.

La Paysan Nantais (Nantes). Regional organ of the FNSEA in
 Loire-Atlantique.

Témoignage chrétien. Left-wing Catholic weekly.

Of the general works on French peasant problems, a half-dozen
stand out as particularly valuable: Michel Augé-Laribé, *La Politique
agricole de la France de 1880 à 1940* (Paris, 1950), the standard
account by France's most prolific agricultural historian; Louis Chevalier, *Les Paysans: Etude d'histoire et d'economie rurale* (Paris,

1947), an unconventional essay by a noted demographer; Jacques Fauvet and Henri Mendras, eds., *Les Paysans et la politique* (Paris, 1958), chapters on political, syndical, and religious currents in the countryside, most of which were read at the annual meeting of the French political science association in 1956; Serge Mallet, *Les Paysans contre le passé* (Paris, 1962), a collection of lively and perceptive *rapportages* by an able young left-wing journalist; Henri Mendras, *Sociologie de la campagne française* (Paris, 1959), a brief but provocative essay by France's leading rural sociologist.

Several other books of broad sweep have also been useful: e.g., Jean Chombart de Lauwe, *Pour une agriculture organisée: Danemark et Bretagne* (Paris, 1949), an analysis of agrarian structure by a noted agronomist; F. Dovring, *Land and Labor in Europe, 1900–1950* (The Hague, 1956), a broad-gauge comparative study by a Swedish scholar; René Dumont, *Voyages en France d'un agronome* (Paris, 1956), case studies by a noted student of comparative agriculture; Georges Friedmann, ed., *Villes et campagnes* (Paris, 1954), proceedings of a congress of French sociologists; Roger Grand *et al.*, *Questions agricoles* (Paris, 1936), papers read at a conference of agricultural specialists in 1935; Gaston Lecordier, *Le Monde rural en marche* (St.-Etienne, 1954), a thorough survey of recent trends by a Catholic publicist; Roland Maspétiol, *L'Ordre éternel des champs* (Paris, 1946), a massive historical analysis by a leading exponent of "peasantist" doctrine; Jules Milhau and Roger Montagne, *L'Agriculture aujourd'hui et demain* (Paris, 1961), a comparative analysis with many French examples; Charles K. Warner, *The Winegrowers of France and the Government since 1875* (New York, 1960), a painstaking study of an important though somewhat atypical segment of the peasantry.

Supplementing these general works, a large number of more specialized books have provided detailed information or have suggested avenues of approach:

CHAPTER ONE. Michel Augé-Laribé, *L'Evolution de la France agricole* (Paris, 1912); Michel Augé-Laribé, *La Révolution agricole* (Paris, 1955); Jean Chombart de Lauwe, *Bretagne et pays de la Garonne: Evolution agricole comparée depuis un siècle* (Paris, 1946), a remarkable study contrasting an advancing region with a declining one; A. Labat, *L'Ame paysanne* (Paris, 1919), a classic essay on the pre-1914 peasantry by a country doctor; Gabriel Le Bras, *Introduction à l'histoire de la pratique religieuse en France* (Paris, 1942–45), by the founder of French religious sociology; Albert Soboul, "The French Rural Community in the 18th and 19th Centuries," *Past and Present*, No. 10 (Nov. 1956), pp. 78–95, an essay by a Communist historian; Albert Soboul, "La Question paysanne en 1848," *La pensée*, Nos. 18, 19, and 20 (1948), pp. 55–66, 25–37, and 48–56.

CHAPTER TWO. Michel Augé-Laribé, *Syndicats et coopératifs agricoles* (Paris, 1938); Michel Augé-Laribé, *Le Paysan français après la guerre* (Paris, 1923); Pierre Caziot, *La Terre à la famille paysanne* (Paris, 1919), an influential tract by a leading "peasantist"; A. Compère-Morel, *La Question agraire et le socialisme en France* (Paris, 1912), an analysis of pre-1914 trends by the Socialist Party's agrarian experts; "Paul Delourme" [Abbé Félix Trochu], *Trente-cinq Années de politique religieuse* (Paris, 1936), a study by the first crusader for peasant syndicalism in Brittany; Daniel Halévy, *Visites aux paysans du centre, 1907–1934* (Paris, 1935), impressionistic sketches by a well-known essayist-historian; Theodore Sands, "Corporatism in French Agriculture" (unpublished dissertation, Univ. of Wisconsin, 1950).

CHAPTER THREE. Michel Augé-Laribé, *Situation de l'agriculture française, 1930–1939* (Paris, 1941); Marcel Braibant, *L'Agriculture française: Son tragique déclin; son avenir* (Paris, 1936), a popularized account by a leading agricultural publicist; Henri Dorgères, *Haut les fourches!* (Paris, 1935), a propaganda tract by the Greenshirt leader; Henri Dorgères, *Au XXᵉ siècle 10 ans de jacquerie* (Paris, 1959), Dorgères's retrospective account of the great crusade of the 1930's; L. Gabriel-Robinet, *Dorgères et le Front Paysan* (Paris, 1937), a sympathetic pamphlet by a Parisian journalist; Henri Noilhan, *La République des paysans* (Aurillac, 1931), a collection of newspaper pieces by a leader of the Parti Agraire; Henri Pitaud, *La Terre au paysan* (Paris, 1936), a left-wing Catholic activist's account of agrarian movements in the depression era; R. G. Tugwell, "The Agricultural Policy of France," *Political Science Quarterly*, XLV (1930), 214–30, 405–28, 527–47; *Vers la corporation agricole* (Paris, 1934), proceedings of the UNSA's first congress dedicated to the corporative ideal; "Jean Yole" [Léopold Robert], *Le Malaise paysan* (Paris, 1930), a book that helped to make its author, a country doctor in the Vendée, a senator.

CHAPTER FOUR. Marcel Braibant, *La Tragédie paysanne* (Paris, 1937), a book by the Popular Front's leading agricultural publicist; René Dumont, *Misère ou prosperité paysanne?* (Paris, 1936), a vigorous pamphlet advocating rural modernization; Rémy Goussault *et al.*, *Union nationale des syndicats agricoles: Congrès syndical paysan, Caen, 5–6 mai 1937* (Paris, 1937), proceedings of the UNSA's most important congress; Neil Hunter, *Peasantry and Crisis in France* (London, 1938), a useful survey by a left-wing British journalist, sympathetic to the Popular Front; Georges Monnet, "The Place of Agriculture in the Economic Policy of the French Government," *International Affairs*, XVI (1937), 418–39, an essay by Blum's Minister of Agriculture; Jean Moquay, *L'Evolution sociale en agriculture* (Bordeaux, 1939), thesis on the farm labor legislation of the Popular Front; Suzanne Sailly-Laisné, *Orage sur le moisson: Le Drame vécu par les jeunes paysans* (Paris, 1941), rural conditions in 1938–39, based on JAC questionnaires; Louis Salleron, *Un Régime corporatif pour l'agriculture* (Paris, 1937), a study by the leading exponent of agrarian corporatism.

CHAPTER FIVE. Marcel Braibant, *La France, nation agricole* (Paris, 1943), a glorification of France's new role in Nazi Europe, by the onetime Popular Front publicist; Pierre Caziot, *Au Service de la paysannerie* (Paris, 1941), selections from the writings of Pétain's Minister of Agriculture; Michel Cépède, *Agriculture et alimentation en France durant la IIe guerre mondiale* (Paris, 1961), the best account of the Vichy era, by a Socialist-oriented agronomist; Mgr. Chaptal, *Lettres à un curé de campagne* (Paris, 1942), a representative tract preaching the conservative-Catholic line of the Vichy era; Henri Dorgères, *Révolution paysanne* (Paris, 1943), Pétain's agrarian policies, viewed by a hero-worshiper; Father N. Drogat, *La Corporation paysanne* (Paris, 1942), a more restrained pro-Pétain tract by a Jesuit agrarian specialist; Father Michel-Dominique Epagneul, *Missionnaire en France* (Paris, 1944), a study by the founder of the Frères Missionnaires des Campagnes; Louis Salleron, *Naissance de l'état corporatif: Dix Ans de syndicalisme paysan* (Paris, 1942), selections from Salleron's writings before and during the Vichy era; Louis Salleron *et al.*, *La Corporation paysanne* (Paris, 1943), a mine of information on the achievements, structure, and prospects of the Corporation, critical of the state's attempts to dominate the Corporation.

CHAPTER SIX. M. Artaud, *Métier d'agriculteur* (Ecully, 1944), the first postwar appeal for rapid mechanization of agriculture, written by a pioneering farmer of the Catholic left; L. Brasse-Brossard, *Le Destin de l'agriculture française* (Paris, 1949), an agronomist's plea for moderate reform; René Colson, *Motorisation et avenir rural* (Paris, 1950), a tough-minded analysis of the modernization problem by the former secretary-general of the JAC; René Dumont, *Le Problème agricole français* (Paris, 1946), Dumont's reform program, as presented to the Planning Commission; Henry W. Ehrmann, "The French Peasant and Communism," *American Political Science Review*, XLVI (1952), 19–43; Father Jean Serve, *Le Syndicalisme agricole* (Paris, 1945), a short pamphlet by a Jesuit agronomist attacking the government's post-liberation policies; S.F.I.O., *La Renovation paysanne: Programme socialiste* (Paris, 1945), the Socialist Party's postwar reform plans; Pierre Tanguy-Prigent, *La Terre aux paysans* (Paris, 1946), a pamphlet in defense of Tanguy's achievements at the Ministry of Agriculture; Maurice Thorez, *Une Politique agricole française* (Paris, 1948), the Communists' proposals for agrarian reform in the postwar years.

CHAPTER SEVEN. Abbé F. Boulard, *Essor ou déclin du clergé français?* (Paris, 1950), a study by a pioneering religious sociologist; Abbé F. Boulard, *Problèmes missionnaires de la France rurale* (Paris, 1945); René Chatelain, *L'Agriculture et la formation professionnelle* (Paris, 1953), the most thorough study of specialized agricultural education; Jean Chombart de Lauwe, *Les Possibilités de la petite entreprise dans l'agriculture française* (Paris, 1954), an empirical study of small-peasant farming in the west; Adrien Dansette, *Destin du Catholicisme français 1926–1956* (Paris, 1956), an excellent account of new currents in the Church; Father N. Drogat, *Civilisation rurale de demain: Guide de culture paysan* (Paris, 1950), a handbook for rural Catholics; *Esprit*, Vol. XXIII (1955), special issue on peasant problems; Jean Fauchon, *Economie de l'agriculture française* (Paris, 1954), a useful compendium by an agronomist; Lucien Gachon, "Evolution de l'agriculture française depuis 1940," *Revue économique*, VI (1955), 35–55, the peasantist view restated by a conservative geographer; Marc Latil, *L'Evolution du revenu agricole* (Paris, 1956), an economist's attempt to clarify the controversial issue of rural incomes (broader than its title); Henri Mendras, "Les Organisations agricoles et la politique," *Revue française de science poli-*

tique, V (1955), 736–60; Société Française d'Economie Rurale, *L'Economie agricole française 1938–1958* (Paris, 1959), contributions by leading specialists.

CHAPTER EIGHT. Raymond Cartier, *France, quelle agriculture veux-tu?* (Paris, 1960), a book by the editor of France's biggest mass-circulation weekly, *Paris-Match*; Marie-Joseph Durupt, "Action catholique et milieu rural" (draft of thesis to be presented at the Institut d'Etudes Politiques in Paris), a remarkable analysis based on extensive travel and interviews; Françoise Langlois, *Les Salariés agricoles en France* (Paris, 1962), an up-to-date study of the farm workers; Henri Mendras, *Les Paysans et la modernisation de l'agriculture* (Paris, 1958), an analysis of attitudes, based on study of a small sample; Gilbert Mury, *Essor ou déclin du Catholicisme français* (Paris, 1960), a sustained attack on Catholic rural activities, by an ex-Catholic Communist; *La Nef*, new series No. 11 (1962), special issue entitled "L'Agriculture en France," with contributions by a number of young farm syndicalist leaders; Georges Suffert, *Les Catholiques et la gauche* (Paris, 1960), a study by a Catholic intellectual of the left; P. Toulet *et al.*, *Les Chrétiens dans le monde rural* (Paris, 1962), a thorough survey.

French geographers, political scientists, and anthropologists (together with a few pioneering foreigners) have been producing a steady flow of careful regional or local studies of rural evolution, structure, and political behavior. They are essential to offset the distortions of any study that attempts to generalize about the peasantry. Representative examples of these monographs are the following: Philippe Bernard, *Economie et sociologie de la Seine-et-Marne* (Paris, 1953); Lucien Bernot and René Blancard, *Nouville: Un Village français* (Paris, 1952); Paul Bois, *Paysans de l'ouest* (The Hague, 1960); Michel Chevalier, *La Vie humaine dans les Pyrénées ariègeoises* (Paris, 1956); S. Derruau-Boniol, "Le Département de la Creuse: Structure sociale et évolution," *Revue française de science politique*, VII (1957), 38–66; Henri de Farcy, *Paysans du Lyonnais: La Vie agricole dans la vallée de l'Yséran* (Lyon, 1950); Lucien Gachon, *Une Commune rurale d'Auvergne du XVIIIe au XXe siècle* (Clermont-Ferrand, 1939); Joseph Garavel, *Les Paysans de Morette: Un Siècle de vie rurale dans une commune de Dauphiné* (Paris, 1948); François Goguel *et al.*, *Nouvelles Etudes de sociologie électorale* (Paris, 1954);

P. Guichonnet, "La Géographie et le tempérament politique dans les montagnes de Haute-Savoie," *Revue de géographie alpine*, XXXI (1943), 39–86; Paul Guiot, *Thurino: Démogéographie d'une commune rurale de l'ouest lyonnais* (Paris, 1949); Count de Neufbourg, *Paysans: Chronique d'un village du Xᵉ au XXᵉ siècle* (Paris, 1945); Henri Mendras, *Etude de sociologie rurale: Novis (Aveyron), Virgin (Utah)* (Paris, 1953); Jean Pataut, *Essai sur la sociologie électorale de la Nièvre au XXᵉ siècle* (Paris, 1956); André Siegfried, *Tableau politique de la France de l'ouest sous la troisième république* (Paris, 1913); André Siegfried, *Géographie électorale de l'Ardèche sous la IIIᵉ république* (Paris, 1949); Roger Thabault, *Mon Village* (Paris, 1945); Alain de Vulpian, "Physionomie agraire et orientation politique dans le département des Côtes-du-Nord, 1928–1946," *Revue française de science politique*, I (1951), 110–32; Laurence Wylie, *Village in the Vaucluse* (Cambridge, Mass., 1957); Laurence Wylie, "Social Change at the Grass Roots," in Stanley Hoffmann *et al.*, *In Search of France* (Cambridge, Mass., 1963), pp. 159–234.

Several valuable recent studies deserve to be listed here, though they were published too late to be used in the preparation of this book: Michel Debatisse, *La Révolution silencieuse: Le Combat des paysans* (Paris, 1963); Jean Meynaud, *La Révolte paysanne* (Paris, 1963); Louis Prugnaud, *Les Etapes du syndicalisme agricole en France* (Paris, 1963); Gérard Walter, *Histoire des paysans de France* (Paris, 1963).

Index